The Village.

The Village.

by Matt & Lentil

GROWN & GATHERED

plum. Pan Macmillan Australia

The Village.

by Matt & Lentil

GROWN & GATHERED

Dedication.

This book, in a way, is not complete within itself. It's the next step—of our life and our lessons—and a continuation of our first book. As we said then, we are forever learning. The ideas in this book represent only what we know now. Our truth in *this* moment. Until the next chapter.

We have written this from our hearts, from our warm home, within our village. May your home be full of people, home-cooked meals and a touch of chaos.

This book is dedicated to making change, through embracing our friends and our families—taking care of them, nurturing them and allowing them to nurture us. By living a full life, one with all of the chaos, the good food, the love and the emotion. A life with all of the 'mess', because that is a full life. And it brings with it so much that is good, nurturing and beautiful.

To your well-stocked pantries, simmering pots on the stove and abundant gardens. To your homes and villages.

With our love. We wrote this for you.

*As with our first book, we have printed this in the most sustainable way we could, knowing full well that the most sustainable thing to do would be to not print a book at all. We hope, once again, that the good it brings outweighs the harm it has caused.

Contents.

PART 1.

Return to the village.

Introduction.

We believe in really *experiencing* our food—growing our own vegetables, gathering from the wild, sourcing produce from local farmers and making big, beautiful meals with all that we have found—and these are such joyful experiences for us. But what makes them even better is doing them with other people. Growing, gathering, preserving, pickling, cooking and eating are all *so much* better when shared with your village. In fact, *most* of the experiences that life has to offer are better when shared with the people you love! It's the sharing that brings maximum joy. It's the sharing that makes these experiences matter, that gives them meaning and brings about feelings of happiness and belonging.

These are the kind of feelings that *truly* nourish us. They are about food, but beyond food also. They do something for your soul. Like when you share a big, beautiful, fresh meal with friends, with a warm fire in the corner and the dog on the couch. Or when you go to a friend's house and they anticipate your needs, greeting you with a freshly-baked cake, a hot pot of coffee and a salad from their garden. When you sit with family, laughing, arguing and sharing a meal. When you walk the streets of a small village where everyone waves hello, and the shopkeepers give you freshly baked goods because they just want you to have it, to try it—they want to *share* it with you. Or when you are *so* tired and someone makes you a simple, wholesome, home-cooked meal, a cup of tea, and tucks you into bed.

It's the feeling you get when someone welcomes you as their own, feeds you as though they have known and loved you forever and it's as if they grew their whole garden just to nourish you. That feeling. It's a feeling that sits somewhere deep within your heart.

And it's a feeling that might be so much more important than we previously thought. Studies now show that when we feel safe and nurtured, when we have abundance and security (as compared to feeling like our resources are scarce and the future is uncertain), our brains function the equivalent of 14 IQ points higher! Having a village support system contributes massively to feeling safe and secure. Because a loving village brings meaning to one's life, creating strong bonds and a security in knowing that there are others around who will 'catch' you if you find yourself with little food or money. In a loving village, there is always abundance to share.

We met a man named Joe at a public spring water fountain in Sardinia, in one of the longest-lived villages on the planet. He wore a torn, white singlet, raggy, once-black pants, dusty shoes and an enormous, slightly toothless grin from ear to ear. We guessed he was about 75.

'I am so poor, but I am so rich, because I have my village, good food and this good water [pointing to the fountain]. I am very lucky.'

Joe had basically no possessions but the clothes on his back. But he had a simple house in the village, access to an abundance of simple, nourishing food and he had *that* water.

He smiled.
He was positive.
He was fed.
And he had community.
What more do you need?

No matter *who* makes up your village, sharing life with loved ones has been shown, time and time again, to have a more extraordinary impact on longevity than so many other factors that you'd think would just *have* to have a greater effect. It's been shown to be more powerful than maintaining a healthy weight, than living amongst a pristine environment, than avoiding substance abuse, than having access to healthcare—the list goes on. In fact, after accounting for all the multitude of variables from one person's life circumstances to the next, people who consider themselves to have strong connections with others can expect to live at least 26% longer than those who don't! So the need for all of us to seek out a village, *our* village, is one of the most crucial things not only for our health, but also to live a life that is long, happy and full of meaning.

The village that surrounds *you* will be different from ours, different for every person—and we often have several 'villages', or communities, that are important to us. Whatever the case, surround yourself with the people who fit *your* idea of the village. People who make you feel as though you aren't just *anyone*, but you are the *whole world*. People who make your soul feel full, as though you've just received the warmest hug in the world. People who are *your* people, who make you feel complete and that you fit. Embrace these people—they are your village.

~~~

I must divulge that so much of what I personally learnt of community growing up was largely from a family of dysfunction. At the dinner table we didn't discuss the weather or politics, and there was little that went unsaid. There was wine, chaos, arguments and more food than we knew what to do with. You always kept it a secret if you were going to visit my Maltese grandmother ('Mumma'), because if she knew you were coming she would cook for days in anticipation of your arrival. And my aunty would *always* burn the food because she would have too many wines and be talking with her hands and getting distracted by any number of things in the room.

As a child, I compared this to other families and concluded that my family, this part of my village, was in fact abnormal. But now as an adult I see that this is the *full* life. I see that life is the *full* cuddle—not the one you give awkwardly and then walk away wondering what just happened. It's the celebrating, the laughing, the fighting and the intensity that comes with being a human. It's the play, the stories, the sharing, the delicious food, the loving freely, the chaos, the mess. *This* is where the joy lives, in all these moments. It's about embracing it all.

~~~

If we go back to the beginning, back to when humans began, we see that this is all deep in our genetics. Humans evolved the way we did because of our ability to gossip, to tell stories, to connect. We roamed in small, exceptionally intimate groups of just 140 people or so, possessing only the most essential items (those easiest to carry on our backs—it's not surprising we get so overwhelmed trying to manage all our thousands of things these days!) and moving every month, every week, sometimes every day. We went our entire lives surrounded by just this small group of close family and friends and were only very rarely exposed to other humans outside of the group. It was a 'good' number. A balanced number. For us, and for nature. Everything was done with some, often all, of this community, and we thrived within this structure.

The traditional village model, likewise, rarely exceeded a few hundred people who knew intimately and supplied readily the needs of their community. We are, quite simply, designed to rely deeply on our village. And we have visited many villages, throughout the world, that still operate on this exact same principle.

I believe that if we all connect with our villages and we *nurture* those villages (and allow them to nurture us) the world will be well. That if we do, we will all have more meaning and therefore be healthier, happier and have a real chance at living the longest and most fulfilled lives we can. And I also believe that the re-emergence of the village mindset is what our *planet* needs. Because when we all care for our little piece of the planet, the whole planet is nurtured.

With this book, we share moments from *our* village. Moments that make us feel nurtured, fulfilled, happy and loved. We wrote it for you, from our hearts, because it is something that we believe in. We want you to use this book in your real life, in your villages, to feel nurtured and loved and to make others feel nurtured and loved. To connect. Because we all deserve it. Because it's a part of being human. A part of being healthy.

To everyone who wants to live the full version of life, with all of its mess, love and passion. We wrote this for you.

–Lentil

1. What is 'the village'? And why health, happiness and longevity are all about relationships.

Community, or 'the village', is something we should all have. Most people have several communities that are tied together by common interests, shared values or heritage. Then there is the literal village that we live in, where you are all tied together by the fact that you live and coexist in one location. Each village should nurture you and you nurture it. If not, it's not a strong, functioning village, and it's not going to make you happier or healthier, or help you to live longer.

Traditionally, the village was at the core of the human experience. Eating, celebrating, growing, gathering and nurturing were done together. And this togetherness is the foundation of human existence—it gives us all our human experiences, which give life meaning, which makes us happy.

This is what we have experienced firsthand. We love growing, gathering and cooking, but it's always better when we do it with others. It's the *togetherness* of these experiences that make you feel happiness. And it's how humans have evolved (see page 12). It is at our core. So, we take these lessons, and apply them to today—traditional living made modern.

Living for a long time (longevity) does not just come down to—some of you may be surprised, so please take a seat—what you eat. In fact, research now shows that living for a long time comes down to having meaningful relationships and especially to the community that we have around us.

People who have more meaning in their lives outlive those who don't. And what leads to more meaning? People! Community. Your village. Meaning isn't complicated. Meaning is as simple as having community. It's all about sharing life and its experiences with *other* people. This is what leads to more happiness—not money, not things, but community and the experiences that come with it. Studies suggest that community is number one on the list. All the other things follow, such as having relationships with nature, heritage and tradition, our physical constitution, food. Community = meaning. Meaning is always tied to others, to connectedness. Put simply, people who develop meaningful relationships live longer!

What's this about longevity?

Research actually shows that those with a high rate of life-meaning have a far greater chance (57% higher) of outliving those with a low rate of meaning. In a nutshell, meaning and meaningful relationships are linked to higher levels of happiness, healthiness and longevity.

More specifically, they have been found to correlate with a healthy mental state, fending off physical pain, helping to delay mental and physical decline, and are better predictors of longevity than socio-economic status, IQ, genetics, even smoking. Seems you can eat as healthy as you want and be as sober as a nun, but it doesn't necessarily lead to longevity. Sorry.

So, lean into your community. Nurture it, and let it nurture you. Enjoy *all* the moments within your village. This is what matters. This is where the meaning of life lies, somewhere in here is the secret to happiness and health.

For us there is so much inspiration in traditional villages that have survived into this era, despite our rapidly evolving modern world. These villages are full of people living the longest lives on the planet, and not only long lives, but such happy and fulfilled lives. So, we went to some of these places to observe, to learn. Not just for ourselves, but for you too.

2. Our observations: the traditional village—simple secrets to longevity and why your everyday experiences matter.

We have read so much about the traditional villages of the world, the places that have the highest rates of longevity. But we wanted to go and see them for ourselves, and observe for ourselves. What are the simple secrets? What magical things make you live forever? Well, the secret is there is no secret. It's about the simple life, the one right in front of you—you just have to reach out and grab it. And it's *all* about community.

We want to share some thoughts and observations from our time in those villages. The things we noted, what stood out to us. Like in our last book, when we shared some of our observations of nature, these are our observations of people at their natural *best*. People living for very a long time, and loving it.

We visited several of the 'blue zones' of the world and stayed for a length of time in villages that are considered to have some of the longest-living populations in the world. *Exact* towns and locations don't matter—we want to share the *lessons* and look at how to apply these to our own lives. Each place was different in so many ways, but they all had similarities. The people always seemed so young, their skin healthy, their cheeks plump, and they laughed out loud, as if they had never laughed before. There was a kindness, a care, an easy nurturing that we had been longing for—like a big cuddle after a long day. They were generally upfront and said what they meant and meant what they said. And most of all, everything was centred around their village—their friends, the way they ate, what they ate, the things they did. Seldom did they leave the village, and seldom did they do anything alone. Actually, we laugh as we remember a time we asked a local woman if she could take us to see something. She said yes, and then arrived with four other people—her cousin, her cousin's wife and a friend—and we all climbed into a tiny car. It is always like this. There are always more people than you think there will be, everyone is invited.

At the time, we noted that obviously we couldn't account for the impact genetics had on these people. Maybe they just had amazing genes that made their skin taut and life jovial. But after further research, we now know that life-meaning and community outweigh all other factors for longevity, even genetics. So, these observations stand alone, they speak to what factors lead to meaning for people in these traditional villages, people who live for a long time. Let's take these observations, learn from them and apply these lessons of meaning to our own lives.

Everyday routines.

Stress. Time and time again, we noticed how no-one seems particularly stressed or time poor.

Online time. Seldom do you see people on their phones or computers in public.

Everyday routines and rituals. There are plenty of these. Work, meal and general routines. For example, every afternoon people meet in different parts of town to talk, laugh and hang out. They gossip and just sit together.

Meaningful work. They all seem to have meaningful work, but they don't work for long, excessive hours. Work happens as it happens, in their own time, when they can do it. They often start work early, finish at lunch and then have a siesta. Most people are gardeners, farmers, shepherds or work in the local stores.

'Meditating'. You often see people just sitting. At first, we thought 'What is that person doing?' because it was so odd to see someone just *sitting*. They often just sit, for an hour or so, every day. We named it 'contemplation hour'. They don't call it meditation, but is this what it is? Sometimes you see people sitting alone, sometimes with others, but always the sitting.

No hurry, no worry. Once, we booked an apartment in a tiny town. It was late when we arrived at a mutually agreed upon check-in time. They weren't there. Thirty minutes later, still not there. Forty-five minutes later, they arrived, as if nothing odd had happened. What could be the problem? What's the hurry—life is good.

Sleep. They sleep and rest a fair bit. Some places have siesta time every afternoon, and all the stores are closed from 1:30–5 pm(ish). We met a 97-year-old man in one of these towns, and we asked him the secret of life. He shrugged and said, 'Good sleep, meaningful work'. That was his secret.

Personality traits.

They say it like it is. They say what they mean and mean what they say.

Generous and giving. People are generous and giving. So much so that if you say you like something, they often want you to have it.

Curious. They are deeply curious and genuinely interested in *everything*.

Traditional. Traditional ways, food and routines are very important. Much more than the latest trends.

They don't take much seriously. They may look like they do, but they don't. Yes, some people may experience anxiety, but they aren't generally worried about much. They laugh a lot. They smile a lot. They are positive and easy-going. Again, why would you worry? Maybe it's because these areas have experienced so much upheaval and war. There is a truly ancient undercurrent of unrest throughout the Mediterranean. *Real* hardship is in their blood. So, in this time of relative peace and calm, what could a resilient people like this possibly worry about?

They aren't rich. They aren't rich, but most people own their own homes as often children build above their parents' house or are given the upper levels. They have security in that. And food in their gardens and fields and hills and bellies. So they don't rely so much on money anyway. And they don't strive for it. In the West, we often tend to have this perspective that our kids should 'earn their place', that we should all go through the stress of accumulating enough wealth to be comfortable. That this makes us better, more rounded people. In comparison, in these villages, the family home is available, or another family-owned home is available. Families share wealth. It's all in. Needs are met. Desires are irrelevant. And life is focused on life.

Roles. People generally have their 'roles', whether it be the cook of the house, or the 'breadwinner', so to speak.

Food and health.

Olive oil. They use it in everything. A little bit of butter, but mostly olive oil.

Good fats, oils and animal fat. Every meal has so many good fats, oils and animal fat.

Cream. They love cream.

Salami or cured meats. Many people cure their own meats, and they eat salami or a cured meat almost every day.

Cheese. They eat a lot of cheese, mostly goat's or sheep's.

Almonds. Most sweets are made from or are a celebration of almonds.

Honey. Honey is usually abundant and used as the primary sweetener.

Local everything. Almost everything they eat is local. It's not even a thought, it's just what they do.

Breakfast. They only have biscotti/pastry and coffee for breakfast, or something that is similarly small.

Alcohol. They drink wine, beer and sometimes spirits, but not often in excess, and mostly with food.

Sweets. This is the one thing that is slightly odd and stands out among the rest. Pretty much everyone eats sweets of some form (biscotti, tiramisu), but never too much, and they are always homemade from simple, natural (refined, yes, but only natural) ingredients—butter, honey (or sugar), flour. No preservatives or artificial colours or flavours. Things are what they are.

A respectful approach to meat and dairy. There is always meat and dairy on the table, and everyone, even the children, understands where it comes from. It doesn't shock them. We don't have to explain why we eat wild meat, or older, rather than younger, pigs, sheep or cows. And the animals at the market still have their heads and feet on so that people can utilise the whole animal. They get it. They know what it takes to raise animals sustainably. And, as always, there is a tradition of moderation.

Waste not want not. It is so rare to see food left on people's plates at the end of a dinner. You eat it. All. And you will never see food scraps going in the bin.

An abundance of fresh produce. From their backyards or the market (there are always local markets). And the village stores sell everything local. It's always seasonal. And there is only about 5% non-local/seasonal foods in their diet.

Not too much. This seems to be the key. Yes, they may drink alcohol. They may drink coffee. They may eat sweets. But they're living for a long time because it's not too much. It's just a little every day. Moderation, with the occasional debaucherous celebration!

Little bits of daily exercise. They do small bits of exercise, every day. Their days aren't sedentary. They do things like cook or garden, and often walk everywhere they need to go in town. But you don't often see someone out for a run. Mostly they walk. They walk the mountains or to get from place to place, up hills, around town—they could walk all day.

Fasting. They fast, but not intentionally. Because breakfast is not a big deal—just coffee and a cookie or pastry—everyone basically fasts from dinner to lunch each day. About 15 or 16 hours!

Four-course meals. Especially if you go out or have celebrations, dinner (and even lunch) always involves four courses. Bigger meals, less often.

Sleeping off meals. Often they sleep after a meal (lunch and dinner). People say that you should let dogs rest after they have eaten—is it the same for us?

The most important thing: community.

The literal village. They live in a literal village, which is generally isolated in some way from everything else.

Older people are celebrated. They meet in the streets every afternoon. They have community. They aren't locked away somewhere separate from everyone else.

Security. They don't seem to have many worries or cares—everyone seems safe within their community. Daily life follows a fairly predictable and sure progression of events.

They are always together. There is always someone hanging out a window talking to someone else. They're always feeding someone. There are always people sitting together. There are always people talking in the street.

Meals are always to share. They eat cheese. They eat salami, lots of tomatoes, meat and vegetables. They eat bread, and some more cheese. And they do it *together.*

They never eat or drink on the move. There is no such thing as 'takeaway'. You either stand and take your coffee and snack at the bar, or you sit with others. One day, we were walking along and eating something. So many people stared. And then we realised it was because we were walking *and* eating—the two are mutually exclusive in village life.

Village culture. As we travelled, without any planning, in almost every town we found ourselves in genuine, traditional village culture. Always at a food market or a flea market, watching a performance for children, surrounded by a village wedding or baptism, or stumbling across a travelling van selling something from a neighbouring area, like meat or bread. At the very least, there was always a village store, with multiple local products—cheese, meat, wine. And if you couldn't see something on display, if you asked, it was often hidden away somewhere. Actually, often the best products were hidden for only those who knew to ask—like the homemade, all-natural salamis!

Communal spaces. In each village, there were always communal spaces, and they were constantly used. Whether it was the square or the bar, these were used by everyone and used as meeting places.

There is so much more to it than food. The food is important, for sure. It's local, it's traditional and it's made from whole, natural ingredients, as we have always known to be important. But it's also beyond that. It's more than that. It's about *sharing* that food. It's about meaning. It's about community. It's the village.

3. To nurture is our nature.

When I think of my Grandma ('Mumma'), I think of her roast potatoes and the tiny cherry tomatoes she always had growing wild in her backyard. Of hot summer days, crisp grass and family lunches. This is a part of *my* village story of community, sharing, celebrating, growing and cooking.

To be nurtured is to feel warmth, to be somewhere where people love you, to have homemade food, some gentle organised chaos around you, people talking, listening to or playing music they love, planting, harvesting, eating.

Nurturing involves all the messiness of real life. It's not this *idea* of calm and quiet, where everyone is so stressed trying to stay calm that they become *more* stressed. Or where you drink green smoothies all day, when in fact your body needs and is craving warming stews. To be nurtured, or to nurture, isn't academic. There is no one-size-fits-all doctrine. It's just real. It's family, whether blood-related or not. And it changes as your needs change. The shape it takes will grow with you, as your needs grow, as the needs of those around you grow. Just like nature.

When we take care of our community, it takes care of us. We nurture our villages, and they nurture us back. It works in balance. And it is not only important to be nurtured and to nurture others, but also to nurture ourselves. Nurturing ourselves can be as simple as embracing what we *do* have—appreciating and cherishing that. In other words, allowing ourselves to be content. And in every long-living village we visited, there was an appearance of lack, but a *reality* of abundance. People had little in terms of material possessions, but actually they had more than they needed, and they always gave generously. They were content. Now *that* is the good life.

Yes, there is merit to the 'eat a restricted healthy diet with moderate exercise' argument. We just don't believe that's the full story. Food is at the core of it all. We grow food to share with each other, and we cook nourishing food to look after ourselves and others. It's always all about food. But, we're saying that it also goes beyond food, much less about what we *do* with that food, and much more about who we do it *with*.

And if someone doesn't have enough, you welcome them. You act as a village, where no-one goes hungry, where everyone feels safe, where everyone has enough. We've seen it—this is the kind of world you want to live in. One where you take care of your village, and it takes care of you. And if everyone just did that, we would all be the better for it.

To nurture is our nature. We need to be nurtured, and we need to nurture. When we all function together, it's like a little circle, perfectly symmetrical. A nice little moving circle, where you do this, and I do that, just like dancing with nature. And we've seen that it's a dance that is crucial to thriving health, happiness and a long and fulfilled life.

-Lentil

4. Bringing it back to food and sustainability.

Traditional food cultures were *all* about nurturing each other. Dishes were developed using what was local and abundant and designed so families had variety in what they ate. It was always about using what you had around you. There weren't such things as supermarkets or grocery stores, and we've seen villages, islands and communities that still live like this.

Traditional food was about feeding many mouths, feeding not only your family, but also your neighbours and *their* neighbours. It was about having lots of food, without having a lot, using what was in season, what was in your garden, what you could trade with your neighbour. And because of all this, traditional food cultures were, and still are, incredibly sustainable.

So, sustainability isn't complicated. It's very simple—traditional food, traditional living, your village. We believe that the way to change the world isn't simply by changing the type of light globe you use. Rather, it's about nurturing your community and your local environment. When you care for your community and it cares for you, you have all that you need, and you don't need to look beyond that. You have meaning. You feel happier, more satisfied and want for less. If we all look after our little part of the world, the whole world is looked after. *That* is true sustainability.

And we as humans are healthier and live for longer as a result. We are sharing abundances, sharing skills, sharing experiences. We are growing our own food together, cooking together, celebrating and trading together. There is naturally less waste. We are focused on necessities, not looking for more 'stuff'. And we are co-operating with our community to nurture the environment. These are the lessons of the traditional village.

The way to change the world is in the smallest things. It's to nurture each other, to eat from each other's gardens and cook in each other's kitchens. It's to feel content with what we have. *That* is the key to sustainability.

We hope we can inspire you to experience all of this for yourself. We look to the traditional village, evolution and what we know today and try to bring these lessons into *our* life, so that we may live the longest, most fulfilled life *we* can. And we truly wish the same for you. There is no world where it is all sunshine, rainbows and lollipops (we don't even like lollipops!), but the good life does exist.

We are certain that a well-functioning village, in whatever form that takes for you, is *the* key component to winning at life. We've seen so many incredibly long-living villages, and it was always about more than what they ate, what exercise they did, what genes they had. Feeling nurtured and safe within your village was *always* what mattered most. Perhaps that's really *all* that matters.

So, embrace *your* community, your traditional village, whoever they are. And maybe we'll see you in ours one day.

PART 2.

Grow.

Mastering the basics to feed your village.

Plantless or perfectly manicured backyards, cleared land and empty balconies. That's no fun. Life is for all the things, the chaos and people … *and* plants. Without plants, we have none of it.

You can grow plants, wherever you are. There is a misconception that to farm or grow produce you must have a large holding of land. This is untrue. *Wherever* you are, you can grow *something* to nurture yourself and your village. This chapter is here to inspire you—no matter what space you have—to grow. Because we have been all over the world, and growing an abundant harvest is where joy lives. It's where the most joyous homes and people are, and it just feels good, it feels right. Spaces where plants are abundant are spaces that can always nurture. In such spaces there is always a fruit tree to harvest, a pot of bountiful herbs or flowers to pick, even the 'weeds' become mostly edible after years of cultivation. And, not by chance, these are often where the longest-living people live—alongside these gardens. This is what we want to cultivate. Many, many homes like this. Because growing nourishes a home, it nourishes community and it is in *all* of us, ready to be explored.

Within the experience of growing plants is life, is meaning, is happiness. Together and shared. When we step into our garden and feel abundance, when someone hands us their homegrown produce or cooks it to share with us, these are the moments that we feel the most fully nourished and nurtured. So we want to share with you the simple secrets of mastering the basics to feed yourself and your village. And it *is* simple. Follow these steps and you too will be nourished and nurtured.

First things first.

Make it yours. Grow what you and your community love, and love to eat. Nothing else. Why would you?

Start slow. Take your time filling your space, however big or small. First, fill just one spot with as many of the things that you love as will fit. When that's under control, go bigger. Then bigger again. No need to do it all at once.

Share it. The harvest from even just one apple tree can be completely overwhelming. But with a village, such harvests are a joy.

Try and fail, together. With trying comes failure, and with failure comes experience and learning, and often great memories. And doing it better the next time. And eventually, it leads to a thriving garden.

Make growing a joyous everyday routine. Check on your garden each morning (or whenever works for you each day). What is it doing, what has sprouted, what is in or out of balance? Then do a little dance with it, gently nudging things towards where you want them to go. Within this routine lies the most beautiful parts of growing, of being connected with nature. The pure joy when seeds sprout; the realisation that within a few weeks your seedlings will become abundant, harvestable plants; the moment where your fruit tree grows its first little fruit (in these cases, we often literally dance); or the pure disappointment when a slug eats the young leaves that held so much promise. With patience, good observation and the right preparation, you will soon be dancing each day. A dance through *your* beautiful, abundant garden, a garden grown to feed *your* village, however you like it.

And actually, our gardens *need* this kind of regular attention if they are going to produce as abundantly as possible. If we don't harvest our vegetables regularly, pick our herbs and flowers regularly and cut our greens regularly, they tend to shift their metabolism and focus on setting seed or going dormant. A rocket patch can provide you with greens for 6 months (see page 66) when carefully tended to and harvested regularly, but left to simply grow, you can be sure it will be flowering and setting seed, its lush leaves giving way to woody stalks, in only a month or two.

All you need are the basics to begin. We are going to arm you with the basics to make your garden a thriving, natural and abundant world, no matter what shape that space takes, and no matter what plants you want to plant. Learn the eight steps to natural garden success (starting page 33) and make your space yours. You do you. Beyond that, look to the wild and the seasons for inspiration. If you see something growing in the wild, often (though not always) you can grow it too. And watching the seasons is where so many simple lessons live. Work with them. Beyond that, experiment, try, fail, try again, succeed, observe and learn. With others, if you can. Gardening is in you, it's in *all* of us. And it's always better when we do it together!

You've got this—it's in your DNA.

For our entire human history prior to the First Agricultural Revolution (which is some 2.5 million years of evolution!), every single one of our ancestors fed themselves exclusively on plants, animals and fungi that lived and bred without intervention. Put simply, they ate wild food. Then, around 12,000 years ago, the agricultural revolution began. We all learn this (or a very similar fact) in school, but what is rarely emphasised is the importance of the word *began*. Actually, it wasn't until just a few thousand years ago that the shift from most people living as hunter-gatherers (who ate only plants, animals and fungi that grew wild) to most people living as farmers/herders (who predominantly ate plants, animals and fungi that they cultivated) occurred.

This means that for 99.9% of the time humans have existed—humans carrying *your* DNA—they have had to know exactly what grows when, how and where, and exactly what to do to sustainably forage and hunt these seasonal abundances year after year after year. Even for the last few thousand years, after the agricultural revolution had run its course and we transitioned to settled agriculture, your ancestors remained incredibly in touch with their natural environment. Almost everyone knew how to milk a cow, or raise a seed from germination to harvest, or heal the sick with various medicinal herbs, or indeed to continue to follow and harvest the wild food abundances that still thrived around them.

It wasn't until just the last 250 or so years that we began to lose this deep relationship with nature, some time after the beginning of the Industrial Revolution. In short, no matter who you are, and no matter where you live, you are but a few generations removed from a life of complete and joyful cooperation with nature.

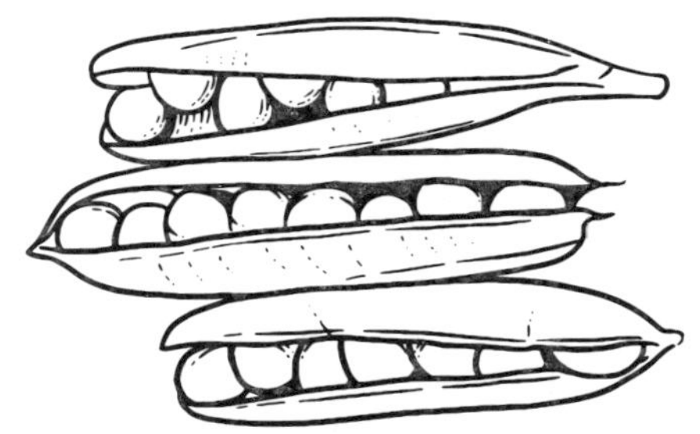

A Sardinian garden (above) and a Pugliese garden (below).

Your abundant village garden.

We want you to know that your abundant village garden, whatever that is, your microcosm of plants and trees and everything growing together, is totally possible. Gardening in our modern world is so often overcomplicated and made to appear as if it's only possible using an unfathomable set of skills and tools, but actually it is the most beautiful and *simple* skill inherent in us all.

Begin to envisage your village garden. The best gardens are always so uniquely beautiful, offering a glimpse into the personality of the gardener—this is when they are at their the best. Just as when you grow older, you become fully you, so does such a garden. Your garden should reflect *you*. If you are wild and free, your garden should be wild and free. If you are calm and orderly, your garden should be calm and orderly. A garden that reflects you will always nurture you and your village. Such gardens, grown using simple, natural methods, are so incredibly satisfying to be in, to work in, and of course to gather and eat from.

Here's a little picture of the abundant village garden in *our* mind, from a diary excerpt during one of our trips to Italy. Why from Italy? Because with their diverse set of truly worshipped, traditional food plants and gleeful predisposition for the good life, we are yet to find another place in the world that nails quite so well the balance between natural wildness, settled village life and the constant pursuit of an abundant harvest.

Matt—Italy, early summer 2017

'There are always common elements in these gardens. A lemon tree, all the old stone-fruit varieties, like flat peaches, mini-apricots and a couple of black cherry trees, several olive trees, multiple orange varieties (red fleshed, navel, valencia), several almond trees and usually also a pecan, a hazelnut, a walnut, a bay laurel. Perhaps a white or pink grapefruit sitting over in the corner. And a row of enormous, ancient rosemary, plus smaller holdings of thyme, various oreganos, winter tarragon, sage.

'Lavender is always somewhere tucked away (the smell!), and a sizeable patch of parsley seems to be in harvestable condition year round. Flat, white and brown cipollini (chip-oh-lee-nee) and large red tropea (trop-ee-ah) onions adorn all the winter patches, beside generous rows of garlic.

'Then there are the broad beans and the poppies, always growing wildly together (the broad beans planted, the electric red poppies just coming up all on their own). And always rows of potatoes, already thriving by mid-spring, with tomatoes, eggplant, capsicums and chillies not far behind them.

'Zucchinis (pale, dark and round) and cucumbers (Lebanese and a furry variety we've never seen elsewhere) are standard. Plus, cucumber melons, a special treat alongside watermelons, green melons and rockmelons. Pumpkins sprawl and kiwi and grapevines creep around the edges, on the fences and over all kinds of simple timber arbours. The artichokes and cardoons are towering by now. Soldier-like grids of lettuces and basil plants stand to attention.

'And the weeds are most often just wild edible plants, such as amaranth, chard, wild garlic and fat hen gone rogue.

'It's a magical, layered world. And it's thriving.'

Natural gardening 101.

Eight steps to natural garden success.

1. Soil—create healthy, living soil.

We begin with soil, because soil is *the most* important element for growing, and soil life is the *key* to the health of your plants. It is not a fixed element like the other all-important factors for gardening success, sun and water. Rather, it is a combination of several incredibly diverse and varied elements. Soil varies greatly depending on where you are, and therefore it is the element that needs the most work to 'get right'. So, what makes a good soil for growing food?

First, look at your soil. Natural, healthy soil has a *look*. An experienced gardener can spot it a mile off. You can gently push a garden fork into it, no effort required. When you wet it, the water soaks in, rather than pooling on the surface or running off. It stays moist, rather than dehydrating too quickly or becoming waterlogged and sticky. When you get close, you can smell it, and it smells fantastic, like a forest floor. When you squeeze healthy, moist soil in your hand, it both holds together *and* crumbles (see Simple mineral component test, page 37). And tiny creatures wriggle through your fingers. Natural soil is both very alive and a very powerful thing.

Natural, healthy soil is made up of various amounts of sand, silt and clay (the mineral components), decayed plant and animal matter, which we call humus (or, more commonly in a garden setting, decomposed compost, manure and mulch), and a great deal of air and water. It is also teeming with microorganisms, mycorrhizal fungi, worms and all manner of tiny (and sometimes not so tiny) insects that are all constantly at work actively decomposing freshly added plant and animal matter, and aerating your soil in the process.

There is a great deal of wiggle room and no fixed recipe or ratio when it comes to creating natural, healthy soil. Plants all over the world grow in all kinds of variations of it every day. But to approximate: **Air and water** make up about 25% each of your total soil structure; **Worms** and all the life *plus* **Humus** make up just 5% combined; and **The mineral components**—sand, silt and clay— make up the final 45%. But these are not fixed percentages. Rather, healthy, wild soils vary in almost every way from location to location depending on several natural factors. The most important thing to know is simply that *every* wild, healthy soil contains at least some of *all* the ingredients, *always*. And plants need that whole recipe to grow—all of the mineral components, regular additions of humus, air and water, worms and all the life. All of it. Let's break it down in order of importance.

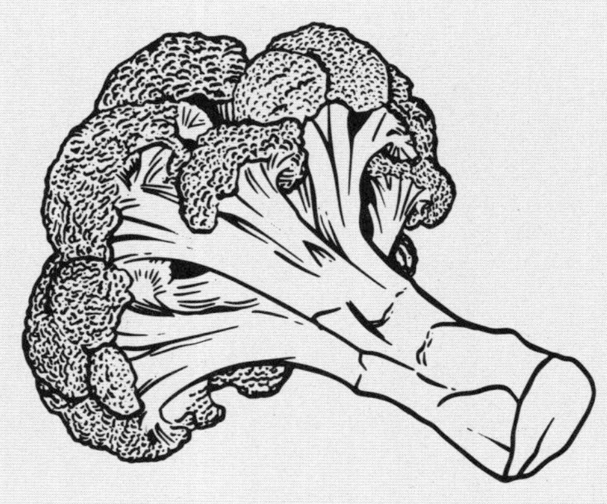

1. Air and water.

Without air and water you have nothing. Well, you have a compacted desert—not ideal conditions for a garden. We have to keep things aerated and moist. Your plants need it and your soil *life* needs it. **Air** is easy—simply keep off your garden beds. Provided you complete all the exercises in this Soil guide, follow the Bed building tips on page 37 and then refrain from placing weight on your beds, air will take care of itself.

For **Water** though, it's important to understand that soil that's been left to get super dry can be quite hydrophobic (water-repellent). You can't plant anything into such a dry soil and it may take a few days to really 'wet down'. The obvious presence of ants or very hard soil are strong signs that your soil is way too dry. In these cases, we need to take steps to *establish* water in our soil when we are starting out. For the *ongoing* water requirements of your garden, see Water, page 50. But first, follow these steps to get your soil wet enough to work with.

Establishing water in your soil.

Day 1. Give your whole garden a really good soak with a gentle overhead sprinkler or hose attachment. You are being the rain. Water, water, water until it just pools on the surface and won't drain away.

Day 2. Dig out a spade's worth of the soil you wet down yesterday. Is it still moist? If it isn't wet below the surface, it probably hasn't been wet for a long time. But now you've at least softened the top crust. Water again until you've reintroduced water deep into your soil and that spadeful is lovely and moist one day after watering. This could take a few days of gentle soaking.

Once your soil is properly wet down, does the water drain away freely, or is the soil getting waterlogged? For waterlogged soils, follow the improvement steps under Condition 3 in the Simple mineral component test on page 37. You will need to build up any poorly draining sections of your garden with lots of compost and manure, and stick to growing shallow-rooted plants, like lettuce and radish, if you want to grow in that soil this season, while the drainage is restoring itself.

2. Worms and all the life.

Once your soil is moist, it's time to bring the *life*. Your soil *needs* life. Castings from worms (and other microorganisms and fungi) are *the most* bioavailable source of nutrients for plants, plus they are the glue that holds the mineral particles of your soil together, allowing them to form what are known as aggregates. These aggregates are like scaffolding in a healthy soil's structure, allowing for a fragile 'openness' to be created by the movement of worms and other microorganisms as they go about their business. That openness—actually a network of tiny capilleries—in turn allows for water to drain freely and air to oxygenate your plants' roots. Without the presence of life in a soil, there are no aggregates thus no structure, nothing to form capilleries thus no openness, no drainage, no breathability. Soil *life* is the key to it all.

Worms are the best indicator of your soil's level of life. Follow these steps to check if they are present and address it if they're not.

Establishing worms in your soil.

You may have answered this during the Establishing water exercise (left). Have you been seeing worms in your moist spadeful of soil? If yes, you've nailed it. Your work is done. If not, read on.

Day 1. Wet a section of your soil one more time as in the water exercise, but this time cover it with a thick layer of straw mulch after you've wet it.

Day 2. Pull back the straw, dig out a spadeful of soil, then go looking for worms in it. The moisture and presence of the mulch should have drawn them to the surface to eat. If you can't find any worms, then it seems your soil has become a bit lifeless. Now that you are activating your soil by following the exercises in this Soil guide, the life will return. But it would be worth adding a box of worms from your nursery or dug out of a friend's compost pile.

Just dig a few holes throughout your garden, each about 30 cm deep, place a handful of worms in each, and gently cover back over with soil.

3. Humus.

Humus comes next because humus is the food that *feeds* your soil life. In the vast majority of cases, we don't believe that soil should be brought into a garden. Rather, we believe that the key to turning the soil you *have* into a thriving garden soil, capable of producing a continuous, abundant harvest, is regular applications of humus, in the form of compost, manure and mulch. Plants are made primarily of carbon and nitrogen, and it is these components that are added when you bring in compost, manure and mulch. When you do so you are reflecting the natural processes of a forest, constantly building upon your soil and giving your worms, microorganisms and fungi the food they need to get to work. It's a cycle, where new humus is added, your soil life transforms it into food for your plants, new plants grow up to feed you, the scraps go into your compost to break down, you add that compost, along with manure and straw mulch back to the garden, and the cycle repeats again:

Establishing humus in your soil.

Playing your part in the humus cycle is simple. Just give your soil an extra generous addition of compost and manure at least once every year. The way we do it is simply to feed the garden with compost and manure every time we replant a given area, and then mulch those new plantings once they are mature enough to do so (more information on mulching, page 53). And for established areas of perennial plants (like fruit orchards and perennial herbs such as rosemary and sage), we simply feed and mulch them once a year, usually over winter (the only season we seem to have the time!).

The manure of grazing animals (cows, horses etc.) is our favourite type of manure as it is most gentle on our plants (and abundant for us locally). And the compost we use always comes from our compost pile, which we feed with kitchen scraps, fallen leaves, chicken manure and straw from when we clean out the chicken hutch and grass throughout the year, but you can also purchase organic compost from your local nursery.

For more extensive guides on the different types of manures and how to successfully and easily make your own compost, please check out our first book.

4. The mineral components.

The final soil ingredients are **The mineral components** —sand, silt and clay. The ratio of sand : silt : clay in your soil is the variable that defines how it will naturally perform. Sand, silt and clay are all of the same origin—formed as rocks break down over time into consecutively smaller and smaller particles. Sand is the largest particle of the three. Silt is finer than sand, and clay is finer than silt. Let's step through each component, one at a time, and then learn a simple test to give you a general picture of your soil's mineral breakdown and how best to work with what you've got:

Sand. Sand doesn't absorb much water, and the large particles also don't fit very neatly together, so particularly sandy soils are naturally very free draining. But sand doesn't offer your plants much nutrition either, as the minerals are bound up in particles too large for them to access. So, particularly sandy soils will require generous applications of manure to bring them to life.

Clay. At the other end of the spectrum, clay is extremely nutrient-rich. The mineral particles are tiny and hugely bioavailable to your plants' roots and soil life, and clay can also absorb and retain a massive amount of water (which is great for keeping a stable, moist environment). But clay particles are *so* fine that, if not treated with care, they can easily clog up those all-important oxygenating/drainage capillaries (see Worms and all the life, page 35).

Also, when wet, clay is extremely malleable (remember art class?) and will easily compress into a solid block when stepped on. And if a clay-rich soil is watered too heavily or with too much force, the tiny particles tend to settle into every little nook and cranny without leaving any gaps, setting the surface like cement.

Silt. Silt has properties somewhere between sand and clay. It is much finer than sand, so offers more nutrition. And it is *almost* as fine as clay, so can absorb and retain a lot of water, but without running the risk of setting hard or waterlogging. Silt is the happy medium.

Simple mineral component test.

It's easy to work out the balance of sand, silt and clay in your soil. Grab a little handful of your garden soil and wet it little by little, kneading it in your palm until it comes together to form a golf-ball sized ball. Then slowly press your thumb into it:

1. It won't even form a ball when sufficiently moist.	Your soil is super sandy. It will require a generous addition of manure and a reasonable addition of compost to bring it to life. This will improve water retention and provide enough fertility for your plants to thrive. You are starting with potentially amazing drainage, but poor fertility.
2. When you press into the ball, it crumbles quite completely.	Your soil is sandy and likely quite silt-heavy, but clay-poor. A good base, but not super fertile. It will require a reasonable addition of compost and manure in equal parts to improve structure and moisture retention. You are starting with a potentially great all-round soil, it just needs a bit of a lift.
3. When you press into the ball, it makes a perfect indentation without even thinking about cracking. It's like art class all over again.	Your soil is clay-heavy and will require a generous addition of compost to improve drainage and stop the surface from setting hard when it dries. We would also recommend introducing a lot of worms—especially if they weren't obviously present in the Establishing worms exercise on page 35—and some manure. The worms will get to work forming healthy capillaries to assist drainage even further and they (and other bugs) love manure. You are starting with potentially amazing fertility, but poor drainage.
4. When you press into the ball, it cracks but holds together.	You've hit the jackpot. You have a great balance between sand, silt, clay and humus. This is exactly where you want to start out. Seems you (or someone else) has been gardening here for a while. Keep doing what you're doing.

Final step: you are now ready to build your garden beds.

Firstly, we want to make a quick note regarding soil depth. It is super important that the soil in your garden beds is readily workable to a depth of at least 40 cm. When we say readily workable, we mean that a garden fork will happily slide in when you lean forward with your body weight. Without at least this much room to move, your plants' root systems simply cannot grow as they need to.

Below the 40 cm should be more soil for your plants to tap into, but that can be firmer (not rock hard—it still needs to drain water away!). It's just the top 40 cm that needs to be easily workable. Follow these steps to make it happen. But if your soil is simply too hard to obtain this kind of performance, or if you live in an area that has hardly any soil to work with at all (such as particularly rocky areas), that would be the only time we would encourage a one-off bulk addition of topsoil to establish your growing beds.

1. You want to form new garden beds so that they are at least slightly higher than the surrounding area to improve drainage. For the main section of your garden, these surrounding ditches will become your pathways.

2. Define your bed area (don't form any beds wider than you can comfortably reach halfway into to weed), then fork over the whole space deeply (push in a fork, pull it backwards, at about 15-20 cm intervals—a broadfork is particularly helpful here). Include 0.5 m around the space for a perimeter pathway).

3. Top-dress with compost and manure.

4. Dig out soil from around the bed spaces (the paths) and turn that soil onto the beds, to form shallow ditches around your beds and increase the depth of the beds themselves.

5. Rake the surface and edges even. Remember you are aiming for a working depth of at least 40 cm of soil. If this method hasn't created enough workable depth in your bed, you may need to bring in some topsoil to achieve it.

2. Sun—position your garden in the sun.

Basically, every food plant likes full sun. Simple as that! They will grow best with full-on heat. *Some* flowers might burn, but the *plants* love the sun! So, position them in it. A plant that receives zero direct sunlight will grow unfathomably slowly. Such shady places are for rainforest-type house plants only. Unfortunately, this means that if your only outdoor area is a south-facing balcony in the southern hemisphere (or a north-facing balcony in the northern hemisphere) house plants are your only option.

If you find that your plants are standing tall but their flowers are getting burnt by the sun, provide shade with shade cloth or tall-growing plants around them, such as sunflowers or corn. You can also spray a natural sunscreen on your plants' leaves and flowers by diluting fine clay (potter's clay) in water until it forms a milky liquid (note that this will add a milky tint to your flowers!). Incidentally, this is also a great caterpillar deterrent.

If your plants' leaves are thin, wilted, dry or parched, check out the first troubleshooting tip on page 98. You have a lack-of-water problem, not a too-much-sun problem—you're just not watering enough.

3. Plan—lay out your garden like they do in the traditional village.

Village gardens (see diary entry, page 31) are human-sized gardens that get squeezed into every single vacant plot of earth possible. In fact, sometimes it feels as if entire villages are organised on the same organic principle as a forest: fill every space possible in some useful way. In these places, no matter how small a space, you will witness someone lovingly carve out an edible garden, always a beautiful combination of orchard and vegetable patch—the trees and the plants as one single edible landscape. Here's how.

Placing your productive trees/vines in and around your garden.

First, we establish our 'structure' by deciding on where to place our trees and vines, the largest and longest-living members of the garden. Scatter your choice of fruit and nut trees/vines, bay laurel, lemon verbena and the like throughout your space at least 3 m apart from each other (see planting tips, page 46). They can be espaliered along fence lines, against walls and on all kinds of trellises and arbours (vines are especially fantastic for this), but make sure you always observe the minimum 3 m rule. By spacing trees and vines at least 3 m apart in every direction (further apart is fine, just not closer), we allow them to grow large while still allowing plenty of space between and beneath for lower-growing plants to thrive.

Importantly, while your vegetables will take as much sun as they can get, they will still do very well when planted under trees in this way, because the movement of the sun means they will still get plenty of direct sunlight. It is totally normal for plants to grow under trees—it is the law of the jungle.

Trees towards the edge of your garden can be allowed to grow larger than those in the middle, which otherwise may shade out the plants below. Trees placed to the south of your garden in the southern hemisphere, or the north in the northern hemisphere, can be allowed to grow the biggest of all because they can only shade out plants directly below them. Evergreens, like citrus, olives and bay laurel are best planted to the edges of your garden because they tend to be quite shady, but this won't be a problem if kept small. The only exceptions to all of this are the large nut trees: walnut, chestnut, hazelnut and pecan. Unless you have a larger space, these trees are best avoided. See Seasonal planting charts, page 79.

Monty, Joe and Raven's garden in Melbourne (top left); a little garden of lettuce, parsley, onions and pumpkins in Calabria (top right); and Julia and Klaas's garden in Tasmania (bottom).

Placing your bushy perennial plants in and around your garden.

Then come the perennial plants (plants that live for many years). Perennial plants maintain a natural, healthy order, and are thus absolutely key to natural gardening success. Perennial plants, like rhubarb, globe artichokes, cardoons, asparagus, rosemary, oregano, thyme, sage, marjoram, lavender and flowering fennel (see Seasonal planting charts, page 79), should take the form of wild clusters of plants, planted closer to the edge of your space, leaving the main area open for the more labour-intensive annuals. Perennials planted 'off to the side' like this will:

Give you flexibility. You will still be able to weed, fork over or even completely renovate the main space without disturbing your perennials.

Provide habitat. They will provide consistent habitat for small reptiles, amphibians and birds who are your main allies when it comes to natural pest control.

Attract all the good bugs. They will consistently attract good bugs and distract or repel pests (especially true for your perennial flowers and herbs), helping to protect your annual crops when they are in their fragile early stages of growth.

Provide a buffer. If you don't establish this outer ring of protective plants, your garden is thrown completely out of balance every time you turn it over to plant a new crop. They are the nonnas and nonnos of the garden, keeping everything steady.

Placing your annual crops in your garden.

Your annual crops are all the vegetables, herbs and flowers that live less than a year, and so have to be planted anew every season (which includes most of the vegetables, herbs and flowers that we all know and love!). Between and beneath your trees, vines and perennial plants, it's time to define your pathways and build up your garden beds (see Building garden beds tips, page 37). Your beds will likely take the form of irregularly scattered blocks placed wherever there is open space and formed into whatever shape that open space takes.

Plantings into these beds will usually take the form of neat little blocks of neat little rows, but there are no fixed rules—the idea is simply to fill the bed spaces up (if you don't, nature will—with a weed), without *overfilling* them. The most successful plantings in your annual beds will be spaced 'just so'—so that when everything matures, there is really no space between each plant at all, and everything has been able to grow to its full size (follow the steps on page 46 when transplanting delicate seedlings). Every plant has its specific spacing needs based on the size it will grow to (see Plant specifics charts, page 84). At the beginning, there might be quite large open spaces between your seedlings that you will have to maintain and weed, but after the initial growth period is over and the garden has settled in for the season, there is little space for weeds to take hold, and very little maintenance.

To help you fill out your new annual space, here's what *we* do, as an example. See the Seasonal planting charts on page 79 for all your options, including how to adapt the planting times to suit your climate.

LATE WINTER

As winter nears its end we begin a new growing season. In the greenhouse we plant trays of lettuce, basil, kale, tomatoes, chillies, capsicums and eggplants, plus loads of beneficial flowers like Queen Anne's lace, marigolds, calendula, cosmos, violas, borage and more. We tidy the garden and sow our first little patches of carrots, beetroot and radish, plus little rows of peas, dill and chard here, coriander, spinach and parsley there.

EARLY SPRING

Just a few weeks later, it's time for more seedling trays to be filled. This time fast-growing zucchini, pumpkin, cucumber, corn, beans, zinnias, nasturtiums, cosmos and sunflowers. Our first plantings are up and running—and growing fast. Actually, the radishes are growing so fast they will be ready to harvest in just another week or two!

LATE SPRING

After the danger of frost has passed it's time for all of our summer seedlings to go into the ground. In go the tomatoes (see page 66), chillies, capsicums and eggplants. A block of corn goes here and a block of sunflowers there, the corn with beans (see page 61) at their base to climb up over them all summer. In, too, go our dahlia tubers.

More roots get their own little patches. Some carrots here, more beets there, sprouting potatoes in one corner, a sweet potato crate (see page 73) in another. A plot of cucumbers with an angled trellis to creep up on and some parsley underneath (so their fruits will dangle down for easy picking while their leaves shade the parsley from the fierce summer sun). A couple of pumpkin plants are set to climb up ladders all the way to the top of the shed and all over that too! And zucchinis (see page 66) and melons sprawl and shade the base of our fruit trees.

In all the gaps we plant more soft herbs like dill, parsley, basil and coriander, all the greens like lettuce, chard, rocket (see page 66), mizuna, tatsoi, amaranth and Portuguese summer—or 'tronchuda'—kale and, perhaps most importantly, all the pest-distracting and good-bug attracting flower seedlings from the greenhouse.

EARLY SUMMER

In early summer we are already getting started on our winter plantings, starting seedling trays of the very slow growing celery, celeriac and brussels sprouts. The garden is really filling out now and our early planted crops are in full harvest.

LATE SUMMER

By late summer, such a garden is a wilderness. It's time to prepare the main winter crops. We start seedlings of broccoli, cauliflower, winter kales, cabbages, foxgloves, poppies and snapdragons. We've been regularly planting little patches of radish, lettuce, dill and coriander and the harvest of everything is in full swing.

EARLY AUTUMN

When autumn arrives, things are complete chaos in our garden (in a good way!). This is the most abundant time, so much is in season and we are preserving like mad for winter. We make space to plant our seedlings of celery, celeriac, fennel, brussels sprouts, broccoli, cauliflower, kale, cabbage, foxgloves and snapdragons. We fill any gaps with onions, French shallots and garlic, and plant new root seeds. We plant climbing peas and sweet peas at the base of the climbing beans and around the base of the sunflowers too, so they will climb up and over the dried stalks of summer's corn and sunflowers as vigorously in the cooler months as the beans did in summer. And we sow fennel, lupins, larkspur and yarrow.

LATE AUTUMN

Just before winter, the first frosts arrive, marking the end of our summer crops. The garden has seen an explosion of life. The winter crops are nearly mature and ready to sit and feed us over winter, the dead zucchinis, cucumbers, tomatoes, capsicums and eggplants have been cleared, pumpkins and beans harvested and broad beans and poppies (see page 62) planted in their place. Our trees and vines are a year older and going dormant. Everything settles for another year, a time for rest.

~~~

Just like in the wild, diversity is king and there is always something to harvest.

Follow these basic principles and you too will be rewarded with a highly productive, healthy space, no matter how big or small, with your trees and plants sharing root zones happily. Despite often challenging conditions and limited space, it filled us with joy, over and over, to see how abundantly such gardens yielded all over the world and how happy they made their gardeners and their villages.
~~~

It took the two of us just six days over a couple of months to establish this garden, including raising all the seedlings in our makeshift greenhouse, forming the beds, laying irrigation, planting everything and mulching (the pears were already established), then 5–10 minutes a day since to maintain. You can do this!

4. Plant—handle seedlings and young trees/vines with care.

This point is all about you, the gardener. Something we've always found really difficult to communicate is how important it is to *feel* plants when you're working with them. We cannot stress enough how vital it is to handle plants with soft hands. To take your time and tend to your garden with care. We don't believe anyone has a greener thumb than anyone else. It all just comes down to taking the time to pay attention, really experiencing the process each time and improving your understanding of your plants a little more with each interaction.

Use soft hands when transplanting seedlings and young trees. Handle those young plants like you would handle any young life—with care and attention. Support them fully. Move gently. There is nothing worse for a young plant than to be handled brutally. It is such a fragile stage of life, and root systems just aren't designed to be exposed to the air, let alone handled, so we need to do everything we can to reduce the damage. It's a joy to watch the tender love and care of an older gardener at work, handling and tending to their young plants. We believe we all have this soft touch within us. Channel that. Embrace it. There's wildness in gentleness. And nature is rarely in a hurry.

To successfully plant a seedling.

1. Always gently water young plants and seedlings, and the soil they are being transplanted into, immediately before and immediately after you perform a transplant.

2. Plant young seedlings deep in the ground, so that the most upper part of their root system is at least 4–5 cm beneath the surface of the soil, at least up to their first set of true leaves—bury the cotyledons.

3. Press firmly around your newly planted seedling so it is supported, then form an earth rim around the outside of it, so that the seedling is sitting in a little crater. This will help to retain moisture and make for easy watering.

4. Immediately water your seedling in with a generous, gentle watering. This will help to settle moist earth around its roots, preventing shock from the exposure to air.

To successfully plant a fruit or nut tree/vine.

1. Dig out a hole that is at least twice as wide and deep as the pot your tree/vine is in.

2. Place composted manure from a grazing animal (cow, sheep, horse etc.) in the bottom of the hole.

3. Water the hole and water the tree/vine, which eases root shock dramatically.

4. Carefully place the tree/vine in the hole and backfill it with the soil you removed. The young tree/vine trunk should now be sitting lower in the soil than it was in the pot. The soil level that was previously the top of the pot should now be 10–15 cm beneath the earth to ensure the fragile roots nearest the suface have plenty of protection.

5. Press firmly around your newly planted tree/vine so it is supported, then form an earth rim around the outside of it, so that your tree/vine is sitting in a little crater. This will help to retain moisture and make for easy watering.

6. Immediately water your seedling in with a *generous*, gentle watering. This will help to settle moist earth around its roots, preventing shock from the exposure to air.

Marchela's cranberries in Veneto (top); Roberto's black cherry tree in Puglia (bottom); and our dahlias on the farm (opposite).

5. Water—you can't not water.

Throughout the hottest months of the year in our temperate climate, we water our garden throughout the day via an automatic drip system. It delivers just 2–3 minutes of water drips every hour on the hour, from sunrise to sunset, quite literally drip-feeding our plants the moisture they need only *when* they need it, and directly to their roots *where* they need it most.

Our drippers emit 900 ml of water each per day when set to 3-minute bursts during the peak watering period in summer, so that's 330 litres per day during this rainless period for our incredibly abundant two-person, 75 m^2 garden. That may sound like a lot, but over the course of the year (accounting for cooler weather and rain) it averages out to just 80 litres per person per day. Just four buckets of water per person per day to raise all of the food plants you need. Unfortunately though, many people really underestimate how much water their food plants need to thrive, and under-watering is for sure the top problem we diagnose in people's ailing gardens.

Your food plants need access to water *whenever* the sun is shining down on them. Mature plants and trees have deep roots, and provided that deep root zone is getting replenished with moisture every few days, they will be fine. But young and small plants have only small root systems, so you can't expect them to thrive unless they are given frequent waterings during hot, dry weather—at least one generous watering each morning or, even better, multiple tiny waterings throughout the day.

Watering by hand is fine, just water each plant at its base with a gentle flow of water, like the shower setting of a spray gun. But we always recommend drip lines and an automatic system for larger gardens, or if you are time-poor. They reduce water use so much, and make life so much easier.

If you don't have access to a water source, have limited water, or need to plant out a remote part of your space, away from your normal watering setup, see page 65 for our favourite dry-climate loving plants, trees and vines that require little water. These are all super hardy, abundantly productive plants, even when treated harshly, and we've witnessed them *thriving* in the most improbable of places.

But assuming you have access to *some* water (see note on town water, opposite, if that's your only option—provided it's not overly chlorinated, it's still a good option), let's look at some watering basics.

Water needs vary massively throughout the year. Let's step it out.

When to water.

If you live in a temperate or cooler/mountain climate, mid-spring to mid-autumn is watering time. If you live in the tropics, the dry season is your watering time. If you live in the subtropics, and experience abundant summer rains and mild winters with regular rains also, you may not water much at all.

No matter where you live though, the rule is the same: once the day's peak temperatures begin to surpass 25°C in the shade, any plant growing in your garden needs a daily watering equivalent of 5 mm rain (the rainfall equivalent to the drip system descibed opposite). Plants will happily withstand the hottest sun, provided they have this water to draw upon. But if their leaves look floppy and thin, they are dehydrated, overheating and burning.

Your plants should never look wilted in the sunshine. Ever. If you receive more than 5 mm of rain on a hot day, then there's no need to water. If not, water. You are watering enough if your plants are still looking good during the peak heat of the day. It's that simple.

Watering in cooler weather.

In our temperate South-East Australian climate, we find we don't water at all from about mid-autumn until well into spring because the sun's ferocity has begun to ease and these are *usually* our wettest times of the year.

But we do still water *some* plants in autumn and spring. These are still times of planting, and we still baby our little seedlings while they establish themselves. We keep freshly planted seeds or seedlings moist with a little watering every day until they are up and running. In the case of seedlings, water daily until their leaves have darkened to a deeper green (this means that they are 'tapped-in', i.e. they have grown new roots and are now drawing nutrition and water from your soil).

And if you're in an area that experiences dry winters, you may even still need to water your *mature* plants during this time. Plant vigour is always the measure. Always provide enough water so that your plants look happy (not floppy) in the sunshine.

Quick water troubleshooting guide.

1. If your plants look floppy/curled in and thin, water more.

2. If your plants keep bolting to flower instead of being the leafy greens and herbs they should be, water more.

3. If your soil is dry 5 cm under the surface, water more.

4. If your fruit trees are hardly setting any fruit, water more.

5. If your fruit trees are dropping all their fruit, water more.

6. If your zucchinis/cucumbers aren't uniform in shape, water more consistently.

7. If your tomatoes keep splitting, water more consistently.

8. And the rare one: if your plant's leaves look curled in but not thin, check for standing water under the surface of the soil, as your plants may be waterlogged.

See page 98 for further troubleshooting tips regarding both under-watering and over-watering.

A little note on the cost of town water.

A 150 m^2 garden is capable of providing a family of four with all the vegetables they could possibly need. This is no small veggie patch, but even that, in the peak of summer, paying full urban water prices and not recycling any greywater or capturing any rainfall, would cost less than three dollars to irrigate each day. If we average the cost over the *entire* year, it equates to not even two dollars per day (less than fifty cents per person!), or just over ten dollars per week for four people. In rural areas, water prices are lower, and so the cost would be even less. No matter which way you look at it, it's a very small price to pay for all the fresh organic produce you can eat!

6. Mulch—to ease the pressure.

Exposed, dry soil in a field quickly loses its rich upper layer (or 'topsoil') simply by it blowing or washing away. These are the processes of erosion and desertification at work, and modern farming has gone a long way to encouraging them by relentlessly ploughing fields, leaving the surface unvegetated and vulnerable. In contrast, in a forest, more and more topsoil is constantly being *created*, as leaves fall from trees to form a natural mulch layer on the forest floor, and worms, microorganisms and fungi get to work decaying that plant matter, building soil humus in the process (see page 34). A home garden is far less exposed than an open field, but still there are many lessons from this comparison. Here's why mulching is key to gardening success.

It stops weeds. Mulch prevents weeds from competing with your plants during their main growth stage.

For moisture. Mulch retains so much moisture.

For your worms. Mulch both cools the soil and provides a food source, allowing worms to get to work producing castings and aerating the soil right up in the top of your plants' root zones.

For added humus. Mulch adds a whole lot of carbon to your garden soil, the key building block of life (see Humus, page 36).

Mulch with: straw, pulled weeds (before they've set seed!) or leaves (natural, soft debris, just like the falling leaves of a forest), rather than woodchips (this kind of mechanically created hard debris is far less beneficial to your garden). You can also mulch with manure from horse stables, which will often dry to form a wonderful thick but water-penetrable layer when exposed to the sun. Or you can mulch with composted grape marc (the dried skins, pulp and seeds left over after winemaking).

If you have a balanced soil structure, even if a little clay heavy (see Simple mineral component test, page 37), you can also just carefully maintain the upper layer of soil *as* a mulch. This will form a breathable crust if watered directly and then left undisturbed. Such an earth-mulch can still retain a great deal of moisture, despite the garden looking unprotected (see picture opposite). However, this technique offers no weed or wind protection, so it only really works well in very established, protected gardens.

7. Allow wildness—to create balance.

Nature isn't about being perfect, and neither is gardening. Your garden doesn't always need to be perfectly weed free and manicured. In nature, there is always something flowering, something creeping, something shading this or overrunning that. Here's how you can allow wildness in your garden to make life a whole lot easier.

Allow self-seeding. Let all kinds of vegetables shoot to flower and even set seed in the garden. This provides nectar for your bees and attracts all the good bugs, which in turn creates balance and a buffer against pest attack. One of our main aims in starting a *new* garden is to actually establish our very own 'food weeds'—edible plants, normally looked upon as domesticated, that have found their own sustainable routine of appearing and growing each season with less and less input from us. We allow the following plants to go to seed in the garden, and they happily reseed themselves year after year: parsley, chervil, leek, lettuce (we transplant self-seeded lettuce seedlings throughout the garden to grow out), amaranth, potato, Jerusalem artichoke, cape gooseberry, tomatillo, poppies, sweet peas, nasturtium, dill, borage and Queen Anne's lace. See Seasonal planting charts, page 79.

Embrace wild-like flowers. Let your garden be full of wild-like flowers (flowers that grow tall and wild and exceptionally beautifully), like dahlias, zinnias, sunflowers, violas, cosmos, scabiosas, forget-me-nots, marigolds, calendula, nasturtium, Queen Anne's lace, borage, foxgloves, yarrow, sweet peas and snapdragons. They bring in the good bugs, add loads of colour and just make you feel good (see guide on page 74).

Grow your own spice seeds. Wild-like spice plants are also fantastic. Think coriander, mustard, sesame, poppy, love-in-a-mist (nigella), anise, cumin, caraway, dill, fennel and celery. Aesthetically, they're amazing. Bee and bug-wise, they're amazing. And in your dinner, they're the *most* amazing. See Seasonal planting charts, page 79.

Allow natural growth. Let things crawl and creep all over each other, up each other and around each other, allowing everything to kind of merge into everything else. It's the natural way and will foster a teeming support crew of insects, birds, amphibians and reptiles to keep everything healthy and in balance.

Embrace your weeds. For sure you are the curator of your garden, and it is your job to foster the plants *you* want, and literally weed out the competitors (most weeds can be pulled and simply laid about as mulch). But there are some wonderful edible weeds you can leave to grow in the garden, especially in the cooler months. Our favourites are fat hen, mallow, wood sorrel, stinging nettle, dandelion, shepherd's purse and wild radish.

A diverse garden, allowed to grow naturally and a little wildly, will be a healthy garden every time. And the healthier the garden, the less maintenance required. The daily dance should be just a little massage of this here, an adjustment of that there. Not some back-breaking endeavour every day to control natural processes. Once your garden has an established element of wildness and has settled into that balance, the 'work' gets easier and becomes less with every passing season. Nurture that wildness. Embrace it.

8. Control pests and problems *naturally*.

Gardening the natural way creates incredibly robust plants. But that doesn't mean a natural garden is impenetrable. Here are our top tips for keeping everything in great health and as bulletproof as possible. If you're experiencing a particular garden dilemma, head to our Natural 'pest' control chart (page 98). It includes all of the most common garden ailments that we've encountered along the way, either in our garden or someone else's. But first, these are the key things applicable to all gardens, in no particular order. Follow these 'rules' and your garden will thrive.

Don't use chemicals.

Yeah, we know you're not into that stuff, but seriously. Don't use slug baits. Even if they say they are natural, they're not—how do you think they kill the slugs? Don't go anywhere *near* glyphosate to control creeping grasses like couch. And not just in your food garden, *anywhere*—it will wreak havoc on your soil life, and remember soil life is *the* key to the health of your plants (see Worms and all the life, page 35). Don't use synthetic fertilisers, or petroleum oils like white oil, or purified mineral compounds like wettable sulphur and copper sulphate. None of these are in any way at home in a garden. Just because they are naturally occurring or naturally derived, doesn't mean they are a natural addition to your *garden*. They all rapidly accumulate in soil, and the imbalance can take years to break down. You would never encounter them in a wild forest—they just don't belong.

Diversity is key.

The more diverse the plants in your garden, the more forest-like it is, the more balanced and robust it will be (see page 54). Monocultures (just growing one variety of plant) are severely unstable. Embrace plant diversity, and *always* plant beneficial flowers, such as Queen Anne's lace, cosmos, nasturtiums, borage, marigolds, dill, coriander, garlic chives and calendula (see full list of beneficial flowers, page 93), as well as powerful and useful perennials, like rosemary, wormwood and lavender throughout or nearby your garden. They not only attract beneficial insects (your most powerful ally in controlling pest insects), but they also distract pest insects away from your food plants and provide shelter for small birds, amphibians and reptiles (your second most powerful ally in controlling pest insects). Bushy natives and fruiting creepers, like kiwi, passionfruit, grapes and the various berries, are also a fantastic addition to the garden. All are ideal for attracting small-bird populations (see Placing trees/vines and bushy perennial plants, pages 40–42).

Nutrition is key.

A healthy garden is a happy garden. Plants that are exceptionally healthy will not succumb to common garden ailments. It's all about the cellular level. If you can make your plants robust on a cellular level, many diseases and tiny pests just won't be able to penetrate them. Fungal diseases, for instance, work by infiltrating your plants' cells and proceeding to feed parasitically off them. If those cells can't be infiltrated, the fungal disease can't take hold. That's why some zucchini/summer squash plants succumb to powdery mildew, while others don't, and some stone fruit trees succumb to leaf curl, and others don't. There is nothing inherently wrong with the variety of zucchini/squash or fruit tree, or the genetics of the ailing specimens, they are just, in that moment, run-down and thus not vigorous enough to keep out the fungus. Plants that are generously fed with composts and manures (especially from grazing animals, like cows, horses, sheep etc.—see Soil, page 34), and that are neither under-watered nor waterlogged (see Water, page 50), will be very unlikely to succumb to diseases and small pests. And pests will *always* destroy the least-healthy plants first—seems it's the order of the jungle. So, if a plant is being attacked, consider that it might not be doing so well health-wise and try to address that first.

Of course, if it's the fruit of a vibrantly healthy tomato plant or peach tree being eaten, there is nothing wrong with your plant/tree—head straight to page 99 for our tips on controlling hungry birds and possums!

Don't get disheartened when starting out.

We recently moved and started *another* farm (this will be our fourth), and it was a great reminder of how hard it can be to establish balance in an empty garden. When we first turned over our new garden, it was like every bug in the world had been waiting for that day. It was spring, it was moist and everything we put in the ground got eaten, by slugs especially, over and over again. They were far less reckless than you'd think. In fact, they quite naturally would focus all their attention on the weakest plants and lowest leaves, leaving the growth points untouched. So, they didn't usually *kill* our new plantings, but the natural order of the garden was still way out of balance, so it really slowed down initial growth.

It reminded us how hard it can be in the beginning, to be patient in these early stages and to not give up! In fact, it will only ever take a month or two to establish a natural balance in a brand-new garden (remember, balance is the key!) if you simply follow the eight steps to Natural gardening success outlined in this chapter and the troubleshooting techniques in the charts beginning on page 98. Once your plants mature, they won't be too fussed by the early damage, we promise. In short, keep an especially close eye on young, fragile seedlings, and just keep working on creating natural balance—once you are established, life is good.

A note on patience and observation.

We humans seem geared to overreact. It's like that pot on the stove, when the recipe tells you not to stir, and all you want to do is stir that pot. Well, we urge you to fight that feeling. Just as we urge you to allow things to grow a little more wildly and fend for themselves a little more, the same goes for responding to perceived pests—watch before you *do* anything.

Sometimes, an apparent insect infestation that looks like it just *has* to be eating everything, isn't actually causing any damage at all. Sometimes, there is indeed damage occurring, but it is really nowhere near enough to warrant intervention—healthy, mature plants can withstand a lot, and pests will only go for the weakest plants. Other times, the threat is indeed real, but within a few days nature will step in and restore balance without you having to lift a finger.

We once experienced an infestation of grey aphids on our newly planted and just flowering peach trees. They were all over the trees and beginning to suck the life out of all the tender, new growth. We wanted to panic. But instead we waited. And just two days later, the ailing trees were recovering. Turns out the local ladybug population had become aware of the problem before us, a mass of ladybug larvae had been hatched and before we knew it the problem was gone. The new ladybugs dispersed to do other great work throughout the new garden, and every year after that the aphids never even got a chance to breed—the ladybugs were all over it. Nature is intelligent beyond our comprehension. Always be patient, step back and give it a chance first. Then be there to help only when needed.

Planting projects.

Eight fun ideas to inspire you and show you how to use different growing methods to fill the extra space in *your* village garden.

NOTE.

These projects are based on our temperate South-East Australian climate, but the majority are fantastic for all climate zones. See the chart on page 79 for information on how to adapt planting times to your climate.

1. Beans for a year.

Growing your own 'dried' beans, such as borlotti beans, cannellini beans and kidney beans, is next-level delicious. In Australia, it's difficult to buy these fresh at markets, and our farmers just don't grow enough beans. So we've taken to growing our own! You can also grow and dry your own peas, broad beans and chickpeas super easily.

Key tips.

Choose climbing bean varieties. Climbing varieties are the way to go, as they will give maximum yield in a given space.

Yields to expect. Climbing beans yield about 1 kg of dried beans per 8 m row of plants spaced 10–15 cm apart.

Provide a trellis. Climbing beans will climb on pretty much anything you give them to climb on (over water tanks, on fences, up walls), and reach as high as the trellis/mesh you provide. You can also plant tall annual crops for them to climb on. For example, plant beans with corn in a richly compost-fed bed, and the corn will provide a natural trellis for the beans as they grow.

Their ability to climb makes them a fantastic choice in small spaces as you are utilising as much vertical space as possible!

Planting companions. Other great bean companions are potato and zucchini, as both of these low-growing plants will shade the earth at the base of the beans. Just let the beans get going before planting the companion crop (to prevent the companion crop from smothering the bean plants in their early stages of growth).

Plant direct for maximum yield. For maximum yield, plant beans directly into the garden from seed. Plant seeds in late spring, one week before the danger of frost has passed. If you are a bit late to get started though, beans can also be planted as seedlings. Plant bean seedlings *after* the danger of frost has passed.

To eat fresh. Pick when the beans inside the pods are plump and ready. Simply pod and they're ready to cook right away (there's no need to soak freshly podded beans before cooking).

Freshly podded beans also cook much faster than dried beans and will be extra butter-soft and delicious when ready to eat. We pick, pod, cook and eat fresh beans like this throughout the season.

To store. Let the beans dry on the plant, then harvest them all at once. Place all your harvested beans in a sack and hit the sack all over with a heavy stick to break the dry pods apart. Carefully, pour the beans out of the sack (they should come out first because they are heavier than the dry pods), then pick out any bits of dry pod that came out with them, and store the beans in sealed jars on the shelf.

2. A field of broad beans and poppies.

These little fields were the most incredible sight in Italy. This is super clever, because they're two plants that can be left to grow wild and self-seed year after year. Additionally, growing broad beans (or other pulses) underneath perennial plants like fruit trees and vines, gives an awesome boost of nitrogen into the soil—so this is a fantastic project underneath an established fruit orchard or vineyard. This is our favourite 'wild' patch, and it is super abundant. There are also lessons you can take from this for your garden in general as you watch the two plants grow alongside each other, complementing each other, as other plants can too.

1. Plant. Unfortunately neither broad beans nor poppies will do well in the tropics. But in all other climates, plant your broad beans and poppies, from seed, at the same time in autumn.

Space broad beans 15 cm apart, in furrows spaced about 50 cm apart, then very lightly broadcast (scatter) your poppy seeds over the top of the area. Rake the entire area over to cover with soil, then generously water in.

2. Grow. Keep your broad bean and poppy field moist until the seeds germinate and the plants are up and strong, then the patch should be fine to take care of itself with the help of autumn/winter/spring rains (we'll leave that to your judgement though—if they look like they need water, water—see Water, page 50).

3. Harvest. Harvest both broad beans and poppies in spring (you can also leave the poppies to form dry seed heads to harvest for an abundance of homegrown poppy seeds for the year!).

A huge caper bush sprouting from a wall in Greece (top left); a five-metre tall kiwi vine and chickpeas growing in the field in Puglia (top and bottom right); and an ancient olive tree in Calabria (bottom left).

3. Dry-loving plants.

Limited water and hot, dry summers? Grow capers (so underrated!) and other hardy, dry-climate-loving plants, like olives, chickpeas, globe artichokes, cardoons, grapes, pomegranates and kiwifruit. Even on the moon-dry, kiln-hot Greek islands, we witnessed these staple foods growing in lush abundance, without irrigation. It inspired us in a whole new way. The fact that *anything* grows there is amazing. And it was a reminder that when you work with nature you can grow things anywhere.

Lentil—Greek islands, summer 2017

'They use honey, not sugar. Chickpeas, not borlotti beans. Oranges, lemons, grapes, pomegranates and figs, not apples, peaches and berries. Onions, garlic and hardy herbs, like sage, oregano and rosemary. Capers, olives and prickly pear. Sheep's cheese and goat's cheese. No cows. No butter. But a donkey-cart-load of olive oil.

'And we love it. This life. Using only what you have. I mean, chickpeas, oranges, lemons, figs, capers, onions, garlic, sage, oregano, rosemary, olives, pomegranates, prickly pears, feta, yoghurt, honey and wine? No complaints. When you adapt what you grow, how you cook and what you eat to your environment, it's always amazing.'

Key tips.

When to plant. Capers, olives, figs, globe artichokes, cardoons, grapevines, pomegranates and kiwifruit vines are all perennials. Plant them in late spring to give them plenty of time to establish themselves before their first winter. Chickpeas are an annual crop, and grow fantastically well underneath all of these dry-loving perennials. Plant chickpeas in spring to harvest in summer. Sow direct, spacing seeds 15 cm apart, or place a few seeds in each hole every 30 cm. Water in generously, and then keep moist until they germinate.

Water until established. Once established, all these plants have enormous root systems and need little irrigation. But keep an eye on them in the early days, and if they look floppy, give them some water.

Water a *little* for the best yield. For the *best* yield, chickpeas will need infrequent watering throughout the growing season. Figs, kiwifruit, pomegranates and grapes will all benefit from some watering also, especially when flowering, to maximise fruit set.

Groundcover alternatives. Cucumbers, zucchinis and bush beans also make brilliant groundcover under olives, figs, grapevines, pomegranates and kiwifruit vines. But these groundcover plants are unlikely to thrive unless irrigated (which you may say defeats the purpose of choosing dry-loving plants in the first place!).

Surprisingly at home. Capers do especially well on rocky outcrops even with virtually no access to water all summer. They are truly amazing plants once established.

4. Grow an abundance!

Grow enough to share with your village. We've found tomatoes, zucchini/summer squash and rocket to be some of the most abundant producers in the garden, and they're all extremely easy to grow.

Key tips—tomatoes.

Start early. Start tomato seedlings in a greenhouse in late winter, then plant advanced tomato seedlings in late spring, after the danger of frost has passed. Plant in 90 cm intervals in a double row—rows spaced 30 cm apart (see opposite). In just 15 m² you can fit 28 plants in two beds!

Provide support. Erect a vertical mesh trellis along each row of tomatoes in the first month after planting. Then simply weave the branches back and forth through the trellis each week as they grow—tomatoes love to climb, but they're not good at it, so we need to help! Any branches growing directly into the path that are too hard to weave can be snipped off near the main stem.

Yield big. Grown on this system, one healthy tomato plant can yield 15–20 kg in a season. That's 420–560 kg of tomatoes from a 15 m² patch! Should be enough to feast on tomatoes all summer, put away all the passata you need and share plenty with your village!

Key tips—zucchini/summer squash.

Just 1–3 plants! For a household, plant just one to three plants in late spring, after the danger of frost has passed. Choose a mix of varieties (striped zucchini and yellow squash are our favourites). Some varieties 'creep' and others will remain a 'bush'. We choose bush varieties for inside the garden and creeping varieties for the perimeter.

Plant young. Plant from seed or as young seedlings with just one set of crinkly leaves—more mature seedlings don't do well. Space 90 cm apart—they'll get enormous!

Harvest regularly. Check for harvest-sized fruits daily (zucchini fruit can grow up to 3 cm a day!). Regular harvest will ensure continuous growth all season until frosts (if you get them) kill the plants. In frost-free areas, a healthy zucchini can live for months upon months.

Nurture. Spray leaves every few weeks with worm tea or a seaweed/kelp/fish emulsion to protect them from powdery mildew (see page 103 for more information). And lay compost around the plants halfway through the growing season to guarantee strength long into autumn.

Key tips—rocket.

Rocket is our favourite salad green. One small patch of rocket (60 cm x 60 cm), planted twice a year, is all you need for a constant supply of lush greens year-round.

Sow. Sow rocket seed in shallow furrows, cover back over with soil and keep moist until the cotyledons appear. Sow a patch in early spring and another in early autumn.

Water. Water rocket every day, as consistent watering is key for it to sit all year, without bolting to flower.

Harvest. Once leaves reach salad size, cut as needed, starting at one end of the row and working your way along. Cut with a knife, 5 cm from the base of the plant. More leaves will grow and be ready to cut in just 3 weeks.

Repeat. You can harvest your rocket this way over and over. A consistently watered patch that has enough nutrition in the soil will continue to grow from spring through to autumn, through several cuttings, and your second patch from autumn to spring again.

5. Small spaces—growing in pots (and jars).

Have only the most limited space? Grow in pots and jars! We grow heaps of things in pots, even though we have space, just because we love it. If you only have a small space, there's no reason you can't still grow something. Provided the pot gets some direct sun every day, things will grow happily. And growing in pots is a great first step to gardening.

Key tips.

Pots need holes in them! You can't grow a plant in a bucket! Remember, soil should be moist but not wet. Use pot bases to catch excess water, holding a little in reserve for your plants throughout the day.

Water daily. Watering your potted plants every day will ensure the absolute best health. Large pots only need about a cup of water a day, smaller pots, equivalently less. So, be careful not to over water and drown the roots! Just a little water, once a day. Watering your pot plants is a beautiful routine to start the day with.

Size matters. Make sure the pot is big enough for the plant. A plant's root system basically reflects its foliage, so compare the two constantly. When the plant has outgrown the pot, it's time to 'pot it up' into a bigger pot. Double the pot size each time.

Or keep small. Alternatively, just keep plants to the size of the pot. Annual herbs, like basil and parsley, can be continuously picked to keep them within size. Flowers can also be continuously pruned.

Tricking your potted plants. The trick to getting a plant to outgrow its pot without having to pot it up is to feed it with worm tea or seaweed/kelp/fish emulsions. It's like adding extra nutrition to the pot in liquid form, rather than as soil.

Careful not to over-pick. If you are growing a plant to harvest, like herbs, take care not to over-pick them. Always leave a significant cover of foliage or the plant may take a very long time to recover or not recover at all.

Our favourites. Our favourite things to grow in pots are: herb and spice plants, chillies, radishes, turnips, lettuce, rocket and other salad greens like raddichio, nasturtiums, marigolds, violas, tomatoes and strawberries. See Seasonal planting charts, page 79, for information on what to plant when.

It's all about the soil. Soil is still the key to a plant's health in a pot. So, be sure to follow all the tips in Soil, page 34, to achieve the healthiest potted plants possible.

Growing in jars! You can also grow things like avocado seeds (they take approximately 8 weeks to sprout) and sweet potato sprouts (page 73) in jars of water (see picture opposite). They have so much stored energy in their seeds/tubers that we've maintained cute little bonsai-like plants this way in the same jar of water for over 12 months! Amazing. Just make sure to top up and refresh the water regularly.

6. The essentials—garlic and onions.

Garlic and onions go into almost every dish we eat. So, every year we try to grow all the onions and garlic we need. Growing both plants in your garden is super easy—you can even grow new onions from old onions (although we usually start onions from seed because we've eaten them all!) and new garlic from old garlic. And there is really nothing like the taste of your own homegrown essentials.

1. Prepare beds. Prepare fresh garden beds in late summer (see Bed building, page 37). To grow all your garlic, build a bed that's about 1.1 x 2.2 m. Make a second bed the same size for onions, and if you want to expand your onion production next time—go bigger!

2. Start your onion seedlings. Start your onion seedlings in early autumn. Form one shallow furrow lengthwise on one edge of the bed and sow thickly with seed. Cover the furrow back over with soil and keep moist until the seeds germinate.

3. Plant your garlic. At the same time, plant 200 cloves of organic garlic in a 10 cm grid, with the pointy tips facing up. Mulch the bed with grain or pea straw immediately, fluffing it up to allow the new garlic shoots to push up through it (don't worry, they're strong!).

4. Plant your onion seedlings. Once your onion seedlings reach pencil thickness, plant out in a 10 cm grid. To do so, gently pull up a few at a time, plant them out in the grid, water in, pull out a few more etc., until they're all spread out!

5. Grow. Now watch your garlic and onions grow. Look after the patch as you do the rest of your garden, keeping it moist and mainly weeded (they can handle a little competition). And when the onion shoots seem sturdy enough, spread some mulch in between them too.

Flower/scape harvest. As they approach maturity, both your onions and garlic may grow beautiful flowers. These make for wonderful cut flowers and also delicious garnishes. Some garlic varieties will grow scapes instead—curious, pointy heads on long stalks. Cut the long scapes as they appear and cook like asparagus. A spring treat!

Garlic harvest. Your garlic will be ready to harvest in the first weeks of summer. When the very lowest set of leaves turn yellow, stop watering the crop. About a week later, when the lowest *few* sets of leaves have turned yellow, pull up the whole crop, brush away any excess dirt and lie on racks in the shade to cure for a week.

Then hang in bunches of ten in a dry, airy place. Store as is, or the tops can be removed after a few weeks of drying and the harvest brought inside.

Set aside the biggest 30 or so bulbs to plant out next year—the biggest cloves will grow the biggest bulbs!

Onion harvest. Your onions will be ready to harvest a little later when most of the tops have fallen over. When this happens, stop watering for a week, then pull up the whole crop, brush clean and cure and store as per the guide for garlic above.

PAJERO

7. Sweet potato crates.

Growing your own sweet potatoes is so much fun. And all you need is a couple of organic sweet potatoes to start things off! This is how you do it.

1. Sprout sweet potato tubers. This happens inside in late winter. Often, they'll sprout all on their own in a warm, dark cupboard. If one has sprouted all on its own, go straight to the next step. If not, place a few tubers in a tray of soil, half-buried, half-exposed. Water the tray generously and place in a greenhouse or very warm, sunny window. Keep the tray moist, and eventually your sweet potatoes will sprout (see picture opposite, top left). The sprouts are called 'slips'.

2. Grow out your slips. As your slips get to about 10–15 cm tall, break them off at their base near the tuber and place in a glass of water for 2–3 days. They will sprout beautiful white roots (tray-grown slips will already have some roots, but still follow this process—it strengthens them) and will then be ready for planting.

3. Plant out your slips. If the risk of frost has passed, you can plant your slips straight out into a deep, well-manured garden bed. Space them about 45 cm apart in all directions.

But if there is still a risk of frost, plant them in little pots and place in a greenhouse or inside by a warm window while you wait for it to warm up outside, then plant them out when the risk of frost has passed in late spring.

Or (our favourite sweet potato growing method) as soon as your slips are ready, set up a mini-greenhouse/planter/sweet potato crate (pictured opposite, top right)! It's super simple: fruit crate + soil + irrigation + old perspex sheet = boom! Ideal, frost-protected sweet potato planter. You can place a few bricks in there to hold the sun's heat from the day and keep the soil warm overnight. Just be sure to remove the perspex sheet in early summer, to avoid burning your plants.

4. Grow. Your sweet potatoes will grow like crazy all summer and into autumn. Just let them grow as much as they can before the frost fries their leaves (or into late autumn in warmer, frost-free areas). If their runners get a bit too exploratory, you can break them off and cook the leaves just like spinach.

5. Harvest. After the frost kills the leaves (or in the last weeks of autumn in warmer areas), harvest all your sweet potatoes (if you leave them in the ground over cold, wet winters they will rot).

Your sweet potato planter or bed should be loaded with huge tubers! Stop watering for at least a week before harvesting and also try to harvest during dry weather. Dig the tubers out carefully to avoid breaking them or damaging their skins, spray clean with water and dry briefly on racks in the sun.

6. Cure. Cure the harvest in the hottest, most sauna-like room you've got. We place them in cardboard boxes in the laundry and seal all the doors and windows. You're aiming at temperatures of 25–30°C, with humidity of 80% for ten days to two weeks. A heater may be required, and wet towels can be used to increase the humidity. If your curing room is a little cooler, cure for a little longer.

7. Store. After curing your sweet potatoes, wrap tubers individually in newspaper. Store in a dark cupboard, or cardboard box with a lid, in a cool place (around 10–15°C). The tubers are best eaten after at least 6 weeks storing because this allows time for the sugars to simplify (so they will taste much sweeter). Tubers should keep like this all winter.

8. A wildflower patch.

We love planting a wildflower patch next to our garden. It's all about growing beautiful wild-like flowers, to be fantastic garden companions (see page 54) and bring in all the good bugs. And often the patch will just self-seed if you let the seeds drop, and then continue to grow wild, all on its own! Grow things that have a double purpose, like vegetables and herbs that also have great flowers—this way you will always have flowers to cut *and* food to harvest from your wild patch.

Flowers grown like this have so much personality. Each flower has a different direction—its *own* direction—with stems all curious and curly. This is really how we like to grow flowers, letting them grow however they want, not trellised to be straight and perfect. If you have the space, plant wild. Here's how.

1. Prepare a fresh garden bed (see page 37).

2. Carve out some shallow furrows in the soil.

3. Broadcast (scatter) a mix of fun flower, herb and vegetable seeds all over the bed, then rake flat to cover with soil and *generously* water it all in.

4. Keep the bed moist until everything has sprouted and then take care of your wild patch just like the rest of the garden, but without weeding or mulching.

5. After the flowers mature, let the seeds drop. Fingers crossed next time they will sprout all on their own!

What to grow in your wild patch.

Vegetables and herbs. Carrots, cardoons, artichokes, amaranth, celery, fennel, dill, mint, coriander, chamomile basil and all the alliums and brassicas all make *great* flowers. Cherry tomatoes are also amazing in vases.

Flowers. Flowers that love the wild patch are cosmos, calendula, larkspur, sweet peas, borage, scabiosa, Queen Anne's lace, nasturtiums, foxgloves, dahlias, sunflowers, poppies, yarrow, snapdragons, forget-me-nots and lupins.

Melons and pumpkins. These love to grow in the wild patch. They run all over the place wherever they want and form a groundcover to keep the soil cool. And while they do, they grow you beautiful fruits!

See Seasonal planting charts, page 79, for information on what to plant when and page 54 for more information on cultivating wildness in your garden.

Some quick tips on cutting flowers to last.

How to cut. Use sharp snips and cut on an angle, then place directly into a bucket of fresh, cold water.

When to cut. Cut stems in the morning, before it's hot. After cutting, store in a cool, dark place until you put them out on display.

Perking up. Some flowers will droop. As a general rule, cut stems again on an angle and place the cut end in boiling water for about 20 seconds, then return to cold water. They should perk back up! This doesn't work for *every* flower, but it does for most. Experiment!

Garden charts.

150 plants to fill your village garden. When to plant them, how to plant them and what to do if you run into problems.

150 plants to fill your village garden.

There is an *enormous* range of food plants out there to choose from. This chapter is all about introducing you to as many of them as possible, focusing on the most common temperate-climate food plants, plus a few of our favourite good-bug attracting plants and flowers. Although these plants are classed as temperate-growing, they are equally great for cooler/mountain, warm-temperate and subtropical climates and most can even be grown in the tropics.

We have tried to keep the information on a need-to-know level for success: when things grow, how much space they need, which plants do and don't get along, and a few other key tips, plus natural pest control and garden troubleshooting tips. You don't need to read *every* line of every chart in this chapter. They are simply here as a reference to help you learn more about the plants *you* want to grow and hopefully introduce you to a few new favourites. The chapter is divided into three sections:

1. **Seasonal planting charts**—what to plant when, opposite.
2. **Plant specifics charts**—spacing, companions, enemies, key tips, page 84.
3. **Natural 'pest' control charts**—a garden troubleshooting guide, page 98.

1. Seasonal planting charts.

What to plant when. We plant into and around our garden from the very end of winter all the way through to the beginning of the next winter. There are so many options of what to plant, no matter what the season, and these charts are all about both inspiring you to try new things and to plant the things you already know and love at the right time for the best growing success. Exactly *what* you plant when is up to you. Remember, your garden is yours. You do you.

There are seven planting times:

1. Late winter.

2. Early spring.

3. Late spring.

4. Early summer.

5. Late summer.

6. Early autumn.

7. Late autumn.

And then we rest.

The beginning of winter (well, most of winter really) is a time of rest in our temperate climate. It is far too cold for anything to grow at any sort of appreciable rate, so it's not a time for planting or large harvests. Instead, all of our mature winter plants just sit happily, feeding us through the cooler weather in a state of semi-dormancy, until everything begins to warm up again in spring. If you are prepared for this seasonal shift with a fully stocked, mature winter garden, it is a wonderful time of feeling nurtured by your garden without having to give back. Of course, if you live in a warmer climate, continue winter plantings as desired based on the following chart.

Adapting the charts to suit your climate.

Cooler/mountain regions. If you live in a cooler/mountain region, your growing season is shorter than ours. You'll need to delay everything by at least four weeks until late summer, then bring everything forward four weeks for the rest of the planting season to beat the winter frosts.

Warmer frost-free and subtropical areas. If you are in an area that doesn't get frosts at all, or if you are in the subtropics, you can bring everything forward half a season until late summer, and then delay/extend plantings by at least half a season through to winter. In these areas, ignore notes to plant 'in a greenhouse', just plant everything out in the open. Many plants will enjoy a much longer growing season in these areas because the frost won't get them.

Tropical areas. If you live in the tropics, you may find it difficult to grow some of these plants, but the vast majority of plants listed under late spring and early summer should do very well when planted at the beginning of the cool, dry season.

Late winter (risk of frost).

Sow seeds in the garden.

Vegetables.
Beetroot
Bok choy/choy sum
Bunching onion
Carrot
Chard/silverbeet
Chicory
Collard greens
French shallot (bulbs)
Japanese turnip
Leek
Mibuna
Mizuna
Mustard greens
Parsnip
Radish
Rocket
Shelling peas
Snow peas
Spinach
Sugar snap peas
Tatsoi
Turnip
Upland cress

Herbs and spices.
Anise (for seed)
Caraway (for seed)
Chervil
Chives
Coriander
Dill
Cumin (for seed)
Garlic chives
Mustard (for seed)
Parsley
Poppy (for seed)

Beneficial flowers.
Lupin
Poppy
Sweet pea
Viola

Plant seedlings/young trees/plants in the garden.

Fruits and nuts.
Almond
Apple
Blackberry
Blueberry
Boysenberry
Chestnut
Cranberry
Currant
Fig
Gooseberry
Grapes
Hazelnut
Mulberry
Pear
Pecan
Persimmon
Pistachio
Pomegranate
Quince
Raspberry
Rhubarb
Stone fruit, various
Strawberry
Walnut

Vegetables.
Asparagus
Cardoon
Chicory
Endive/escarole
Fennel
Globe artichoke
Lettuce
Onion

Herbs and spices.
Bay laurel
Garlic chives
Lavender
Marjoram
Mint
Oregano
Rosemary
Sage
Savory (winter type only)
Thyme
Wormwood

Beneficial flowers.
Foxglove
Viola

Start seedlings in pots/trays in a greenhouse.

Fruits.
Cape gooseberry

Vegetables
Asparagus
Cabbage
Capsicum
Cardoon
Cauliflower
Chicory
Chilli
Eggplant
Endive/escarole
Fennel
Globe artichoke
Kale
Kohlrabi
Leek
Lettuce
Potato (start to sprout tubers)
Sweet potato (start to sprout tubers)
Tomatillo
Tomato
Tronchuda kale
Wombok

Herbs and spices.
Basil
Chamomile
Garlic chives
Lavender
Love-in-a-mist (for nigella seed)
Marjoram
Oregano
Rosemary
Sage
Savory (winter, summer)
Tarragon
Thyme
Wormwood

Beneficial flowers.
Calendula
Cornflower
Dahlia (from seed)
Forget-me-not
Foxglove
Larkspur
Love-in-a-mist
Lupin
Queen Anne's lace
Snapdragon
Sweet pea
Viola
Yarrow

Early spring (risk of frost).

Sow seeds in the garden.

Vegetables.
Beetroot
Bok choy/choy sum
Bunching onion
Carrot
Chard/silverbeet
Chicory
Collard greens
Japanese turnip
Leek
Mibuna
Mizuna
Mustard greens
Parsnip
Radish
Rocket
Shelling peas
Snow peas
Spinach
Sugar snap peas
Tatsoi
Turnip
Upland cress

Herbs and spices.
Anise (for seed)
Caraway (for seed)
Chervil
Chives
Coriander
Cumin (for seed)
Dill
Garlic chives
Love-in-a-mist (for nigella seed)
Mustard (for seed)
Parsley
Poppy (for seed)
Sesame (for seed)

Beneficial flowers.
Calendula
Cornflower
Forget-me-not
Love-in-a-mist
Lupin
Poppy
Queen Anne's lace
Sweet pea
Viola
Yarrow

Plant seedlings/young trees/plants in the garden.

Fruits and nuts.
Almond
Apple
Blackberry
Blueberry
Boysenberry
Chestnut
Citrus, various
Cranberry
Currant
Fig
Gooseberry
Grapes
Hazelnut
Kiwifruit
Mulberry
Pear
Pecan
Persimmon
Pistachio
Pomegranate
Quince
Raspberry
Rhubarb
Stone fruit, various
Strawberry
Walnut

Herbs and spices.
Bay laurel
Chamomile
Garlic chives
Horseradish
Kaffir lime
Lavender
Love-in-a-mist (for nigella seed)
Marjoram
Mint
Oregano
Rosemary
Sage
Savory (winter and summer)
Thyme
Wormwood

Vegetables.
Asparagus
Cabbage
Cardoon
Cauliflower
Chicory
Endive/escarole
Fennel
Globe artichoke
Kale
Kohlrabi
Leek
Lettuce
Potato
Tronchuda kale
Wombok

Beneficial flowers.
Calendula
Cornflower
Forget-me-not
Foxglove
Larkspur
Love-in-a-mist
Lupin
Queen Anne's lace
Sweet pea
Viola
Yarrow

Note.

Most herbs and spices and a few vegetables (for example, amaranth, the allium family, carrots and cardoons) also produce wonderful flowers if left to do so.

Start seedlings in pots/trays in a greenhouse.

Fruits.
Cape gooseberry
Melon, various

Herbs and spices.
Basil
Chamomile
Garlic chives
Lavender
Love-in-a-mist (for nigella seed)
Marjoram
Oregano
Rosemary
Sage
Savory (winter, summer)
Tarragon
Thyme
Wormwood

Beneficial flowers.
Borage
Calendula
Cornflower
Cosmos
Dahlia (start from seed)
Forget-me-not
Gomphrena
Love-in-a-mist
Lupin
Marigold
Nasturtium
Queen Anne's lace
Scabiosa
Snapdragon
Sunflower
Viola
Yarrow
Zinnia

Vegetables.
Amaranth
Asparagus
Beans
Capsicum
Cardoon
Chicory
Chilli
Cucumber
Eggplant
Endive/escarole
Fennel
Globe artichoke
Leek
Lettuce
Maize (including popping) corn
Potato (start to sprout tubers)
Pumpkin
Sweet corn
Sweet potato (start to sprout tubers)
Tomatillo
Tomato
Tronchuda kale
Warrigal greens
Zucchini/summer squash

Late spring (risk of frost has passed).

Sow seeds in the garden.

Fruits.
Melon, various

Vegetables.
Amaranth
Beans
Beetroot
Bok choy/choy sum
Bunching onion
Carrot
Chard/silverbeet
Chickpeas
Collard greens
Cucumber
Japanese turnip
Jerusalem artichoke (tubers)
Leek
Maize (including popping) corn
Mibuna
Mizuna
Mustard greens
Parsnip
Pumpkin
Radish
Rocket
Sweet corn
Tatsoi
Tronchuda kale
Turnip
Warrigal greens
Zucchini/summer squash

Herbs and spices.
Anise (for seed)
Basil
Caraway (for seed)
Chives
Coriander
Cumin (for seed)
Dill
Garlic chives
Love-in-a-mist (for nigella seed)
Mustard (for seed)
Parsley
Sesame (for seed)

Beneficial flowers.
Borage
Calendula
Cornflower
Cosmos
Dahlia (tubers)
Gomphrena
Love-in-a-mist
Marigold
Nasturtium
Queen Anne's lace
Scabiosa
Snapdragon
Sunflower
Viola
Yarrow
Zinnia

Plant seedlings/young trees/plants in the garden.

Fruits and nuts.
Almond
Apple
Blackberry
Blueberry
Boysenberry
Cape gooseberry
Chestnut
Citrus, various
Cranberry
Currant
Fig
Gooseberry
Grapes
Hazelnut
Kiwifruit
Melon, various
Mulberry
Olive
Passionfruit
Pear
Pecan
Persimmon
Pistachio
Pomegranate
Quince
Raspberry
Rhubarb
Stone fruit, various
Strawberry
Walnut

Herbs and spices.
Bay laurel
Capers
Chamomile
Garlic chives
Horseradish
Kaffir lime
Lavender
Lemon verbena
Love-in-a-mist (for nigella seed)
Marjoram
Mint
Oregano
Rosemary
Sage
Savory (winter, summer)
Tarragon
Thyme
Wormwood

Vegetables.
Amaranth
Asparagus
Beans
Cabbage
Capsicum
Cardoon
Cauliflower
Chicory
Chilli
Cucumber
Eggplant
Endive/escarole
Fennel
Globe artichoke
Kohlrabi
Leek
Lettuce
Maize (including popping) corn
Potato (sprouting tubers)
Pumpkin
Sweet corn
Sweet potato (slips)
Tomatillo
Tomato
Tronchuda kale
Warrigal greens
Wombok
Zucchini/summer squash

Beneficial flowers.
Borage
Calendula
Cornflower
Cosmos
Dahlia (seedlings grown from seed)
Forget-me-not
Gomphrena
Love-in-a-mist
Lupin
Marigold
Nasturtium
Queen Anne's lace
Scabiosa
Snapdragon
Sunflower
Viola
Yarrow
Zinnia

Start seedlings in pots/trays in a greenhouse or outside.

Fruits.
Melon, various

Vegetables.
Beans
Cucumber
Leek
Lettuce
Maize (including popping) corn
Pumpkin
Sweet corn
Tronchuda kale
Warrigal greens
Zucchini/summer squash

Herbs and spices.
Basil
Chamomile
Garlic chives
Lavender
Marjoram
Oregano
Rosemary
Sage
Savory (winter, summer)
Tarragon
Thyme
Wormwood

Beneficial flowers.
Borage
Calendula
Cosmos
Gomphrena
Marigold
Nasturtium
Queen Anne's lace
Scabiosa
Sunflower
Yarrow
Zinnia

Early summer.

Sow seeds in the garden.

Vegetables.
Amaranth
Beans
Beetroot
Bok choy/choy sum
Bunching onion
Carrot
Chard/silverbeet
Chickpeas
Collard greens
Cucumber
Japanese turnip
Leek
Maize (including popping) corn
Mibuna
Mizuna
Mustard greens
Parsnip
Radish
Rocket
Sweet corn
Tatsoi
Turnip
Warrigal greens
Zucchini/summer squash

Herbs and spices.
Anise (for seed)
Basil
Caraway (for seed)
Chives
Coriander
Cumin (for seed)
Dill
Garlic chives
Mustard (for seed)
Parsley
Sesame (for seed)

Beneficial flowers.
Borage
Calendula
Cosmos
Marigold
Nasturtium
Queen Anne's lace
Sunflower
Yarrow

Plant seedlings/young trees/plants in the garden.

Fruits.
Blueberry
Cranberry
Currant
Gooseberry
Melon, various
Rhubarb

Vegetables.
Amaranth
Beans
Capsicum
Cardoon
Chilli
Cucumber
Eggplant
Endive/escarole
Globe artichoke
Leek
Lettuce
Maize (including popping) corn
Pumpkin
Sweet corn
Tomato
Tronchuda kale
Warrigal greens
Zucchini/summer squash

Herbs and spices.
Basil
Bay laurel
Capers
Chamomile
Garlic chives
Lavender
Lemon verbena
Marjoram
Oregano
Rosemary
Sage
Savory (winter, summer)
Tarragon
Thyme
Wormwood

Beneficial flowers.
Borage
Calendula
Cosmos
Gomphrena
Marigold
Nasturtium
Queen Anne's lace
Scabiosa
Sunflower
Yarrow
Zinnia

Start seedlings in pots/trays outside.

Vegetables.
Beans
Brussels sprouts
Celeriac
Celery
Cucumber
Leek
Lettuce
Maize (including popping) corn
Sweet corn
Tronchuda kale
Warrigal greens
Zucchini/summer squash

Herbs and spices.
Chamomile
Garlic chives
Lavender
Marjoram
Oregano
Rosemary
Sage
Savory (winter type only)
Tarragon
Thyme
Wormwood

Beneficial flowers.
Calendula
Cosmos
Queen Anne's lace
Sunflower
Yarrow

Late summer.

Sow seeds.

Vegetables.
Amaranth
Beetroot
Bok choy/choy sum
Bunching onion
Carrot
Chard/silverbeet
Chicory
Collard greens
Japanese turnip
Leek
Mibuna
Mizuna
Mustard greens
Parsnip
Radish
Rocket
Shelling peas
Snow peas
Spinach
Sugar snap peas
Tatsoi
Turnip
Upland cress

Herbs and spices.
Anise (for seed)
Caraway (for seed)
Chives
Coriander
Cumin (for seed)
Dill
Garlic chives
Mustard (for seed)
Parsley

Beneficial flowers.
Calendula
Forget-me-not
Foxglove
Queen Anne's lace
Sunflower
Sweet pea
Viola
Yarrow

Plant seedlings/young trees/plants in the garden.

Fruits.
Blueberry
Cranberry
Currant
Gooseberry
Rhubarb

Vegetables.
Amaranth
Beans
Brussels sprouts
Cardoon
Celeriac
Celery
Cucumber
Endive/escarole
Globe artichoke
Leek
Lettuce
Maize (including popping) corn
Sweet corn
Tronchuda kale
Zucchini/summer squash

Herbs and spices.
Bay laurel
Chamomile
Garlic chives
Lavender
Lemon verbena
Marjoram
Oregano
Rosemary
Sage
Savory (winter type only)
Tarragon
Thyme
Wormwood

Beneficial flowers.
Calendula
Cosmos
Queen Anne's lace
Sunflower
Yarrow

Start seedlings in pots/trays outside.

Vegetables.
Broccoli
Cabbage
Cauliflower
Chicory
Fennel
French shallot
Kale
Kohlrabi
Leek
Lettuce
Onion
Radicchio
Shelling peas
Snow peas
Sugar snap peas
Witlof
Wombok

Herbs and spices.
Chamomile
Garlic chives
Lavender
Marjoram
Oregano
Rosemary
Sage
Savory (winter type only)
Thyme
Wormwood

Beneficial flowers.
Calendula
Forget-me-not
Foxglove
Queen Anne's lace
Scabiosa
Snapdragon
Sweet pea
Viola
Yarrow

Early autumn (risk of frost).

Sow seeds in the garden.

Vegetables.
Beetroot
Bok choy/choy sum
Broad beans
Bunching onion
Carrot
Chard/silverbeet
Chicory
Collard greens
French shallot (seeds)
Garlic (cloves)
Japanese turnip
Leek
Mibuna
Mizuna
Mustard greens
Parsnip
Radish
Rocket
Shelling peas
Snow peas
Spinach
Sugar snap peas
Tatsoi
Turnip
Upland cress

Herbs and spices.
Chervil
Chives
Coriander
Dill
Garlic chives
Parsley
Poppy (for seed)

Beneficial flowers.
Calendula
Cornflower
Forget-me-not
Foxglove
Larkspur
Lupin
Poppy
Queen Anne's lace
Scabiosa
Snapdragon
Sweet pea
Viola
Yarrow

Plant seedlings/young trees/plants in the garden.

Fruits.
Blueberry
Cranberry
Currant
Gooseberry
Rhubarb

Vegetables.
Broccoli
Brussels sprouts
Cabbage
Cardoon
Cauliflower
Celeriac
Celery
Chicory
Endive/escarole
Fennel
Globe artichoke
Kale
Kohlrabi
Leek
Lettuce
Onion
Radicchio
Witlof
Wombok

Herbs and spices.
Bay laurel
Chamomile
Garlic chives
Lavender
Lemon verbena
Marjoram
Mint
Oregano
Rosemary
Sage
Savory (winter type only)
Thyme
Wormwood

Beneficial flowers.
Calendula
Forget-me-not
Foxglove
Queen Anne's lace
Scabiosa
Snapdragon
Sweet pea
Viola
Yarrow

Start seedlings in pots/trays in a greenhouse.

Vegetables.
Chicory
French shallot
Leek
Lettuce
Onion
Radicchio
Shelling peas
Snow peas
Sugar snap peas
Witlof

Herbs and spices.
Chamomile
Garlic chives
Lavender
Marjoram
Oregano
Rosemary
Sage
Savory (winter type only)
Thyme
Wormwood

Beneficial flowers.
Calendula
Cornflower
Foxglove
Larkspur
Lupin
Snapdragon
Sweet pea
Viola
Yarrow

Late autumn (risk of frost).

Sow seeds in the garden.

Vegetables.
Bok choy/choy sum
Broad beans
Bunching onion
French shallot (bulbs or seeds)
Garlic (cloves)
Leek
Mibuna
Mizuna
Mustard greens
Radish
Rocket
Shelling peas
Snow peas
Spinach
Sugar snap peas
Tatsoi
Upland cress

Herbs and spices.
Chervil
Chives
Coriander
Garlic chives
Parsley
Poppy (for seed)

Beneficial flowers.
Cornflower
Larkspur
Lupin
Poppy
Snapdragon
Sweet pea
Viola

Plant seedlings/young trees/plants in the garden.

Fruits.
Blueberry
Cranberry
Currant
Gooseberry
Rhubarb

Vegetables.
Cardoon
Chicory
Endive/escarole
Globe artichoke
Leek
Lettuce
Onion
Radicchio
Witlof

Herbs and spices.
Bay laurel
Chamomile
Garlic chives
Lavender
Lemon verbena
Marjoram
Mint
Oregano
Rosemary
Sage
Savory (winter type only)
Thyme
Wormwood

Beneficial flowers.
Calendula
Cornflower
Foxglove
Larkspur
Lupin
Snapdragon
Sweet pea
Viola
Yarrow

Too late in the season to raise seedlings.

Early winter.

Put your feet up. It's time for a well-earned break.

2. Plant specifics charts.

Spacing, companions, enemies and key tips. This chart is to help you plant what you want in the best way possible. In all cases, be sure to create healthy soil first and proceed through the other key steps outlined in Natural gardening 101 (page 33). See Seasonal planting charts (starting page 79) for accompanying planting times and the chart on page 79 for information on how to adapt them to suit your climate.

To make use of the companions/enemies tips in these charts just make sure to plant companions ('likes') literally next to each other and enemies ('dislikes') far away from each other.

The charts are broken up into four sections:

1. Annual vegetables and herbs.
2. Perennial vegetables and herbs.
3. Beneficial flowers.
4. Fruits and nuts.

Annual vegetables and herbs (A–Z).

Plant.	Space required.	Likes.	Dislikes.	Key tips.
Amaranth	10-15 cm spacing; rows 30 cm apart	Beans, cucumber, corn, peas	None	Amaranth definitely grows best when planted directly from seed. Be careful not to leave plants in the garden too long as they will readily self-seed (unless that's what you want—see page 54!). If growing for seed, cut full plants before seeds release and hang for final stages of drying.
Anise	30 cm spacing; rows 30 cm apart	Coriander	Basil	Brilliant and simple seed plant to grow. Very good for attracting good bugs and deterring bad ones, especially during flowering.
Basil	30 cm spacing; rows 30 cm apart	Asparagus, cucumber, fennel, tomato, chives, garlic chives, potato, bok choy/choy sum, broccoli, brussels sprouts, cabbage, cauliflower, collard greens, kale, kohlrabi, mibuna, mizuna, mustard greens, radish, rocket, tatsoi, turnip, wombok, olives, capsicum, chilli, tomatillo, blueberry	Chard/silverbeet, anise	Can be tricky to germinate, so sow one tray thickly in a greenhouse in late winter to plant out from late spring. To harvest, break off stems below the first two or three sets of leaves. This will prevent the plant from flowering and encourage continuous, vigorous bushy growth—it's called 'tipping-out'.
Beans, all	15 cm spacing; rows 30 cm apart	Carrot, celery, cucumber, chard/silverbeet, eggplant, corn, peas, potato, savory, strawberry, rosemary, sage, parsnip, pumpkin, parsley, celeriac, amaranth, lettuce, spinach, gooseberry, passionfruit, grapes	Beetroot (climbing types only—bush beans not affected), fennel, French shallot, garlic, leek, onion, chives, garlic chives, sunflower, Jerusalem artichokes	Climbing beans are definitely our favourites for small spaces. See page 61 for how to grow all the beans your heart could possibly desire and field notes on page 303 for our favourite way to eat our favourite climbing bean—the snake bean.
Beetroot	10 cm spacing; rows 30 cm apart	Broccoli, brussels sprouts, cabbage, cauliflower, collard greens, French shallot, garlic, kale, kohlrabi, leek, lettuce, mibuna, mizuna, mustard greens, onion, radish, rocket, spinach, tatsoi, turnip, chives, garlic chives, bok choy/choy sum, wombok, olives, chard/silverbeet, cumin	Beans (climbing only—bush beans not affected), tomato	Can be transplanted very successfully as tiny seedlings when the cotyledons first emerge, but before the first true leaves. Or best sown directly as seed and thinned to 6–10 cm apart when the seedlings are between 1–3 cm tall. Harvest just the biggest beets first to allow the remaining beets to grow to size in the spaces created.
Bok choy/ choy sum	10-15 cm spacing; rows 30 cm apart	Beetroot, carrot, celery, chard/silverbeet, cucumber, garlic, lettuce, onion, potato, spinach, basil, dill, oregano, rosemary, sage, thyme, chamomile, marigold, nasturtium, cress, chives, garlic chives, sunflower, Jerusalem artichoke, rhubarb, cumin, chicory, peas, cardoon, globe artichoke, lavender, thyme, borage, gooseberry, lupin	Tomato, strawberry, capsicum, eggplant	Transplant young seedlings or thin directly sown seeds to 6–10 cm apart. Harvest biggest choy plants first by cutting at the base, leaving the remaining plants undisturbed to grow into the spaces created.
Broad beans	15 cm spacing; rows 30 cm apart	Poppy	Fennel, French shallot, garlic, onion, chives, garlic chives, leek	Plant with poppies every year for the most beautiful scene in spring (see page 62). Dwarf varieties fruit earlier and are easier to support. Broad beans do best with a couple of horizontal wires or lines of string around them for support, as the fruit weight can easily topple a plant. Cut off the top 20 cm of growth once the plants reach 1 m tall to encourage plants to focus their energy on maturing fruit (beans). These cut 'tips' are delicious sautéed, steamed or fried.
Broccoli	45 cm spacing; rows 30 cm apart	See bok choy/choy sum	Tomato, strawberry, capsicum, eggplant	We prefer Calabrese/sprouting varieties for their longer season. Harvest the main floret before it starts to grow leggy and flower, then continue to harvest all the side shoots (broccolini) long into spring.

Annual vegetables and herbs (A–Z).

Plant.	Space required.	Likes.	Dislikes.	Key tips.
Brussels sprouts	45 cm spacing; rows 30 cm apart	See bok choy/choy sum	Tomato, strawberry, capsicum, eggplant	Brussels sprouts seedlings must be started the week before Christmas (or the second last week of June if in the northern hemisphere) and planted out late summer to mature enough before winter sets in. Follow this timing to guarantee lush sprouts every year. When planting out seedlings, plant them deep, up to the second set of true leaves.
Bunching onion (immature onion)	3 cm spacing; rows 30 cm apart	Beetroot, broccoli, brussels sprouts, cabbage, carrot, cauliflower, collard greens, kale, kohlrabi, lettuce, mibuna, mizuna, mustard greens, parsnip, radish, rocket, tatsoi, tomato, turnip, marjoram, rosemary, savory, fruit/nut trees/vines, chamomile, bok choy/choy sum, wombok, rhubarb, spinach, dill, potato, gooseberry, celery, celeriac, zucchini/summer squash, spinach, tomatillo, cress, strawberry, kaffir lime	Beans, broad beans, peas, Jerusalem artichoke, sunflower	Plant seed directly in the garden in short drills. Successively plant throughout the planting season for a constant supply of bunching onions. Harvest when shoots are finger thick. Harvest the largest, thickest shoots first, leaving the remaining shoots to grow to size in the spaces created.
Cabbage	45 cm spacing; rows 30 cm apart	See bok choy/choy sum	Tomato, strawberry, capsicum, eggplant	When planting out cabbage seedlings, plant them deep, up to the second set of true leaves. Harvest when heads are rock hard.
Capsicum	60 cm spacing; rows 30 cm apart	Carrot, parsnip, tomato, basil, parsley, marigold, rhubarb, tomatillo, eggplant, chilli	Fennel, potato, bok choy/choy sum, broccoli, brussels sprouts, cabbage, cauliflower, collard greens, kale, kohlrabi, mibuna, mizuna, mustard greens, radish, rocket, tatsoi, turnip, wombok	Requires staking for support before getting too leggy and starting to set fruit, or will topple. Can be grown as perennial in areas that don't get frosts. Really needs full sunny position and to be planted as an advanced seedling as soon as the risk of frost has passed if you are to obtain a good yield of ripe fruit.
Caraway	30 cm spacing; rows 30 cm apart	Peas, strawberry	Fennel, dill	Brilliant garden friend, especially when flowering. Plant a few plants each year for a generous seed harvest.
Carrot	5 cm spacing; rows 30 cm apart	Beans, French shallot, garlic, leek, lettuce, onion, peas, radish, chives, garlic chives, parsley, rosemary, sage, tomatillo, coriander, chard/silverbeet, chilli, capsicum, bok choy/choy sum, broccoli, brussels sprouts, cabbage, cauliflower, collard greens, kale, kohlrabi, mibuna, mizuna, mustard greens, radish, rocket, tatsoi, turnip, wombok, asparagus	Parsnip, coriander, dill, tomato, celeriac, celery, potato	Soil must be friable to at least 40 cm for carrots to grow straight and long. Keep soil just moist, not wet, or thick lateral roots will form off the main tap root. Must be sown directly into the garden as seed because transplanting will deform the root. Then, carefully thin seedlings to 3–5 cm apart when they are between 1–3 cm tall.
Cauliflower	45 cm spacing; rows 30 cm apart	See bok choy/choy sum	Tomato, strawberry, capsicum, eggplant	Ensure you grow the right variety for the time of year. A winter variety will struggle in summer and vice versa. After main head is harvested, plants left in the soil will often grow delicious side shoots.
Celeriac	20 cm (diameter)	Beans, French shallot, garlic, leek, onion, tomato, chives, garlic chives	Carrot, corn, parsnip, potato	Seedlings can be slow to grow, so start in early summer to be planted out in late summer. Give them plenty of space.

Annual vegetables and herbs (A-Z).

Plant.	Space required.	Likes.	Dislikes.	Key tips.
Celery	30 cm spacing; rows 30 cm apart	Beans, broccoli, brussels sprouts, cabbage, cauliflower, collard greens, cucumber, kale, kohlrabi, mibuna, mizuna, mustard greens, radish, rocket, spinach, tatsoi, tomato, turnip, dill, marjoram, cosmos, marigold, nasturtium, snapdragon, bok choy/choy sum, wombok, chickpeas, onions, garlic, leek, chives, garlic chives, French shallots, chard/silverbeet, peas, cucumber, olives	Carrot, corn, parsnip, potato, lettuce	Seedlings can be slow to grow so start in early summer to be planted out in late summer. Harvest outer leaves of celery weekly once they've plumped up for a continuous harvest from late autumn through to mid-spring.
Chard/ silverbeet	15 cm spacing; rows 30 cm apart	Beetroot, carrot, celery, lettuce, parsnip, bok choy/choy sum, broccoli, brussels sprouts, cabbage, cauliflower, collard greens, kale, kohlrabi, mibuna, mizuna, mustard greens, radish, rocket, tatsoi, turnip, wombok, beans, coriander, olives	Basil	Incredibly hardy, frost-tolerant greens. Plant seeds or seedlings in early spring and late summer and pick only the largest outer leaves each week for constant harvest year round. Italian taglio ('cutting') chard is our go-to variety. An incredibly prolific and abundant year-round vegetable.
Chervil	15 cm spacing; rows 30 cm apart	Lettuce, radish, coriander, dill, parsley, yarrow, parsnip	None	Hardy performer when planted with parsley in late summer for harvest from late autumn through to spring. An often forgotten winter herb, especially brilliant with eggs in the morning.
Chickpeas	15 cm spacing; rows 30 cm apart	Celery, savory, grapes, passionfruit, strawberry	French shallot, garlic, onion, chives, garlic chives	Completely underrated garden crop. Great groundcover under vines and fruit trees. Easiest to plant in the garden as seed, a few seeds to each hole. See page 65 for more growing information.
Chicory	15 cm spacing; rows 30 cm apart	Broccoli, brussels sprouts, cabbage, wombok, cauliflower, collard greens, kale, kohlrabi, mibuna, mizuna, mustard greens, radicchio, endive/escarole, witlof, radish, rocket, tatsoi, turnip, bok choy/choy sum	None	Brilliant bitter greens that thrive in cooler months, but we've had very good results with Catalogna varieties in summer too. Harvest whole plant when about 30 cm tall.
Chilli	60 cm spacing; rows 30 cm apart	Carrot, parsnip, tomato, basil, parsley, marigold, rhubarb, tomatillo, eggplant, capsicum	Fennel, potato	Requires staking for support before getting too leggy and starting to set fruit, or will topple. Can be grown as perennial in areas that don't get frosts. Really needs full sunny position to do well. Rocoto variety can be grown as small tree/shrub in frost-free areas and will bear fruit for years.
Collard greens	30 cm spacing; rows 30 cm apart	See bok choy/choy sum	Tomato, strawberry, capsicum, eggplant	Summertime alternative to kale. Will sit happily in hot weather while all your kale has bolted to flower. Regularly pick largest/lowest outer leaves for continual harvest.
Coriander	15 cm spacing; rows 30 cm apart	Carrot, chard/silverbeet, radish, anise, chervil, parsnip, asparagus	Fennel, dill	Readily goes to flower. So, successively plant throughout the planting season for a good supply of herbs all year. Frost tolerant. Great to have some coriander flowering in the garden constantly to attract good bugs.
Corn (sweet, maize, popping)	30 cm spacing; rows 30 cm apart	Beans, cucumber, Jerusalem artichoke, peas, potato, pumpkin, zucchini/summer squash, marjoram, melon, marigold, sunflower, lettuce, dill, amaranth, tomatillo	Tomato, celery, celeriac	Corn is the most fun thing to grow! Always plant each variety in blocks of at least nine plants (3 x 3), as they are wind pollinated. We highly recommend growing your own popping corn (a specific variety of maize)—homegrown popcorn is unbeatable!
Cucumber	15 cm spacing; rows 30 cm apart	Beans, celery, lettuce, corn, peas, dill, rocket, wombok, marigold, nasturtium, sunflower, parsley, cumin, amaranth, olives, basil, tatsoi, Jerusalem artichoke, bok choy/choy sum, broccoli, brussels sprouts, cabbage, turnip, cauliflower, collard greens, kale, kohlrabi, mibuna, mizuna, mustard greens, radish, lupin	Potato, tomato, sage, savory	Grows best when given a trellis angled at 45° to climb on. Fruits hang down for easy picking. Lettuce or parsley can be grown underneath, as they like the shade in peak summer. Plant only young seedlings that have only one set of crinkly leaves, or sow directly from seed.

Annual vegetables and herbs (A–Z).

Plant.	Space required.	Likes.	Dislikes.	Key tips.
Cumin	30 cm spacing; rows 30 cm apart	Likes everything/general garden helper	None	Brilliant garden friend, especially when flowering. Plant a few plants each year for a generous seed harvest.
Dill	15 cm spacing; rows 30 cm apart	Broccoli, brussels sprouts, cabbage, lupin, cauliflower, collard greens, cucumber, asparagus, fennel, kale, kohlrabi, lettuce, corn, mibuna, mizuna, mustard greens, onion, radish, rocket, tatsoi , turnip, bok choy/choy sum, wombok, olives, zucchini/summer squash, parsnip, celery, chervil	Carrot, tomato, coriander, caraway	Brilliant garden friend. Have some growing and some flowering from spring through to winter. Collect flowers and any set seed for cooking and preserving too.
Eggplant	60 cm spacing; rows 30 cm apart	Beans, capsicum, potato, marjoram, spinach, tarragon, chilli	Bok choy/choy sum, broccoli, brussels sprouts, cabbage, cauliflower, collard greens, kale, kohlrabi, mibuna, mizuna, mustard greens, radish, rocket, tatsoi, turnip, wombok, strawberry, fennel	Will fruit much more heartily than capsicum in cooler areas. May require staking. Does best when planted as an advanced seedling as soon as the risk of frost has passed.
Endive/ escarole	10–15 cm spacing; rows 30 cm apart	See chicory	None	Grow spring through to winter. Harvest whole plant like lettuce. Brilliant, mildly bitter green, a great addition to salads.
Fennel	15 cm spacing; rows 30 cm apart	Basil, dill	Beans, broad beans, capsicum, tomato, coriander, lavender, chilli, eggplant, tomatillo, caraway	Best bulbs form when planted in late summer for late autumn/winter harvest, and late autumn for spring harvest. Flowering fennel is great for the garden.
French shallot	20 cm (diameter)	See bunching onion	Beans, broad beans, peas, Jerusalem artichoke, sunflower	Grow French shallots from 'seeds' (they look like tiny French shallots), or simply by planting the smallest French shallots saved from the previous harvest. Each plant will yield several delicious bulbs at harvest. Harvest/store as per onion guide, page 70.
Garlic	10 cm (diameter)	See bunching onion	Broad beans, peas, sunflower, Jerusalem artichoke, beans	See page 70 for complete garlic growing guide.
Garlic shoots	3 cm spacing; rows 30 cm apart	See bunching onion	Beans, broad beans, peas, Jerusalem artichoke, sunflower	Garlic shoots are young garlic, before the bulb starts to form. Sow garlic cloves thickly in a 10 cm furrow in early autumn and cover back over with soil. Keep moist. Harvest through winter and spring when finger thick.
Horseradish	30 cm spacing; rows 30 cm apart	Potato, fruit/nut trees/vines	None	Plant root pieces in deep, friable soil in spring. Dig up after leaves die back in winter to make horseradish condiment. Replant some pieces of root again in spring and repeat. Any roots left in the ground over winter will sprout anew in spring also.
Japanese turnip	15 cm spacing; rows 30 cm apart	See bok choy/choy sum	Tomato, strawberry, capsicum, eggplant	Grow through the warmer months. Fast growing. Brilliant raw or cooked, both tops and roots. Grows well in a deep pot.
Jerusalem artichoke	20 cm spacing; rows 30 cm apart	Broccoli, brussels sprouts, beans, globe artichoke, cabbage, cauliflower, collard greens, cucumber, kale, kohlrabi, corn, mibuna, mizuna, mustard greens, cardoon, pumpkin, radish, rocket, tatsoi, turnip, zucchini/summer squash, melon, bok choy/choy sum, wombok, tomatillo	Beans, garlic, potato, tomato, French shallot, onion, leek, chives, garlic chives	Plant in spring for large brain-like tuber harvest in autumn. From the sunflower family, so also produce beautiful flowers. Plant away from main garden, because once you've grown them, missed tubers are likely to reseed on their own forever.

Annual vegetables and herbs (A–Z).

Plant.	Space required.	Likes.	Dislikes.	Key tips.
Kale	30 cm spacing; rows 30 cm apart	See bok choy/choy sum	Tomato, strawberry, capsicum, eggplant	Will grow brilliant edible shoots if left to flower. A prolific and abundant cooler season vegetable. Pick largest/lowest outer leaves regularly for continuous harvest from autumn to spring.
Kohlrabi	30 cm spacing; rows 30 cm apart	See bok choy/choy sum	Tomato, strawberry, capsicum, eggplant	Easy to grow. Plant seedlings deep in the soil, up to the second set of true leaves. Harvest when stem has swolen to be the size of at least an orange, or—if you're lucky—a grapefruit!
Leek	10 cm (diameter)	See bunching onion	Beans, broad beans, peas, Jerusalem artichoke, sunflower	Plant in spring and again in autumn for year-round harvest. Prolific, year round allium.
Lettuce	20 cm spacing; rows 30 cm apart	Beans, beetroot, broccoli, carrots, sweet corn, maize, onions, peas, radish, spinach, mint, strawberry, marigold, cucumber, lupin	Celery, cress, parsley	Best planted out as seedlings. Will bolt (run to seed rather than creating a lovely head) readily if not given enough space or water. Less prone to bolting in the cooler months.
Mibuna	10–15 cm spacing; rows 30 cm apart	See bok choy/choy sum	Tomato, strawberry, capsicum, eggplant	Easy green for cut salad greens. Leaves can be cut 5 cm from base and will regrow over and over again before the plant bolts to flower. Small greens in just 2 weeks.
Mizuna	10–15 cm spacing; rows 30 cm apart	See bok choy/choy sum	Tomato, strawberry, capsicum, eggplant	Easy green for cut salad greens. Leaves can be cut 5 cm from base and will regrow over and over again before the plant bolts to flower. Small greens in just 2 weeks.
Mustard greens	15 cm spacing; rows 30 cm apart	See bok choy/choy sum	Tomato, strawberry, capsicum, eggplant	Purple-leaf variety happiest in hotter months. Shoots are delicious when it goes to flower. Small greens in just 2 weeks.
Onion	10 cm (diameter)	See bunching onion	Beans, broad beans, peas, Jerusalem artichoke, sunflower	Produce incredibly beautiful flowers if left to do so, which make an excellent spring garnish or cut flower display. See page 70 for complete onion growing guide.
Parsley	15 cm spacing; rows 30 cm apart	Asparagus, beans, carrot, radish, tomato, rosemary, chives, garlic chives, raspberry, cucumber, capsicum, chervil, chilli, tomatillo	Lettuce	Thrives in cooler months but will cope in the garden even in summer in a shadier spot.
Parsnip	5 cm spacing; rows 30 cm apart	Beans, lettuce, onion, peas, potato, radish, chilli, capsicum, chard/silverbeet, chervil, chives, coriander, dill, marjoram, sage, garlic chives, onions, garlic, leek, French shallots	Carrot, celery, celeriac	Needs deep, friable soil, at least 40 cm for good root development. Like carrots, keep soil just moist, not wet, to avoid thick lateral roots and must be sown directly into the garden as seed because transplanting will deform the root. Then, carefully thin seedlings to 5-7 cm apart when they are between 1-3 cm tall.
Potato	30 cm spacing; rows 30 cm apart	Beans, broccoli, brussels sprouts, cabbage, cauliflower, collard greens, garlic, horseradish, kale, kohlrabi, lettuce, mibuna, mizuna, mustard greens, onion, peas, radish, rocket, tatsoi, turnip, basil, marigold, bok choy/choy sum, wombok, corn, cumin, parsnip	Capsicum, carrot, celery, cucumber, tomato, zucchini/summer squash, rosemary, apple, cherry, melon, raspberry, strawberry, sunflower, chilli, pumpkin, celeriac, Jerusalem artichoke, spinach	Plant potatoes away from main garden, as it's impossible not to miss some when you harvest, and they will reseed over and over again. Potato plants are grown from sprouting potatoes. See our first book for our favourite way to grow them—in barrels. Prolific, easy and super rewarding vegetable to grow.

Annual vegetables and herbs (A–Z).

Plant.	Space required.	Likes.	Dislikes.	Key tips.
Pumpkin	90 cm spacing; rows 2–3 m apart	Beans, corn, melon, zucchini/summer squash, marigold, nasturtium, Jerusalem artichoke, sunflower, lupin	Potato	Plant with lots of space away from main garden. Cut off lateral runners when they reach 2 m to encourage fruit development. Plant only young seedlings that have only one set of crinkly leaves, or sow directly from seed.
Radicchio	15 cm spacing; rows 30 cm apart	See chicory	None	Plant in autumn for growth in cooler months to achieve most striking colour and maximum sweetness.
Radish	5 cm spacing; rows 30 cm apart	Beetroot, carrot, celery, chard/silverbeet, cucumber, garlic, lettuce, onion, potato, peas, spinach, basil, dill, oregano, rosemary, sage, thyme, chamomile, marigold, nasturtium, parsnip, cumin, parsley, coriander, chervil, zucchini/summer squash, chives, garlic chives	Tomato, strawberry, capsicum, eggplant	Fastest growing root. Plant in any little gap in the garden. Or grows fantastically in deep pots.
Rocket	10–15 cm spacing; rows 30 cm apart	See bok choy/choy sum	Tomato, strawberry, capsicum, eggplant	Easy green for cut salad greens. Leaves can be cut 5 cm from base and will regrow over and over before the plant bolts to flower. Small greens in just 2 weeks. See page 66 for complete rocket growing guide.
Sesame	30 cm spacing; rows 30 cm apart	Likes everything/general garden helper	None	Super-simple and fun spice to grow. Loves sun!
Shelling peas	15 cm spacing; rows 30 cm apart	Beans, broccoli, brussels sprouts, cabbage, carrot, cauliflower, celery, collard greens, cucumber, kale, kohlrabi, lettuce, corn, mibuna, mizuna, mustard greens, potato, radish, rocket, tatsoi, turnip, zucchini/summer squash, sage, bok choy/choy sum, wombok, parsnip, caraway, passionfruit, amaranth, spinach, cardoon, globe artichoke	Tomato, strawberry, capsicum, eggplant	Grow through the cooler months. Super easy and fast growing. Plants don't like super-hot weather but are happy in frosts. Plants won't *set* peas in frosty weather however, as it burns the flowers.
Snow peas/ sugar snap peas	15 cm spacing; rows 30 cm apart	See shelling peas	French shallot, garlic, onion, chives, garlic chives, tomato	Grow through the cooler months. Super easy and fast growing. Brilliant raw or cooked. Plants don't like super-hot weather but are happy in frosts. Plants won't *set* peas in frosty weather however, as it burns the flowers. The creeping tendrils, or 'pea shoots', are very edible also.
Spinach	15 cm spacing; rows 30 cm apart	Beans, broccoli, brussels sprouts, cabbage, cauliflower, celery, collard greens, eggplant, kale, kohlrabi, leek, lettuce, mibuna, mizuna, mustard greens, peas, radish, rocket, tatsoi, tomato, turnip, melon, strawberry, nasturtium, bok choy/choy sum, wombok, onion, French shallot, garlic, chives, garlic chives, zucchini/ summer squash, beetroot, fruit/nut trees/vines	Potato	Only thrives in spring and autumn. Plant late winter and late summer. Harvest as whole plant.
Sweet potato	45 cm (diameter)	Melon	None	See page 73 for complete sweet potato growing guide.
Tatsoi	10–15 cm spacing; rows 30 cm apart	See bok choy/choy sum	Tomato, strawberry, capsicum, eggplant	Easy green for cut salad greens. Leaves can be cut 3 cm from base and will regrow over and over again before the plant bolts to flower. Or can be cut at base as for bok choy/choy sum. Small greens in just 2 weeks.

Annual vegetables and herbs (A–Z).

Plant.	Space required.	Likes.	Dislikes.	Key tips.
Tomatillo	90 cm spacing; rows 30 cm apart	Capsicum, carrot, chilli, French shallot, garlic, leek, corn, onion, basil, chives, garlic chives, parsley, sage, marigold, nasturtium, sunflower, Jerusalem artichoke	Bok choy/choy sum, broccoli, brussels sprouts, cabbage, cauliflower, collard greens, kale, kohlrabi, mibuna, dill, mizuna, mustard greens, radish, rocket, tatsoi, turnip, wombok, strawberry, fennel	Super fun to grow, harvest and eat! Grow tomatillos like you would capsicums. May benefit from staking to prevent from toppling over/splitting.
Tomato	90 cm spacing; rows 30 cm apart	Asparagus, carrot, celery, French shallot, leek, lettuce, onion, spinach, basil, chives, garlic chives, marjoram, oregano, parsley, borage, dahlia, marigold, nasturtium, tomatillo, capsicum, chilli, parsnip, grapes, celeriac, rosemary, Queen Anne's lace	Beetroot, cucumber, broccoli, brussels sprouts, cabbage, cauliflower, collard greens, fennel, kale, kohlrabi, corn, mibuna, mizuna, mustard greens, peas, potato, radish, rocket, tatsoi, turnip, dill, rosemary, apricot, walnut, strawberry, sunflower, Jerusalem artichoke, bok choy/choy sum, wombok	See page 66 for complete tomato growing guide.
Tronchuda kale	30 cm spacing; rows 30 cm apart	See bok choy/choy sum	Tomato, strawberry, capsicum, eggplant	Wonderful Portuguese summer kale variety. The only kale variety that will sit happily through summer without bolting to flower.
Turnip	10 cm spacing; rows 30 cm apart	See bok choy/choy sum	Tomato, strawberry, capsicum, eggplant	Fun to plant all planting season but for sweetest roots plant in late summer and harvest after first frost because frost sweetens turnips. Can also be grown in deep pots.
Upland cress	15 cm spacing; rows 30 cm apart	Broccoli, brussels sprouts, cabbage, cauliflower, collard greens, French shallot, garlic, kale, kohlrabi, leek, mibuna, mizuna, mustard greens, onion, radish, rocket, tatsoi, turnip, chives, garlic chives, bok choy/choy sum, wombok	Lettuce	Excellent protector of brassica family from white cabbage butterfly grubs (see page 101). Thrives in spring, autumn and winter. The most nutrient-dense green you can grow.
Warrigal greens	30 cm spacing; rows 30 cm apart	Fruit/nut trees/vines	None	Hardy warm-weather green. Actually a succulent, so tolerates dry conditions well. Creeps vigorously.
Witlof	15 cm spacing; rows 30 cm apart	See chicory	None	Best grown in the cooler months, which intensifies flavour and colour. Cover with soil or straw for blanched (white and light yellow-green coloured) hearts.
Wombok	45 cm spacing; rows 30 cm apart	See bok choy/choy sum	Tomato, strawberry, capsicum, eggplant	Grows best when planted in autumn or early spring. Can be grown in the hotter months but tends to bolt more readily. Plant with carrots in late summer for a kimchi harvest with your chillies in late autumn.
Zucchini/ summer squash	90 cm spacing; rows 90 cm apart	Beans, garlic, corn, peas, radish, spinach, dill, oregano, strawberry, borage, marigold, nasturtium, sunflower, Jerusalem artichoke, fruit/nut trees/vines, lupin	Potato	The most fun vegetable to grow. Grows incredibly fast. One to three plants are all most houses will need, as they fruit prolifically. We prefer the bush types to the running/creeping types, as they behave a little more predictably in the garden! See page 66 for complete zucchini/summer squash growing guide.

Perennial vegetables and herbs (A–Z).

Plant.	Space required (diameter).	Likes.	Dislikes.	Key tips.
Asparagus	30 cm	Carrot, tomato, basil, coriander, dill, marjoram, parsley, marigold	None	Takes 3 years from seed or 2 years from crowns before first harvest but will then provide a harvest for 20+ years.
Bay laurel	3 m+	Olives, oregano, rosemary, citrus, pomegranate, lavender	None	Super-hardy perennial tree/shrub/hedge. One plant will provide more than enough bay leaves for a home.
Capers	1 m	Likes everything/general garden helper	None	Incredibly hardy perennial. Does not need irrigating once established. Harvest flower buds to pickle before they open. See page 65 for more growing information.
Cardoon	1 m+	Broccoli, brussels sprouts, cabbage, cauliflower, collard greens, globe artichoke, kale, kohlrabi, mibuna, mizuna, mustard greens, peas, radish, rocket, tatsoi, turnip, tarragon, sunflower, bok choy/choy sum, wombok, Jerusalem artichoke	None	Incredibly hardy plant. Requires no irrigation. Grows huge, so plant off to the side of the garden. Fantastic purple/blue flowers are loved by bees, and they're great for floristry. Cut plants down to their base at end of summer. For the best eating stalks, push early growth down when it reaches 40 cm tall so it's lying flat in a bunch and cover in earth or straw. Keep covered with earth or straw as they grow to create blanched stalks—just as white asparagus or witlof is grown. See page 65 for more growing information.
Chamomile	30 cm	Broccoli, brussels sprouts, cabbage, cauliflower, collard greens, kale, kohlrabi, mibuna, mizuna, radish, rocket, tatsoi, turnip, mustard greens, bok choy/choy sum, wombok, chives, garlic chives, olives, leek, onion, garlic, French shallot	None	Frost tolerant perennial or annual. Great creeping groundcover under fruit trees. Makes brilliant tea—just harvest the flower buds and dry in the sun. Self-seeds readily.
Chives/ garlic chives	5 cm	Beetroot, broccoli, brussels sprouts, cabbage, carrot, cauliflower, collard greens, kale, kohlrabi, mibuna, mizuna, lettuce, mustard greens, parsnip, radish, rocket, tatsoi, tomato, turnip, basil, cress, marjoram, rosemary, savory, chamomile, parsley, wombok, strawberry, marigold, bok choy/choy sum, spinach, gooseberry, rhubarb, tomatillo, fruit/nut trees/vines	Beans, broad beans, peas, Jerusalem artichoke, sunflower	Super-hardy, frost-tolerant perennials once established. Divide clumps and spread through the garden every few years to encourage vigorous growth. Great garden friends. Flowers make delicious garnishes.
Globe artichoke	1 m+	See cardoon	None	Super-hardy perennial. Needs no irrigation but lots of space. See page 65 for more growing information.
Kaffir lime	3 m+	French shallot, garlic, horseradish, leek, lettuce, onion, chives, garlic chives, strawberry, borage, yarrow, nasturtium, zucchini/summer squash	None	Easy to grow citrus tree. Grown for leaves. Can be kept small, so planting in the garden is okay.
Lavender	90 cm+	Broccoli, brussels sprouts, cabbage, cauliflower, collard greens, kale, kohlrabi, mibuna, mizuna, mustard greens, radish, rocket, tatsoi, turnip, bok choy/choy sum, wombok, bay laurel, kiwifruit	Fennel	Hardy perennial. Give lots of space. Needs minimal water and produces fantastic flowers with an even more fantastic scent that bees adore.
Lemon verbena	3 m+	Likes everything/general garden helper	None	Perennial tree said to struggle in frost-prone areas, however we have grown it successfully despite regular winter frosts. Grow near a warm wall for frost protection.
Marjoram	30 cm	Likes everything/general garden helper	None	Hardy perennial herb and brilliant garden friend. Plant throughout the garden.
Mint	30 cm	Olives	Plant away from everything except olives	Incredibly vigorous, creeping herb. Keep out of the garden—plant instead in its own space like a tub or half-barrel. Most easily grown from pulled creeping roots off a friend's plant. Great edible flower too.

Oregano	30 cm	Likes everything/general garden helper	None	Hardy perennial herb. Spreading habit, so plant off to the side in the garden.
Rosemary	90 cm+	Beans, broccoli, brussels sprouts, cabbage, cauliflower, collard greens, garlic, kale, kohlrabi, radish, rocket, mibuna, mizuna, mustard greens, tatsoi, turnip, sage, bok choy/choy sum, wombok, chives, garlic chives, olives, carrot, bay laurel, onion, tomato, leek, French shallot, garlic, lupin	Potato, tomato	Super-hardy perennial herb. Plant with lots of space. Very tolerant of dry conditions once established. Can live for decades. Don't cut back to woody growth. Only harvest stems that are still green and soft (not woody).
Sage	60 cm	Beans, broccoli, brussels sprouts, cabbage, carrot, cauliflower, collard greens, kale, kohlrabi, mibuna, mizuna, mustard greens, peas, radish, rocket, tatsoi, turnip, rosemary, strawberry, bok choy/choy sum, wombok, olives, tomatillo, parsnip	Cucumber	Super easy to grow. Flowers are great bee forage. Will live for many years. Don't cut back to woody growth. Only harvest stems that are still green and soft (not woody).
Savory	30 cm	Beans, onion, chives, garlic chives, chickpeas, lupin	Cucumber	Totally underrated herb. Summer savory is a frost-sensitive annual. Winter savory is a frost-tolerant perennial. Our preference is the winter variety for its bolder flavour.
Tarragon	30 cm	Likes everything/general garden helper	None	Super-hardy herb in the warmer months. Will die back in winter but should reshoot in summer, especially if mulched to protect roots. French tarragon is by far the tastiest.
Thyme	30 cm	Broccoli, brussels sprouts, cabbage, cauliflower, collard greens, kale, kohlrabi, mibuna, mizuna, mustard greens, radish, rocket, tatsoi, turnip, bok choy/choy sum, wombok, olives	None	Super-hardy perennial herb. Will live for many years. Don't cut back to woody stem. Only harvest stems that are still green and soft (not woody).
Wormwood	1 m+	Olives	Plant away from everything except olives	Super-helpful perennial herb, but toxic to most vegetable plants if they share its root zone. Plant outside of, but near, the garden.

Beneficial flowers (A–Z, see page 74 for further tips on growing your wildflower patch).

Plant.	Space required.	Likes.	Dislikes.	Key tips.
Borage	30 cm spacing; rows 30 cm apart	Broccoli, brussels sprouts, cabbage, cauliflower, strawberry, collard greens, kale, kohlrabi, mibuna, mizuna, mustard greens, peas, radish, rocket, tatsoi, turnip, tomato, zucchini/summer squash, wombok, bok choy/choy sum, fruit/nut trees/vines	None	Crack for bees. Plant throughout the garden. Plants can get easily 1 m across if left to their own devices. Edible flowers. Great for soil nutrition if you cut leaves and add to soil/compost. Self-seeds readily.
Calendula	30 cm spacing; rows 30 cm apart	Likes everything/general garden helper	None	Plant throughout the garden. Brilliant garden friend. Edible petals. Frost tolerant. Regularly dead-head for continuous growth and flowering. Self-seeds readily.
Cornflower	30 cm spacing; rows 30 cm apart	Likes everything/general garden helper	None	Hardy. Edible petals. Frost tolerant. Regularly dead-head for continuous growth and flowering. Annual and perennial varieties.
Cosmos	30 cm spacing; rows 30 cm apart	Likes everything/general garden helper	None	Easy to grow. Brilliant cut flower and loves heat. Regularly dead-head for continuous growth and flowering.
Dahlia	30 cm spacing for smallest growing varieties up to 90 cm for very large growing varieties; rows 30 cm apart	Tomato	None	An all-time favourite of ours. And tomatoes planted with dahlias really seem to grow and fruit that little bit more heartily in our experience! Lift and divide dahlia tubers after plants die back in autumn, store in damp wood-shavings over winter, then replant after danger of frost passes in spring. Support with horizontally suspended wire mesh.

Beneficial flowers (A–Z, see page 74 for further tips on growing your wildflower patch).

Plant.	Space required.	Likes.	Dislikes.	Key tips.
Forget-me-not	20–30 cm spacing; rows 30 cm apart	Likes everything/general garden helper	None	Hardy. Great for floristry. Self-seeds readily. Doesn't like hot conditions. Annual, biennial and perennial varieties. Can take up to 1 month to germinate.
Foxglove	30 cm spacing; rows 30 cm apart	Likes everything/general garden helper	None	Very attractive for bees. Do not eat flowers/leaves, as they can be poisonous. Self-seeds readily. Up to 20 days to germinate, 5 months to flower! Biennial.
Gomphrena	20–25 cm spacing; rows 30 cm apart	Likes everything/general garden helper	None	Regularly pick/dead-head for continuous growth and flowering and to encourage bushiness. Loves the heat.
Larkspur	30 cm spacing, in clumps; rows 30 cm apart	Likes everything/general garden helper	None	Does best sown directly into the garden from seed, a few seeds per hole. Hardy annual, easy to grow.
Love-in-a-mist	20–30 cm spacing; rows 30 cm apart	Likes everything/general garden helper	None	Beautiful flowers produce nigella seeds for cooking. Super easy to grow, hardy flower. Grows best when sown directly into the garden from seed. Harvest when flower *just* opens for longest cut bloom. Self-seeds readily. Thin self-seeded seedlings to 20–30 cm while plants are still young for best growth. Short flowering so successively plant for continuous bloom.
Lupin	45 cm spacing (diameter)	Cucumbers, pumpkins, zucchini/summer squash, melons, bok choy/choy sum, broccoli, brussels sprouts, cabbage, cauliflower, collard greens, kale, kohlrabi, mibuna, mizuna, mustard greens, radish, rocket, tatsoi, turnip, wombok, lettuce, rosemary, dill, strawberry, summer savory	Tomato, eggplant, capsicum, chilli, potato, tomatillo	Can be annual or perennial. Takes a long time (16–30 weeks!) to bloom. Pick 'in-bud' (just before it blooms) for best cut flower. Grows best when over-sown directly into the garden from seed, then thinned to 45 cm spacing when seedlings are still young. Nitrogen fixer, so great addition to compost when pulled up and improves soil while growing. Annual and perennial varieties.
Marigold	30 cm spacing; rows 30 cm apart	Likes everything/general garden helper	None	Brilliant garden friend. Plant throughout the garden. Edible petals. Annual and perennial varieties but can only be perennial in frost-free areas.
Nasturtium	30 cm spacing; rows 30 cm apart	Likes everything/general garden helper	None	Brilliant garden friend. Plant throughout the garden. Creeping habit. Entire plant is edible.
Poppy	20–30 cm spacing; rows 20–30 cm apart	Likes everything/general garden helper	None	Fun, frost hardy flower. Plant with broad beans in spring (see page 62) and save the edible seeds. Best sown direct from seed. Self-seeds readily. Thin self-seeded seedlings while still young. Cut flowers when just opening in the morning.
Queen Anne's lace	30 cm spacing; rows 30 cm apart	Likes everything/general garden helper	None	The best garden friend, it is actually wild carrot. Plant everywhere. Excellent distractor of harlequin bugs so plant abundantly in orchards and around tomatoes. Self-seeds readily. Biennial.
Scabiosa	30 cm spacing; rows 30 cm apart	Likes everything/general garden helper	None	Brilliant wild flower. Annual and perennial varieties (only some varieties are frost-hardy). Deadhead regularly for continuous growth.
Snapdragon	20–30 cm spacing; rows 30 cm apart	Likes everything/general garden helper	None	Excellent bee forage and cut flower. Great 'wild' flower. Perennial once established.
Sunflower	30 cm spacing; rows 30 cm apart	Bok choy/choy sum, broccoli, corn, brussels sprouts, cabbage, tatsoi, cauliflower, radish, collard greens, kale, kohlrabi, mibuna, mizuna, mustard greens, cardoon, rocket, turnip, wombok, bush beans, cucumber, pumpkin, zucchini/summer squash, melon, apricots, tomatillo, grapes, globe artichoke	Beans, garlic, potato, leek, tomato, French shallot, onion, chives, garlic chives	Some varieties grow over 4 m tall—make for good pea trellises. Save seed by leaving flower head to dry fully on the plant. Quick to flower. Easy to grow. Successively plant for continuous bloom from late spring to mid-autumn.

Sweet pea	15 cm spacing; rows 30 cm apart	Beans, broccoli, brussels sprouts, cabbage, carrot, cauliflower, celery, collard greens, cucumber, kale, kohlrabi, lettuce, corn, mibuna, mizuna, mustard greens, potato, radish, rocket, tatsoi, turnip, zucchini/summer squash, sage, bok choy/choy sum, wombok, parsnip, caraway, passionfruit, amaranth, spinach, cardoon, globe artichoke	French shallot, garlic, onion, chives, garlic chives, tomato	Super easy to grow. Plants don't like super-hot weather but happy in frosts, however frost may burn the flowers. Great 'wild' flower. Soaking seeds overnight prior to planting will dramatically increase successful germination rate. Grow on a fence or other trellis to support climbing habit. Does best when sown directly from seed.
Viola	30 cm spacing; rows 30 cm apart	Likes everything/general garden helper	None	Will continue to flower throughout winter (very frost tolerant), so great for bees. Edible flowers. Does not do well in hot conditions. Most varieties are perennial.
Yarrow	30 cm spacing; rows 30 cm apart	Likes everything/general garden helper	None	Brilliant perennial garden helper. Plant all around the edges of your garden and under fruit trees. Very hardy and tolerant of dry conditions. Also frost hardy. Perennial once established. Deadhead regularly for continuous growth and flowering.
Zinnia	30 cm spacing; rows 30 cm apart	Likes everything/general garden helper	None	Regularly pick/dead-head for continuous growth and flowering and to encourage bushiness. Support with some suspended horizontal wire mesh to prevent toppling. Excellent, super colourful garden flower. So many varieties to choose from.

Fruits and nuts (A–Z).

Plant.	Space required (diameter).	Likes.	Dislikes.	Key tips.
Almond	3 m+	All fruit/nut trees/vines will benefit from the following companions: French shallot, garlic, horseradish, lettuce, mustard greens, spinach, zucchini/summer squash, chives, garlic chives, strawberry, marigold, borage, nasturtium, yarrow, Queen Anne's lace, leek, sunflower, bay laurel, warrigal greens, onion	None	Always net almond trees after the green fruit has formed to avoid bird attack, especially in areas with cockatoos (for further pest control tips, see page 99).
Apple	3 m+	See almond	Potato	Control codling moth with traps and other measures (see page 102) to avoid a serious problem. Thin apples to 15 cm apart after the petals drop (after flowering) and before the fruit reach 1.5 cm across. Thinning encourages even year-to-year fruit set. Up to 5 years before first good harvest. Can store fruit in cool conditions for many months.
Apricot	3 m+	See almond	Tomato	Brilliant, easy fruit to grow. We love small-fruited, early varieties. Will benefit from fruit thinning when fruits are still only 1 cm wide.
Blackberry	1 m	See almond	None	Thornless varieties may be the preferred option. Prune back bush every winter so it doesn't sprawl out of control!
Blueberry	1 m	Basil, cranberry, raspberry, rhubarb, strawberry	None	Requires acidic soil to thrive. Naturally acidify soil by integrating peat moss, aged sawdust and compost, and watering with a little apple cider vinegar (1 teaspoon per 2 litres).
Boysenberry	1 m	See almond	None	Thornless varieties may be the preferred option. Prune back bush every winter so it doesn't sprawl out of control!
Cape gooseberry	90 cm	Currants	None	Give plenty of space for a mass of fruit from summer through to frost. If you don't get frosts, gooseberries can be grown as a perennial—place off to the side with your other bushy perennials.
Cherry	3 m+	See almond	Potato	Most cherry trees require a male and female tree to fruit. Check with your local nursery to make sure you have what you need.
Chestnut	3 m+	See almond	None	Will grow enormous! Plant somewhere with lots of space if you want to allow it to grow naturally, or it will eventually shade out your entire garden. Nuts drop to the ground when ready.

Fruits and nuts (A-Z).

Plant.	Space required (diameter).	Likes.	Dislikes.	Key tips.
Cranberry	1 m	Blueberry	None	See blueberry.
Currant	1 m	Cape gooseberry, gooseberry, marigold	None	See blueberry.
Fig	3 m+	See almond	None	Easiest to grow fruit tree in the world. Super hardy and can grow without much water. Fruits prolifically once established. See page 65 for more growing information.
Gooseberry	1 m	Beans, broad beans, French shallot, garlic, leek, tomato, onion, chives, garlic chives, currants, marigold, cape gooseberry	None	Adding a little fire ash to the soil around your gooseberries will increase flowering and aid fruit set. Begin to pick your gooseberries before they're all really ready. This thinning out will increase later fruit production.
Grapes	3 m+	Beans, mustard greens, tomato, mulberry, sunflower, yarrow, chickpeas	None	Grapevines in the backyard are best utilised as shady arbours and trellised along fence lines. Will grow as tall as the trellis you provide (we've seen one spanning a horizontal trellis 8 m off the ground in Italy!). See page 65 for more growing information.
Grapefruit	3 m+	See almond	None	Hardy, easy to grow, evergreen citrus tree. Can grow very large if allowed to. Plant outside the garden to avoid shading everything out.
Hazelnut	3 m+	See almond	None	Hardy, easy to grow tree. Will grow to be enormous and take many years before the first harvest. Plant outside the garden to avoid shading everything out.
Kiwifruit	3 m+	Zucchini/summer squash, marjoram, fruit/nut trees/vines, lavender	None	Need both male and female vines to fruit. Check with your nursery to make sure you get what you need. One male to up to five females will usually suffice.
Lemon	3 m+	See almond	None	Hardy, evergreen citrus tree. Can be kept small, so good for gardens.
Lime	3 m+	See almond	None	Hardy, evergreen citrus tree. Can be kept small, so good for gardens.
Mandarin	3 m+	See almond	None	Hardy, evergreen citrus tree. Can be kept small, so good for gardens.
Melon, various	60 cm	Corn, sweet potato, tomato, sunflower, Jerusalem artichokes, pumpkin, lupin	Potato	Sprawling, climbing vine. Will grow vertically up trellising/ladders/trees. Harvest when the little curly tendril attached to the stem near the melon has dried. Plant only young seedlings that have only one set of crinkly leaves, or sow directly from seed.
Mulberry	3 m+	See almond	None	Hardy fruiting tree. Tends to fruit biennially.
Nectarine	3 m+	See almond	None	Easy to grow fruit tree, can be kept small so good for gardens. Prone to leaf curl if not properly fed each winter (see troubleshooting chart, page 103, for other preventative measures also).
Olives	3 m+	Beetroot, celery, chard/silverbeet, cucumber, garlic, lettuce, onion, spinach, basil, dill, mint, oregano, rosemary, sage, thyme, wormwood, chamomile, marigold, nasturtium, yarrow, bay laurel	None	Super-hardy, evergreen trees that require minimal water. Great for dry climates and can handle some frost. See page 65 for more growing information.
Orange	3 m+	See almond	None	Beautiful, easy to grow, evergreen citrus tree. Can be kept small, so good for the garden, or allowed to grow very large outside of it.
Passionfruit	3 m+	Beans, peas, chickpeas, marjoram, marigold	None	Hardy evergreen vine, will grow as tall as the trellis you provide. Ensure the rootstock doesn't take over (passionfruit vines tend to always be grown on vigorous rootstocks) by regularly cutting back any suckers that grow from below the graft point.
Peach	3 m+	See almond	None	Easy fruit tree, can be kept small so good for gardens. Prone to leaf curl if not properly fed each winter (see troubleshooting chart, page 103, for other preventative measures also).

Fruits and nuts (A–Z).

Plant.	Space required (diameter).	Likes.	Dislikes.	Key tips.
Pear	3 m+	See almond	None	Easy fruit tree, can be kept small, so good for gardens. Can suffer from codling moth attack (see page 102). Pick when fruit comes away easily from the tree and is still rock hard. Will ripen off the tree in 1 week (or store in cool conditions for many months).
Pecan	3 m+	See almond	None	Hardy, easy to grow tree. Will grow to be enormous and take 6–10 years before first harvest. Plant outside the garden to avoid shading everything out.
Persimmon	3 m+	See almond	None	Easy to grow tree. Can be kept small, so good for the garden, or allowed to grow large outside of it. Astringent and non-astringent varieties. We prefer astringent, which make great date alternatives when dried (called 'hoshigaki'—see our first book).
Pistachio	3 m+	See almond	None	Super-fun to grow. Can be kept small, so good for the garden, or allowed to grow large outside of it.
Plum	3 m+	See almond	None	Super easy to grow in or out of the garden.
Pomegranate	3 m+	See almond	None	Easy to grow. Tolerates dry conditions (a desert plant originally). See page 65 for more growing information.
Pomelo	3 m+	See almond	None	Hardy, easy to grow, evergreen citrus tree. Can grow very large if allowed to. Plant outside the garden to avoid shading everything out.
Quince	3 m+	See almond	None	Very hardy tree, tolerant of dry conditions. Fruits prolifically. Pineapple quince is our favourite variety.
Raspberry	1 m	Parsley, marigold, blueberry	Potato	Thornless varieties may be the preferred option. Prune back bush every winter so it doesn't sprawl out of control!
Rhubarb	60 cm	Broccoli, brussels sprouts, cabbage, capsicum, cauliflower, chilli, collard greens, French shallot, garlic chives, turnip, kohlrabi, leek, onion, radish, rocket, mibuna, mizuna, tatsoi, kale, blueberry, mustard greens, garlic, chives, bok choy/choy sum, wombok	None	Hardy perennial. Divide every few years to encourage vigorous growth. Spray leaves with seaweed/kelp/fish emulsion every 6 months at least. If your stalks are green, that's most likely just the variety—totally normal (see field notes, page 178).
Strawberry	30 cm	Beans, leek, lettuce, onion, spinach, zucchini/summer squash, caraway, chives, garlic chives, sage, borage, blueberry, chickpeas, kaffir lime, fruit/nut trees/vines, lupin	Broccoli, eggplant, bok choy/choy sum, brussels sprouts, cabbage, kale, turnip, cauliflower, tatsoi, collard greens, mibuna, mizuna, kohlrabi, potato, mustard greens, radish, rocket, tomato, wombok	Most varieties fruit from spring into summer. Can be utilised as a vigorous groundcover under fruit trees. Strawberry runners should be cut free from the 'mother' plant regularly and either discarded or planted out to become new plants. That will allow the mother plant to focus on fruiting for you plus you will be expanding your crop! Very happy growing in a hanging basket.
Tangelo	3 m+	See almond	None	Hardy, easy to grow, evergreen citrus tree. Can grow very large if allowed to. Plant outside the garden to avoid shading everything out.
Tangerine	3 m+	See almond	None	Hardy, easy to grow, evergreen citrus tree. Can grow very large if allowed to. Plant outside the garden to avoid shading everything out.
Walnut	3 m+	None	Plant away from everything	Will grow enormous. Plant out of the garden with lots of space around it. Also, because it exudes a poisonous chemical from its roots to prevent other plants growing beneath it once established.

3. Natural 'pest' control charts.

A garden troubleshooting guide. This information is to help you troubleshoot the most common growing 'problems', naturally. All part of the daily garden dance. For sure, these problem-solving tips are far from comprehensive. But if we *have* encountered a problem, either in our garden or someone else's, it is in here. Happy gardening.

Observation.	Solution.
The leaves of my... look thin, fragile and wilted/curled in on themselves. It's sunny. The root zone is dry.	Your garden is badly dehydrated. You're not watering enough. In our experience, *all* plants do best when watered in tiny bursts throughout the day (see Water, page 50). This is the answer to this problem 99.9% of the time (if upon digging around the root zone you find the soil is sodden, however, see next point in the table). - Young plants need to be gently but thoroughly watered at their base, so that the water soaks into the soil, *every* day. - Mature plants and trees can be treated a little more harshly because they have access to a deeper moisture zone, but you still have to replenish that moisture zone. It is highly unlikely in any cooler/mountain or temperate region, in the warmer months of the year, that you will get away with watering your mature plants any less often than once every few days. Trees can be watered deeply once a week, but more regular, smaller waterings are better. In the tropics and subtropics, your cooler, dry seasons will be equivalent. - Your plants should never be wilted. If they are, increase the water. Vegetable gardens require the equivalent of about 5 mm of rain per day. If it hasn't rained that much on average in the last few days, it's watering time.
The leaves of my... seem robust but they're all curled in, like they're dying. The root zone is saturated.	At first sight, a plant that is getting too much water *can* appear like a plant getting too little, but if you gently dig around the plant's root zone and the soil is completely sodden (there may even be standing water present under the surface), then actually your plant is waterlogged. Most likely you have built your garden bed upon a heavily compacted section of earth and have a serious drainage problem. The soil around your plants' roots should always be moist, but *never* wet. A root system cannot continue to grow through water (unless it is an aquatic plant!) because roots can't breathe in water. And if the roots stop growing, so does the plant. - You may simply need to decrease how much you are watering this area. Try to find a balance. - But likely, you will need to completely renovate this section by deeply forking over it to create natural clefts in the dense pan. It will also need to be brought to life with worms and lots of manure and compost (see pages 34–37 for more information). Build your garden bed up high in this section, mulch it generously, and over time the drainage will be restored. In the meantime, use the area to grow only shallow-rooted plants like salad greens, soft herbs, like dill and coriander, and radishes, which should all still do quite well here even during this restoration period (and go easy on the watering during this time). If none of this seems to apply, you may be up against a fungal disease (see point on page 103, 'I have leaf curl on my peach trees...').

Observation.	Solution.
Possums are eating *everything*.	- Leave treats. The simplest and easiest solution, so try this first before netting. We've had amazing results by simply leaving out little offerings of scraps for possums (consistently in the same place) in what they would consider a safe place, away from the garden. The lower risk placement makes the offering extremely attractive to them. This is what we do. - The only 100% foolproof method is to net your entire garden (actually a smaller investment than you think). - Dogs also deter possums. - Large hawk and owl kites (see the next point, 'Birds are eating my leafy greens...') can also sometimes work.
Birds are eating my leafy greens, young seedlings, nuts and fruit.	- Our favourite bird deterrent, and our go-to—for anything from the most insistent blackbirds to the greediest wild ducks—is Harry the Hawk, our hawk kite. It is literally what it sounds like, a kite that is shaped like a hawk. You can make your own simply by cutting the silhouette of a flying hawk out of some robust, flexible material, or they can be readily purchased. It is most effective to string the kite up between trees with fishing line, so that it bobs about 4-8 m above your garden. It will clear an area of 'pest' birds in a heartbeat. - Netting is another obvious solution here, even for greens. For fruit trees, net only when the fruit is getting super close to harvest time. For nut trees, net after the fruit has started to mature but the nut inside is still a while from harvest. For all trees, just don't net too early or you will have a whole lot of trouble removing the net afterwards, because new green branches will have grown through the netting. And remove the netting *as soon* as the harvest is over to avoid the same issue. For greens and other young seedlings, net when you sow/plant and be sure to support the netting off the seedlings themselves with some upturned buckets or pots. - Hanging old CDs and plastic bags in trees also works great but is far from pretty.
Harlequin bugs are sucking the life out of my tomatoes/fruit.	We'd never had a problem with harlequin bugs until the first season in our current village garden. It was as if they'd been breeding in the area for years, feeding off our established orchard (which dropped all its fruit before harvest that year because of the onslaught) and vegetable garden (our tomatoes were being sucked dry). It was clear measures needed to be taken! In our previous market gardens, harlequin bugs were always present, but never caused noticeable damage. We believe it was because we were always growing row upon row of beautiful beneficial flower crops (such as Queen Anne's lace and fennel), right beside our tomatoes and fruit trees. The umbrella-like blooms of these plants would often be *covered* with harlequin bugs, the Queen Anne's lace especially. And these plants are also the best attractors for the natural predatory wasps that feed on harlequin bug eggs. So, when these flowers are in abundance, harlequin bugs aren't able to become established. Once established though, harlequin bugs require active control with the natural pesticide and spray options described on page 100 in, '*Something* is eating my plants' until they are brought into balance. Persistence with these measures will win the day in the end. Be prepared next season by planting a *lot more* umbrella-like beneficial flowering plants at the beginning of the season to ensure they don't become established. Queen Anne's lace, flowering fennel, yarrow, caraway, carrot and celery are all ideal for this specific problem, so plant throughout your garden (specifically around your tomatoes, fruiting trees and vines) or in a wildflower patch (see page 74) *beside* your garden.
A strange fluoro orange/yellow slime kind of thing has grown out of my manure/ compost and is oozing onto my...	This is harmless slime mould. It will soon harden into a crisp honeycomb-like mass, die off, slowly turn brown/ black and then disintegrate. It will not harm your plants. Weird, yes. Problem, no. We've mainly experienced this kind of thing sprouting out of manure from horse stables.

Observation.	Solution.
***Something* is eating my plants.**	- If your plants are being completely beheaded, it is most likely birds. See point, 'Birds are eating my leafy greens...', page 99. - If it's more like chunks, usually round-edged and only from the softest part of the leaves (leaving just the leaf veins or stems), it is most likely slugs or snails. See the next point, 'Slugs and snails are eating my leaves.' - If it's particularly your brassicas (broccoli, cauliflower, cabbage, kale, turnip, radish etc.) see point on opposite page, 'Little green caterpillars are destroying my brassicas...' - If you can see it's caterpillars, see the point below, 'Caterpillars are eating my plants.' - If you think it's something other than all of this, try a homemade garlic pesticide. We've found that most leaf-eaters hate this. Simply crush a few cloves of garlic into a 1 litre or so jar of water and let it steep overnight. Strain into a spray bottle, then spray the affected plants. You can also steep crushed fresh chilli, oregano and wormwood in the mix for added power. And while you're at it, you might as well add in some worm tea or seaweed emulsion to strengthen the affected leaves. Works wonders.
Slugs and snails are eating my the leaves of my plants.	Slugs and snails are some of the most common garden pests, and every gardener we know has had to battle them at some point. They are especially active in spring and autumn, away from the hottest and coldest parts of the year, but can be present all year. We've found they can be especially ferocious in a newly established garden. A new garden is yet to find its balance. It is yet to attract all the little birds and frogs and beneficial insects (see Don't get disheartened when starting out, page 57, and Placing your bushy perennial plants, page 52). In these cases, don't give up hope, just be consistent with the following approach, and within a few weeks balance will begin to establish itself. - Firstly, all snail and slug baits are toxic. Even the ones that say they are pet friendly or non-poisonous. They are not the solution. - Shell grit, ash and other physical deterrents are also a waste of time. - The solution is a combination of beer traps and picking. Beer traps are shallow containers (anything about 5 cm deep and 5–10 cm in diameter) dug into the soil so that the lip is level with the soil, then half-filled with beer. Slugs and snails will be attracted into the traps and drown. If you're lucky, you might be able to get beer 'slops' from your local pub. Place traps in problem spots in your garden, or to protect large areas, place several traps along the bed spaced about 1 m apart. Keep them topped up. Along with beer traps, you can get on top of a slug/snail infestation very quickly as it emerges simply by going out into the garden with a torch at night and picking them off your plants. Feed them to the chickens or squash them (or purge, cook and eat the snails!). - Finally, letting your chickens roam in a mature autumn garden can be a great way to get rid of any slug/snail eggs that have been laid. Chickens *can* also be a bit destructive and will kick mulch all over the place, so use this tip with caution! Guinea fowl and turkeys are less destructive and just as effective.
Caterpillars are eating my plants.	- If the caterpillar is small and bright green, see the next point also. But no matter what caterpillar you're looking at, you actually have a lack of small bird population. The best long-term fix for this is to plant more bushy natives, fruit trees, fruiting creepers, like kiwi, passionfruit, grapes and the various berries (see Placing trees/vines and bushy perennial plants, pages 40–42) and tall-growing flowers, like dahlias, cosmos, cornflowers and scabiosa (see A wildflower patch, page 74). - In the short term, pick off caterpillars by hand, spray with the natural pesticide mentioned above in '*Something* is eating my plants', soapy water (although soapy water can kill some beneficial insects too, so this isn't usually our preference), pure fine clay (potter's clay) diluted in water until it forms a milky liquid, or alternatively dust with ground white or black pepper.

Observation.	Solution.
Little green caterpillars are destroying my brassicas and popping out of my tomatoes. There are little white butterflies everywhere too!	You have a white cabbage butterfly problem (those little green caterpillars are baby white cabbage butterflies!). Firstly, having a garden full of white cabbage butterflies is very different to having a white cabbage butterfly *problem*. Our garden is *always* full of white cabbage butterflies—they are beautiful to watch, and they lay their eggs on everything. But either those eggs are being eaten by our good-bug population, or the little green caterpillars are getting gobbled up as they hatch, because we rarely see the grubs and we rarely see any damage from them. Remember, bugs in a garden are not inherently a problem—your garden should be *full* of bugs! The question is, 'Are they doing damage?' If you genuinely have a problem and they are causing damage: - Follow the tips for other caterpillars in the point on opposite page. - Attract more beneficial insects by planting lots of dill, coriander, fennel, cosmos, parsnip, Queen Anne's lace, nasturtium and garlic chives. Especially when flowering, these plants will bring in all the good bugs that prey on the white cabbage butterfly eggs. - Hang tiny white butterfly shaped kites. Literally cut little butterfly shapes out of white plastic ice-cream containers (or a similar material) and hang them about the affected areas with fishing line. White cabbage butterflies are territorial, so won't lay where another white cabbage butterfly is lingering. - Pick off and squash any of the little green caterpillars that you see causing trouble. - People have noted that purple-leaved varieties of commonly affected plants are far less targeted, so try purple kale, cabbage, bok choy, cauliflower and broccoli varieties. - Dill and nasturtium actually attract the white cabbage butterfly, so they are great sacrificial offerings around your brassicas. - But our favourite helper, and something we always plant with our brassicas in the lead up to autumn, is upland cress. Not only do the white cabbage butterflies prefer to lay eggs on *it* over brassicas, cress also kills the caterpillars as they hatch by poisoning them with the natural chemicals inside the cress leaves as they begin to eat them. A true super plant for white cabbage butterfly control!
Aphids/mites/ mealybugs/thrips are attacking my...	We have sometimes experienced aphid/mite/mealybug/thrip attacks in our roses or fruit trees, but only in new plantings/gardens. We've found that once our gardens are established and blooming with beneficial plantings of things like dill, coriander, fennel, cosmos, parsnip, Queen Anne's lace, nasturtium and garlic chives, there are more than enough beneficial insects and small birds about to keep everything in balance. A newly planted peach tree or rose bush may experience such an infestation in its first season, but in a healthy, balanced garden you should find that the natural predators are ready and waiting the following season. Nature is clever like that. If you are experiencing such an infestation: - The first thing to do is wait and observe. You may find that in just a few days the local ladybugs will swoop in and eat the aphids/mites/mealybugs/thrips without *you* needing to do anything. If this doesn't happen (and the plant in question is robust enough), try simply spraying the pests off with water from a standard garden spray gun. If spraying doesn't work, or the plant is too fragile to withstand such a blast of water, try any of the natural pesticide and spray options described opposite in '*Something* is eating my plants' or try a spray of equal parts milk and water. - Ants could also be the problem. See the sticky sap solution to scale bugs on page 102 in, 'My citrus tree's leaves and fruit have all these little red-brown spots...' - Finally, planting a wild patch of beneficial flowers every spring (see page 74) is the best way to ensure you have an army of good bugs at the ready to deal with these kind of invasions.

Observation.	Solution.
I have codling moth in my apples/pears/ quinces.	Unfortunately, if you are only just realising you have a codling moth problem as you harvest this year's fruit, there's nothing that can be done for this year's crop. But next year you're going to be all over it. - Your number one allies for codling moth control are beneficial insects. So, surround your orchard with, and plant under your trees, good-bug attracting plants, like dill, coriander, fennel, cosmos, buckwheat (especially beneficial for attracting control bugs for codling moth), parsnip, Queen Anne's lace and yarrow and let them flower profusely all year (see page 74). - Codling moth traps will also help. Mix together 1 cup of molasses, 1 cup of apple cider vinegar, 1 tablespoon of sourdough culture (optional but causes more rapid fermentation which attracts the moths) and 2 litres of water. Cut an apple-sized opening in each side of a few used 2-4 litre, wide-mouthed plastic bottles (small buckets work too—no holes necessary because of their open tops), fill the bottles/buckets with 5-7 cm of the trap liquid and hang in the affected trees. Check traps every week to 10 days and refresh them as needed. Traps should be in place from early spring through to winter. - Finally, keep your orchard tidy of fallen fruit and regularly remove any fruit that is affected (any fruit with a pin-sized hole in it). Run poultry under the trees, as they will do the tidying for you, or simply collect fallen fruit and feed it to them. If you don't keep poultry, submerge any removed affected and fallen fruit in a barrel/ bucket of water for at least 1 week before burying or adding to your compost. This will kill any coddling moth caterpillars inside the fruit.
I have fruit fly in my fruiting trees and plants.	Just like codling moth, once a fruit has had fruit fly eggs laid in it (gardeners call this being 'stung'), that fruit must be removed and destroyed. - Control of fruit fly is similar to control of codling moth. Follow the same suggestions above as far as planting good-bug attracting plants, destroying fallen and stung fruits and utilising poultry to keep things tidy. - But fruit flies require a more complex bait. By far the most effective commercially available bait is called Naturalure. It is composed of a protein and sugar solution combined with a natural bacterial insecticide. Spray the bait in patches, directly onto the trunks of your fruit trees, every week and after rains, from the moment the petals drop after flowering all the way through to harvest.
My citrus tree's leaves and fruit have all these little red-brown spots on them, and the leaves have a kind of black soot growing on them (bay laurel trees are also often affected).	You are experiencing a scale bug infestation. The spots are actually tiny bugs that are feeding off your tree and secreting a sticky sap. In a balanced environment, beneficial insects, like ladybugs and lacewings, control scale bug no problem. But what often happens in citrus trees is that ants want to feed off the sticky sap, so they literally farm the scale bugs by picking them up and spreading them all over your trees. The ants then proceed to fight off the good bugs so that the scale bugs live and rapidly breed and can continue to secrete the sticky sap (the ant's food source). The black soot is sooty mould, a mould that also feeds off the sticky secretions. It is just a secondary symptom. - Forget spraying with white oil, it is only treating the symptoms. You must treat the problem—the ants. - The very effective treatment is simply to stop the ants from climbing on your trees. To do this, apply a non-drying, sticky sap (available at all good nurseries under various names) in a ring around the tree's trunk. The sap is a natural, physical barrier that the ants simply can't crawl past. And once the ants are gone, the beneficial insects will be able to eat the scale bugs and will clear up the problem in a matter of weeks. We find it's best to wrap the trunk with tape (builder's tape or masking tape) first and paint the sap onto that. That way, when the sap gets covered with dirt, dust and twigs it can be easily removed and replaced. Check on the sticky barrier every couple of weeks to make sure no leaves or twigs have stuck to it, as these will form bridges the ants can use to cross.

Observation.	Solution.
I have leaf curl on my peach/nectarine trees/ powdery mildew on my cucumbers/pumpkins/ zucchinis/summer squash/melons/some other fungal disease on my...	Fungal problems are super common but they are also super manageable. Actually, all fungal problems are really vigour problems. That is, your plant or tree is run down and so isn't strong enough in this moment to fight off the attacking fungus. The most common fungal problems experienced in the garden are powdery mildew and leaf curl. Towards the end of the season, almost all zucchini/summer squash and cucumber plants tend to succumb to powdery mildew (it looks like white dust on your plants' leaves). Pumpkins, melons and grapevines often suffer from powdery mildew attack also. And *many* stone-fruit trees, especially peaches and nectarines, succumb to leaf curl around flowering each year. Importantly, once the fungus has taken hold, it doesn't mean your plant is done for. Usually a peach tree will fight back against leaf curl all on its own once spring's humidity gives way to the drier summer air, growing a new healthy plume of foliage and thriving. But it is unlikely to successfully grow a crop of fruit that year. And zucchinis/summer squash and cucumbers that have been affected by powdery mildew can be very successfully cut back and treated and continue to fruit and grow for months. But the smartest approach is definitely prevention: **Prevention.** A robustly healthy plant will never succumb to a fungal disease. So, to prevent fungal disease from ever occurring in the first place, we need to ensure our plants are in the best health possible: - Stone-fruit trees should be fed over winter with a generous dose of grazing animal manure (cow, horse, sheep etc.) spread around their base (keep about 10 cm away from the trunk) then mulched over with straw. - When the first leaves appear in spring, spray the leaves and branches with a seaweed/kelp emulsion or a fish emulsion. Worm tea works well too. As does trichoderma, which is an isolated, naturally occurring beneficial bacteria that will populate your tree's leaves and branches, leaving no place vacant for fungal attack. Spray the trees every week or two with one or a mix of these until a couple of weeks after fruit set. - Cucumber, pumpkin, melon and zucchini/summer squash plants and grapevines will benefit from the same treatment at monthly intervals all season, including the manure at the beginning of the season, to prevent powdery mildew from becoming an problem. **Treatment.** If you haven't been utilising the above measures and begin to see signs of fungal disease, there is still lots you can do: - Make a simple spray and spray the affected tree/vine/plant's leaves: 1 teaspoon of bicarbonate of soda, a few drops of soft soap and 2 litres of water. The alkalinity of bicarb wreaks havoc on fungal diseases. - Cooled chamomile tea (literally the same tea you'd make yourself before bed) is also a wonderful natural fungicide. - As is a mix of equal parts milk and water, especially if the milk is raw. - Seaweed/kelp emulsions, fish emulsions, worm teas and trichoderma sprays should also be employed to increase vigour and restore balance.
Tiny grey flies are sucking the life out of my leafy greens.	We experienced this nearly every year during late spring in our previous market garden. Our greens would be lush and healthy one day, then wilting and weird the next. When we brushed our hands through the plantings, thousands of tiny grey flies would take to the air. But then, maybe a week later, they were nowhere to be seen! Nearly every year it happened this way. And as soon as they were gone, the greens returned to health. The old leaves were scarred, but the new growth was perfect. We suspect the resolution each year was really thanks to our beneficial insects (like our lady bugs). The damage was minor, and all plants survived happily every time. It was another good lesson in waiting for nature. So plant yourself a wild patch of beneficial flowers (see page 74) to attract all the good bugs and know that you're covered. If you desperately want to clear them off sooner, employ the same tactics as for aphids (page 101).

PART 3.

Eat.

Nurturing yourself and your village.

Traditionally, food and cooking were seasonal and regional at their core. You took what was seasonal and regional and created variety within it, to nurture and nourish yourself and your village. And to celebrate, feast and share.

Meals were always shared—never did you eat alone. This is how children learnt, how we as people would connect, share stories and show love. It's how we have evolved. It's in us. And, it's how we nurture ourselves and each other.

And not only do we share food, abundant harvests and meals, but we share recipes and our knowledge. Within our families, this kind of sharing deeply connects us with each other, passing on traditions that have nourished bodies like ours for generations. And within the village at large, this kind of sharing is another way to bring us together, to bond, to enhance the experience of nurturing—and being nurtured *by*—the community that surrounds us.

Within all of this, we have meaningful experiences together. We are nurtured and we feel safe. This is what we believe in.

Our top tips to make cooking for your village the easiest it can be, every day.

1. Routines. Have them. For a long time, we thought, 'Routines? Pft!' Then we got a wild duck. Every morning when we let it out of its hutch, it did the same thing—woke, flew around in a circle and then ate some grass. That's when we realised that we are animals too and we all need a routine, whatever that is for you. For example, dedicating a set amount of time each morning or evening for gardening (even just 15 minutes—harvesting, maintaining, planting) will centre you in the day and make growing easy. Or taking time to sit and have a tea or coffee each morning—simple but nurturing. Or setting a time aside each week to preserve something from the garden—your winter shelves will be abundant.

2. Think a day ahead. Think today about what you might eat tomorrow. Prepare what you need.

3. Look inside your fridge. Seriously. People don't look in it. Look in it for food. Cook, preserve and eat that food.

4. Keep the top shelf of your fridge for leftovers and quick meal-makers. This way, they don't get lost.

5. Sundays are for cleaning out your fridge. This is when you make a stew (page 294) or risotto (page 286), cook whatever is over-abundant (suggestions, page 108) and preserve/freeze things you aren't going to eat. Or, if you are traditional, and Sundays are a day of rest, put a chickpea soup (page 280) on the stove on Saturday, so Sunday is easy.

6. Pick a day to cook big. Cook or prepare something for the week ahead—a batch of cookies (page 192), stock (page 341), pesto (page 124), a big salad, bread (page 134), sprouts (page 340), beans (page 339), grains (page 338). This will make eating well all week as easy as possible. You can also double recipes to either have leftovers throughout the week, freeze or give to someone else. Many recipes can be expanded easily, such as stews (pages 294 and 306), soups, baked goods, bread (page 134), muffins (pages 198 and 231), cakes (pages 204 and 328), crackers (page 136) and our chickpea lasagne (page 300).

7. Family meal day. Choose a regular day each week to share a meal. Make it a routine with family or friends.

8. Grow a little bit in abundance. Growing rocket? Grow double for your friend (see Grow, page 27), then trade/share, or use to make pesto (page 124).

9. Freeze excess fruits (and veggies). For adding to smoothies (page 186) and cakes (pages 198 and 204).

10. Preserve any extra harvest *every* week. So that it doesn't build up into a huge insurmountable job!

11. Always have pickles/preserves on the go. Easy, delicious snacks, toppings and salad heroes (see Preserves, page 153).

12. Antipasti boards are the best! This is how you do slowing down, easy food and feeding many right. And cheese boards make the easiest desserts.

13. Don't be scared to ad-lib with recipes. We are massive fans of using what you have.

14. Make staples. The base of easy meals and salads to serve many (see Staples, page 115). Also, cook extra beans, pulses and grains and keep them in the fridge tossed with olive oil and a pinch of salt—ready to add to salads (see salad chart, page 242).

15. Salads are always good. They are easy, balanced and primarily plant-based meals, great in themselves or easy meal additions to share.

16. Prepare your nuts and seeds in advance. Toast batches of nuts and seeds and store them in airtight jars or containers, which saves time when cooking. They make easy and delicious toppings.

17. Make the space. Have a kitchen shelf dedicated to things soaking/fermenting, then your bench will stay clear and everything will feel easy.

18. You don't need a mill to make flour. Rolled grains (like oats), nuts (like almonds) and seeds (like flaxseeds) can be blended in a high-powered blender to make flours. And don't forget, you can roll grains other than oats in an 'oat-roller' too!

Getting the most out of your ingredients.

Using what you've got.

We are all about using what you've got. Here are some ingredients we often use instead of, or in addition to, other ingredients. We know not everyone will have all of these, but if you do, this is a guide on how to use them.

Fresh herbs/seeds/spices: can generally be substituted for their dry equivalents by using three to four times the amount.

Wild fennel fronds or seeds: can be used to add extra flavour to dishes already using fennel, or as a garnish for soups and stews. We also often add them to preserves.

Leek and onion flowers: are a fantastic garnish for soups, stews, pastas and risottos.

Onion shoots/bunching onions/young onions: are all perfect substitutes for spring onions (actually, they're the same thing!).

Garlic shoots: (young garlic before the bulb begins to form) are great in place of mature garlic cloves.

Wild garlic: is also a great substitute for 'standard' garlic.

Chicory and wild dandelion leaves: can both be used instead of radicchio.

Wild mushrooms: work fantastically in place of common mushrooms.

Wild greens: like wild radish, mallow, fat hen, stinging nettles, amaranth and warrigal greens can all be used instead of spinach or chard/silverbeet.

Portuguese 'tronchuda' kale and collard greens: are both excellent substitutes for kale.

Herb flowers: can be used alongside the herb (fennel, coriander, dill, garlic chives, onion, rosemary, sage, basil, oregano and thyme) as well as brassica and leek flowers.

Edible flowers: such as borage, nasturtiums, violas, calendula and marigolds are great for garnishing dishes.

Alternative sweeteners: such as maple syrup, brown rice malt syrup, stevia, agave syrup, yacon syrup or coconut sugar/syrup can all be used instead of sugar/honey.

Plant-based milks: can be used instead of dairy.

Mango: makes a great substitute for apricot.

Our favourite pasta alternatives: are snake beans, julienned zucchini or carrot, fried chickpea pancakes cut into strips (page 218), whole chickpeas and sweet potato gnocchi (page 128).

Seasonal abundances (A to Z).

Throughout the seasons, we find that we are often faced with an abundance of a specific ingredient. Sometimes so much so that we refer to these abundances as our 'burden', because there is such an abundance of something that we don't know what to do with it. So, if you are faced with burdens of your own, here are some ideas for what to do with them. Or, if you don't grow yourself, but see something in season at your local market, use this list as inspiration to make the most of this seasonal abundance.

Almonds. Marmalade and honey biscotti (page 190); almond sorbetto and popsicles (page 331).

Apricots. Spiced apricots with fresh cheese and honey (page 201).

Asparagus. Potato, asparagus and parsley soup (page 278).

Avocados. So simple chocolate gelato (page 319); raw chocolate and espresso mousse (page 322); breakfast bowls (page 206).

Beetroot. Millet and beetroot pilaf (page 252).

Bread. Mumma Michelle's egg and bread muffins (page 231); wild fennel and bread soup (page 272).

Broad beans. Quick-pickled broad beans (page 164).

Buttermilk. Buttermilk, oat and lake salt crackers (page 136).

Capsicum. Capsicums under oil (page 163).

Carrots. Creamy carrot and parsnip soup (page 270).

Cauliflower. Cauliflower wraps (page 133).

Cherries. Natural cherry syrup (page 320).

Cherry tomatoes. Whole cherry tomatoes in brine (page 172); eggplant, cherry tomato and borlotti bean salad (page 297); baked butternut pumpkin and cherry tomatoes (page 255).

Cooking greens (chard/silverbeet, kale etc.). Wild greens with fresh dukkah (page 258).

Corn. Husk-baked cheesy corn (page 244).

Dairy milk. Fresh cheese (page 144); cacioricotta (page 148).

Eggplants. Joe's burnt baba ganoush (page 215); eggplant and chickpea lasagne (page 300); baked eggplant and pear slices (page 239).

Fennel. Wild fennel and bread soup (page 272).

Fruit. Smoothies (page 186).

Grapefruit. Grapefruit, orange and fennel marmalade (page 180).

Grapes. Cold polenta and grape slice (page 334).

Green salad leaves. Family salad dressing (page 244); salad chart (page 242).

Herbs. Basil and rocket pesto (page 124); all the herbs green sauce (page 124); rhubarb, orange and mint cordial (page 178); potato, asparagus and parsley soup (page 278).

Leeks. Nonna's leek and spinach fritters (page 222); leek jam (page 155); sweet potato steaks with leeks and wine (page 264).

Leftover cooked grains. Stuffed quinoa tomatoes in broth (page 290); millet and beetroot pilaf (page 252); breakfast bowls (page 206); salads (salad chart, page 242); honey onion, buckwheat and lentil salad (page 260).

Mushrooms. Creamy mushrooms (page 263).

Olives. Dry-salted olives (page 177).

Oranges. Grapefruit, orange and fennel marmalade (page 180); rhubarb, orange and mint cordial (page 178).

Peaches. Peach and cream slabs (page 316).

Pears. Pear, lemon and chilli jam (page 172).

Plums. Baked plums, sage and warm cheese (page 325).

Potatoes. Potato, asparagus and parsley soup (page 278).

Pulses/legumes. Sprouts (page 340); honey onion, buckwheat and lentil salad (page 260); chickpea soup (page 280).

Pumpkin. Baked butternut pumpkin (page 255).

Quinoa. Stuffed quinoa tomatoes in broth (page 290).

Random mixed fruit and vegetables. Oat, fruit and vegetable breakfast muffins (page 198); salads (salad chart, page 242); smoothies (page 186).

Random mixed vegetables. Mumma's barley stew (page 294); every Sunday freestyle stew (page 306); salads (salad chart, page 242); Lach's brown rice risotto (page 286); egg surprise (page 194).

Raspberries. Four-ingredient walnut cake (page 328).

Rhubarb. Rhubarb, orange and mint cordial (page 178).

Rocket. Basil and rocket pesto (page 124).

Sardines. Sardines under oil (page 166).

Sourdough culture. Leftover-sourdough flatbreads (page 134).

Stale bread. Wild fennel and bread soup (page 272); Mumma Michelle's bread muffins (page 231).

Summer squash. Shaved zucchini and apricot salad (page 250); zucchini pickles (page 170).

Sweet potatoes. Gluten-free sweet potato gnocchi (page 128); sweet potato steaks with leeks and wine (page 264).

Tomatoes. Tomato and brown rice soup (page 268); stuffed quinoa tomatoes in broth (page 290); simplest red sauce (page 312); whole cherry tomatoes in brine (page 172).

Vine leaves. Fermented vine leaves (page 160); dolmades (page 228).

Walnuts. Four-ingredient walnut cake (page 328).

Wombok. Italian kimchi (page 156).

Zucchinis. Zucchini pickles (page 170); shaved zucchini and apricot salad (page 250); zucchini rolls (page 236).

Preparing the most nutrient-rich food possible.

To ensure that our food is as nutrient rich as it can be, we prepare our wholefood ingredients the traditional way, as our ancestors did. They knew how to take raw, unrefined and sometimes quite indigestible foods and transform them into the most nutrient-rich foods possible. Eating in this way means that you need to eat less and produce less, putting the least toll on nature and on you. You are also truly getting the most out of your food. So you are as healthy as you can be, and so is nature.

To do this requires an understanding of each food source, because preparation techniques for each vary. On the following page is a list of some of the key wholefood ingredients that we use in our recipes and some super-quick guides on how to preserve your excesses and best prepare your wholegrains.

And please see the appendix (page 337) for our guides on preparing the most nutrient-dense bone and vegetable stocks, wholegrains, pulses, sprouts and preserves.

Wholefood ingredients.

Cooking with these ingredients will help you to create the same flavours that we achieve in the recipes to follow.

Water. Rainwater or spring water—it is essential to have access to unchlorinated water for your health and the health of your ferments.

Vegetables, fruits, fungi and edible flowers. And lots of them! Grown in nutrient-rich soil or gathered from the wild.

Wholegrains. Soaked or sprouted first, or when flour is required, always milled fresh in a stone mill.

Pulses. Always soaked or sprouted first.

Dairy products. Full-fat dairy! Always use full-fat, pastured dairy products from well-raised animals.

Eggs. Pastured eggs from home-raised or similarly spoilt chickens.

Meat and fish. Gathered from the wild or raised and killed respectfully, naturally and stress free.

Fats and oils. We use extra-virgin olive oil, ghee, butter and lard or other rendered fats, and occasionally cold-pressed seed oils like sesame and sunflower. These are all whole forms of natural fats, which help our digestion, skin and nervous systems, and some contain vitamins and minerals that are otherwise hard to get.

Nut and seed meals/flours. We always grind nuts (like almonds) and seeds (like flaxseeds and sunflower seeds) fresh in our high-powered blender, as they oxidise rapidly once ground and lose their nutritional benefits. If you need to buy pre-ground versions, try to find fresh, refrigerated stock.

Spices. We use the seeds whole or mill them fresh.

Salt. We only use unrefined salt, as refining strips away all of the trace minerals.

Coffee, tea and chocolate. Responsibly sourced from farmers who grow well.

Honey. Unprocessed honey—not heat-treated. Raw honey contains live enzymes, pollen, vitamins, minerals, antioxidants and antifungal properties, which are largely denatured when heat-treated.

Sugar. We always use unrefined sugar unless stated. The person who produces our sugar, juices their sugarcane and dries that juice—and that is our sugar. It's full of all of its natural vitamins and minerals and tastes like nothing else. Or we use rapadura, but even rapadura is still processed, with some minerals stripped. So even 'unrefined' sugars are still processed to some degree.

Why we don't always use everything.

Some people might wonder why we don't use the skin on everything or use juice pulp leftovers. The answer is that it's not wasted, it goes to the compost or the chickens, and that is something we need too. We need compost for our soil to grow more vegetables and flowers. And we love fresh eggs and happy hens! Life is a cycle.

Simple preservation guide.

Have excess? There are five main ways to preserve, which we use throughout the book. They are:

1. Freeze it. We all have freezers these days, might as well fill them. They work a lot more efficiently when they're full too!

2. Dry it. In the sun, or in the oven set between 40 and 50°C. The oldest form of preservation.

3. Cure it with salt or sugar. See sardines under oil (page 166) and dry-salted olives (page 177).

4. Lacto-ferment it. Full of good bacteria (see page 342 for more information). This is our favourite preservation method! See Italian kimchi (page 156) and fermented vine leaves (page 160).

5. Bottle it. Using our heat preservation guide (page 343). See capsicums under oil (page 163), leek jam (page 155), quick-pickled broad beans (page 164), zucchini pickles (page 170), cherry tomatoes in brine (page 172), pear, lemon and chilli jam (page 172), cordial (page 178) and marmalade (page 180).

Simple preparation guide for grains, nuts, pulses and seeds.

Grains, nuts, pulses and seeds are best for your body when they are in their whole form and prepared by soaking, souring or sprouting, which makes their nutrients the most readily available and digestible. Here is a quick reference guide to soaking/souring these foods (1 = least nutrient rich, 6 = best practice).

1. White grains and refined flours: don't need to be soaked or soured because they have already had their digestion-disrupting anti-nutrients (along with most of their nutrients) stripped away in the refining process.

2. Souring wholegrains in the fridge: not as effective at neutralising the anti-nutrients as the next point, but still a huge improvement on unsoaked grains.

3. Souring wholegrains on the bench with an acid: (see page 338) for 4–48 hours (the longer the better!), or soaking nuts and seeds (including beans/pulses) in water with a little salt (see page 339) for 12 hours.

4. Milling your wholegrains to make sourdough: and fermenting for 12 hours (see page 337). Yes!

5. Milling your wholegrains to make sourdough: and fermenting for 24–72 hours (see page 337). Even better!

6. Sprouting your wholegrains, seeds and pulses: (see page 340) the absolute best!

Practicalities.

All our recipes are tested using a fan-forced convection oven. If you are using a conventional oven (not fan-forced), you may need to adjust the temperature by raising it slightly. Our recipes are always tested using metric weights for accuracy, and we recommend that you do the same. We use Australian cups, tablespoons and teaspoons (Commonwealth cups, tablespoons and teaspoons: 1 cup = 250 ml = 8.5 fl oz, 1 tablespoon = 20 ml = ¾ fl oz, 1 teaspoon = 5 ml = ¼ fl oz). For a full metric/imperial conversion chart, see page 351.

Guide to categories.

GF—gluten free

WF—wheat free

DF—dairy free

V—vegetarian

VG—vegan

Su—summer

A—autumn

W—winter

Sp—spring

Adapting recipes to suit your climate.

The abbreviations for summer, autumn, winter and spring that appear above our recipes are a general guide to what is seasonally available in our South-East Australian temperate climate. These seasonal indicators can be adjusted for other climate zones as follows:

Cooler/mountain regions. If you live in a cooler/mountain region, your growing season is shorter than ours. Spring, summer and autumn produce may be delayed by up to a month in comparison, while winter produce will be available sooner and be around for much longer.

Subtropics. If you are in, or nearer to, the subtropics, you can probably expect everything to be available at least half a season sooner from spring through autumn, and you may have to wait the equivalent time for your cool-season goodies to first appear each year.

Tropics. If you live in the tropics proper, you may find it difficult to find some of these plant foods grown locally at all, but the vast majority of those listed under summer and autumn should be readily available through the cool season and likely most of the rest of the year too.

Sourdough rye friselli and bagels, page 141.

Staples.

Store in the fridge or on the shelf for good, quick food. Great for antipasti, easy meals and snacks.

MAKES 1 SCOBY // TIME: 1 WEEK IF YOU'RE LUCKY, BUT UP TO 4 WEEKS

Kombucha scoby from scratch.

- 2 litres unchlorinated water (see notes, page 159)
- 110 g (½ cup) raw sugar
- 4 black teabags (or 1 tablespoon loose black tea)
- 250 ml (1 cup) store-bought plain kombucha (it must be unpasteurised for the fermentation to work)

SPECIAL EQUIPMENT

- 2 litre jar

Kombucha is *everywhere* now! We love it, and it's clear that we're not alone. It's actually so easy to make at home, and we can't recommend it highly enough. It's quick, costs literally next to nothing and it's so fun and rewarding taking part in such a simple and yet utterly complex transformation. It's super easy to get your hands on a kombucha scoby (symbiotic culture of bacteria and yeasts), which is the mother of the fermentation—just like a vinegar mother—and functions like sourdough culture, in that it's the living thing that inoculates (ferments) an infinite number of batches. But it's also very easy to make your own from a bottle of store-bought unpasteurised kombucha. If you love kombucha, make your own scoby for an endless supply!

DAY 1

Boil the water in a large saucepan, add the sugar and stir to dissolve. Add the tea and steep for a few minutes, then remove the tea and leave the mixture to cool to room temperature, which can take a few hours.

Add the kombucha (if there is a little cloudy thing in the bottle, that's a baby scoby, so try to get that in there too, as it speeds up the formation) to the pan, stir, then transfer to a clean 2 litre jar. Cover with a finely woven tea towel that has been doubled over (to keep the bugs out) and secure with a rubber band.

Now simply set aside at room temperature for 1–4 weeks while the scoby grows. Aim for a room that is roughly stable at about 20°C or more for consistent growth. If it is cooler, the process will just take longer. If it is hotter, the process will be quicker. Keep it out of direct sunlight. Over the next few days, a thin film will begin to form on the surface of the liquid, which will then get progressively thicker and more robust.

WEEK 1–4

When the film has thickened to about 4–5 mm, your scoby is ready to inoculate a new batch of kombucha. You have made your first scoby! Now see our recipe on page 118 to make kombucha.

The remaining liquid is basically over-fermented kombucha. It will be super tart. Use it just like vinegar in dressings and for preserving, add dashes of it to your chicken's drinking water, or start your day with a teaspoon in a glass of water.

New scoby after 2 weeks (top left), after 3 weeks (top right) and after 4 weeks (bottom) when it is ready to use!

Making kombucha with your new scoby.

3 litres unchlorinated water (see notes, page 159)

220 g (1 cup) raw sugar (see note)

8 green or black (or a combination) teabags (or 2 tablespoons loose tea)

500 ml (2 cups) kombucha from the last batch (you can also use the over-fermented kombucha from scoby making)

1 scoby (see field notes)

SPECIAL EQUIPMENT

3 litres worth of bottles that can handle pressure (resealable soft drink, sparkling water or beer bottles)

3–4 litre jar

FIELD NOTES.

On scoby care.

Scobys are tough little things. We once forgot a batch and the scoby sat happily atop some very over-fermented kombucha in the fridge for three years! Keeping it in the fridge sealed in a jar with a little kombucha, as described in the recipe, is all you need to do between ferments. This puts it to sleep, just like your sourdough culture. And if you *do* forget about it and it dries out or goes bad, just start a fresh one (page 116). The only other maintenance involved is to remove the bottom layer (your scoby grows in layers–you'll see) occasionally if it's getting too thick. That's it! Happy fermenting.

DAY 1

Boil the water in a large saucepan, add the sugar and stir to dissolve. Add the tea and steep for a few minutes, then remove the tea and cool to room temperature, which can take a few hours.

Add the kombucha to the pan, stir, then transfer the liquid to a clean 3–4 litre jar. Gently slide your scoby into the liquid (clean hands please—good hygiene is key to a successful ferment). Cover with a finely woven tea towel that has been doubled over (to keep the bugs out) and secure with a rubber band.

Set aside at room temperature to ferment for 7 days. Aim for a room that is roughly stable at about 20°C or more for consistent growth. If it is cooler, the process will take longer. If it is hotter, the process will be faster. Keep it out of direct sunlight.

DAY 7

Taste the kombucha for your preferred balance of sweet to tart. If it's not yet tart enough, give it another day and try again until you hit the spot. If it's too tart, proceed to the next step and note that next time you'll want to shorten the fermenting time. When ready, gently remove the scoby (clean hands again!) and place on a clean plate. If you're not making another batch, add at least a cup of the kombucha to a clean jar, slide in the scoby, seal and store in the fridge. If you're making another batch, splash a few tablespoons of kombucha over the scoby, and place in a dark corner of the kitchen while you prepare and cool the new tea.

Transfer the kombucha into three clean 1 litre bottles (or an equivalent number of smaller bottles) using a clean funnel. If you want to add flavours like ginger, strawberries, herbs etc., now is the time—experiment! Seal the bottles and set aside at about 20°C, out of direct sunlight, for 2–3 more days to carbonate, then place in the fridge, which will slow the fermentation (so your bottles don't explode). Kombucha will keep for a very long time, but it will keep fermenting very slowly too, gradually becoming more and more tart.

RECIPE NOTE.

You can use less-refined sugars to make kombucha, but most scobys prefer more refined sugars because that's how they've been bred for centuries. Importantly, most of the sugar is transformed into beneficial goodness during fermentation, so there is very little actual sugar left in the finished kombucha. So we just stick to the tried and true method.

Whipped butter & olive oil for spreading.

MAKES ABOUT 450 G
TIME: 5 MINUTES + COOLING

I seriously love butter. If I could, I would eat it on everything. But that's not how nature works. In so many of our favourite places, butter is in fact a rare commodity. In those villages, you can only access what is in season around you—which is just the best! Living with the seasons in dry areas means there are few cows, so butter is precious. Sheep and goats are more suited, and are milked predominantly to make delicious cheeses. But cows, not so much. So butter, not so much. Fortunately though, there are *so many* olive trees in these places, which means an abundance of olive oil, and I loved this reminder that butter is precious, and to use what's abundant.

So this is my solution to extend the butter and make it into something even more delicious. We use it as a super-spreadable butter replacement, as part of a cheese board, or on crackers (page 136) for aperitivo.
-Lentil

- 250 ml (1 cup) extra-virgin olive oil
- 200 g unsalted butter, at room temperature
- 3 tablespoons full-cream milk
- ¼ teaspoon unrefined salt

FLAVOURING OPTIONS
(the spread is neutral for sweet or savoury dishes, but you could also try one of these)

- 2–3 teaspoons freshly ground black pepper
- 2–3 teaspoons unprocessed honey
- ½ teaspoon ground turmeric (adds incredible colour)
- 1 garlic clove, crushed (amazing for garlic bread)

Pulse all the ingredients in a food processor or blender until well combined, about 1 minute. Pour the mixture into an airtight container or jar and refrigerate until cold. Once ready, it will be set but still spreadable.

The spread will keep in the fridge for 3–4 months.

Fresh dukkah.

MAKES 1 x 500 ML JAR
TIME: 10 MINUTES

We came up with this dukkah recipe while playing around with the wild greens recipe on page 258. We're all about making things from scratch, so nailing this was super rewarding. This nut, seed, spice and herb mix hits all the dukkah notes you've come to expect, but with a freshness from the herbs that really lifts the whole experience. Put it on *everything*!

- 75 g (½ cup) pistachio kernels, finely chopped
- 70 g (½ cup) pumpkin seeds, finely chopped
- 3 tablespoons sesame seeds
- 3 tablespoons cumin seeds
- 1½ tablespoons coriander seeds
- 1 cup oregano leaves, finely chopped
- 1 cup thyme leaves, finely chopped

Dry-roast the pistachios and seeds in a heavy-based frying pan over low–medium heat, agitating the pan regularly, until wonderfully fragrant. You're looking for the sweet spot, so take care not to burn them, but don't be shy—it's worse to under toast them than to have them extra toasty. Under-toasted seeds will mean your dukkah will taste raw.

Meanwhile, combine the herbs in a medium bowl.

As soon as the seed mix hits peak toastiness, add to the bowl and combine thoroughly. The heat from the seeds will release the oils from the herbs and everything will come together nicely. Set aside to cool.

Once cool, store the dukkah in an airtight container or jar in the fridge. It will keep fresh for up to 1 month. It's great with yoghurt-style dressings, or simply serve with olive oil, fresh bread and dip.

MAKES ABOUT 375 ML (1½ CUPS) // TIME: 20 MINUTES

GF | DF | VG

Quick tomato sauce.

When there is no tomato sauce left on the shelves from last season's batch, it makes us feel deeply upset. So this is a recipe for when you didn't bottle enough, or for when you just need it now. This is quick, easy and delicious! We often have it with eggs, or fish and chip pie (page 285). It has natural sweetness from the apple, a bit of acid, and umami from the soy—all the elements of a good ketchup—but it only takes 20 minutes, as compared to hours for the 'real deal'.

PART 1

- ½ onion, diced
- 1 small celery stalk with leaves, diced (if in season)
- 1 small green apple, peeled and diced
- ¼ teaspoon sweet paprika
- ¼ teaspoon ground ginger
- ¼ teaspoon hot chilli powder (optional)
- a big pinch of freshly ground black pepper
- a generous splash of extra-virgin olive oil

PART 2

- 1 garlic clove, crushed
- 3 teaspoons apple cider vinegar
- a splash of tamari
- 1 tablespoon unrefined sugar (e.g. rapadura)
- a big pinch of unrefined salt
- 375 ml (1½ cups) passata

In a small saucepan over low–medium heat, sauté the part 1 ingredients in the oil for about 3 minutes. Add the part 2 ingredients, except for the passata, and cook for 3–4 minutes, stirring often. When ready, the onion should have softened and the garlic should be beginning to turn golden. Add the passata to the pan and stir to combine.

Pour the mixture into a blender and pulse a few times until just combined, then tip back into the pan over a low–medium heat and reduce for about 10 minutes.

Serve the sauce warm or cold. It will keep in the fridge in an airtight container or jar for 1 month or more.

RECIPE NOTE.

If you have chilli, ginger or even paprika growing fresh in your garden, feel free to adjust the recipe using fresh ingredients rather than dried. See Using what you've got on page 108 for how to switch between fresh and dried herbs.

Basil & rocket pesto.

MAKES ABOUT 280 ML
TIME: 5-10 MINUTES

Many years ago, for one of Matt's birthdays, a few of our friends put together a little notebook of their favourite recipes. It turns out that everyone loves pesto. There were about three pesto recipes in there, each a little different. So, this is a combo of theirs and ours, the recipe we now make by default. It's a thick pesto that has no cheese, but tastes so cheesy. We prefer to add our cheese fresh and it's heaps better to freeze pesto without the cheese. This is great with pasta, gnocchi (page 128), roast veggies, soups, breakfast bowls (pages 206 and 209), eggs and salads.

2 packed cups basil leaves
1 packed cup rocket leaves
2 garlic cloves, crushed
60 g (½ cup) almonds, roughly chopped
160 ml (⅔ cup) extra-virgin olive oil (plus extra if storing)
2 ½ tablespoons apple cider vinegar
¼ teaspoon unrefined salt

Pulse all the ingredients in a food processor or blender until fully combined but still a tiny bit chunky. Be careful not to puree—it will taste totally different! That's it—easy as. Add more oil if you like your pesto a bit thinner.

Use now, or store with a layer of oil on top, which will stop it from oxidising, in an airtight container or jar. It will keep in the fridge for up to 1 month (provided the oil layer is maintained), or in the freezer for 6 months.

FIELD NOTES.

On preserving pesto. People always ask about preserving pesto. Turns out the ones on the shelves are done under high pressure, which is not achievable at home (unless you have a pressure canner). So, simply place it in jars or ice-cube trays and freeze. It will last for about 6 months—although we've frozen it for a year or more and it's still been great!

GF | DF | VG Su | A

All the herbs green sauce.

MAKES ABOUT 320 ML
TIME: 5-10 MINUTES

A vinegary, fresh, super-herby and delicious pesto/sauce/salsa—there's really no more that needs to be said, except that everyone should make it once, because you'll be addicted once you do! This is great with eggs, breakfast things, roasted vegetables and salads, like our so good salad (page 304)—it's just awesome with everything.

1½ packed cups flat-leaf parsley leaves and stalks
1 packed cup mint leaves
½ packed cup basil leaves (see notes)
1 garlic clove, crushed
juice of 1 large lemon
160 ml (⅔ cup) extra-virgin olive oil (plus extra if storing)
2 tablespoons water
1 tablespoon white wine vinegar
¼ teaspoon unrefined salt

Blitz all the ingredients in a food processor or blender until well combined.

Use now, or store with a layer of oil on top, which will stop it from oxidising, in an airtight container or jar. It will keep in the fridge for 5–7 days, or in the freezer for 4 months or longer.

RECIPE NOTES.

If you want to make this outside of summer or autumn, you can replace the basil with more parsley and/or mint.

If chilli is your thing, you could add a little of that too.

Gnocchi land.

We are in the far north-east of Italy, staying with Matt's Italian family. We wake up—it's 7 am—to the sound of church bells and Felice (Lucky) the dog 'singing' along with them, almost in time. He does it every morning. This is the wake-up call for the village.

We walk downstairs to the tiny kitchen. There's a wood stove in the corner, a small table that somehow regularly fits about 12 people around it and light streaming through an east-facing window. Matt's elderly cousin Cesarina (Ches-ar-ina) wheels about on her office chair, back and forth from the kitchen table to the stovetop.

She is 81 years old, and is a typical Italian mama, who asks you, 'Aren't you going to eat breakfast?', after you have finished two coffees, two biscotti and a piece of bread with salami and cheese. She tells stories of how some Australian family visited with their children once and the children didn't even eat at the table—can you believe it? And then—it's exactly 9:45 am—she asks if we want a wine. This place is amazing.

Story continued over page →

Gluten-free sweet potato gnocchi.

SOFT IN TEXTURE, NOT STICKY OR DENSE, AND PERFECTLY SWEET.

950 g peeled sweet potatoes, quartered if large, halved if small (see notes)

1 egg yolk

1 tablespoon extra-virgin olive oil

½ teaspoon unrefined salt

190 g fine white rice flour, plus extra for dusting

55 g fine tapioca (cassava) flour

ADDITIONAL FLAVOUR PUNCH
(optional—use one, or keep plain)

½ packed cup spinach or flat-leaf parsley leaves, finely chopped

1 garlic clove, crushed, or garlic shoot, finely chopped

a big pinch of freshly ground black pepper

It's all about butter and gnocchi up here. Cesarina hand-makes us gnocchi for lunch one day. She asks, as always, if it's good. 'Buono?' We answer, 'Yes, amazing!' And the next morning, we ask if we can have it again. She tuts with disbelief—you couldn't possibly have the same thing two days in a row! This made me laugh and reminded me of why traditional cuisines exist—to feed your family variety, based on what is in season.

Being in Italy, and around family, broke the mental block I had with gnocchi, where I truly believed it was a dish that was all too hard, too temperamental. It inspired me to create a recipe for us, and it worked. Amazing. This recipe is a little untraditional, as it has some quirks, like being gluten free (I can just hear the Italians tutting as they read my bastardised recipe). But it's how we like it. And it works.

We love it because it's soft in texture, not sticky or dense, and has an amazing sweetness from the sweet potato. I have tried my hardest to eliminate variables, so that it works every time (and you don't need a potato ricer, because who has one of those?). *–Lentil*

Preheat the oven to 200°C fan-forced.

Place the sweet potato on a baking tray, then pierce the pieces all over with a fork. Dry-roast for about 40 minutes, or until it has fully softened and formed a skin on the outside. Set aside until cool to the touch. Have a glass of wine while you wait.

Squeeze the potato into a medium bowl so that the 'skins' pull away from the flesh and you are left with a super-soft mash. Discard the 'skins'.

Add the egg, oil and salt to the bowl and stir to combine. Add the flours slowly (this is key, as all flours are slightly different in absorbancy and you may not need to add it all) and any additional flavourings (if using), bringing the dough together with your hands as you go, until it is soft but no longer sticky. When you place it on the bench, it shouldn't stick—this is the key test! If necessary, add a tiny bit more tapioca flour until it comes together. Rest the dough for 5–10 minutes. Have another glass of wine.

Very lightly flour the bench. Take a chunk of the rested dough and roll it with your hands into a log about 1.5 cm thick, then cut into 2 cm pieces. (Optional step: take each piece between your fingers and press with a fork or wooden gnocchi tool to leave an impression on top—this is the traditional way!) Repeat for the remaining dough.

Recipe continued over page →

→ **Recipe continued from previous page**

Add all the gnocchi to a large saucepan of boiling salted water (salty enough to remind you of the sea!) and cook until they float, 2–3 minutes. Drain and rinse briefly under cold water to stop them cooking any further. Your gnocchi should hold together, have a soft texture and not be sticky, stodgy or gluey at all.

Serve with your favourite pasta sauce (pages 263 and 312) or pesto (page 124), or for some other ideas see pages 303 and 311. These gnocchi are best when pan-fried quickly before serving.

The dough or the cooked gnocchi will keep in the fridge for up to a week in an airtight container. You can also freeze pre-made gnocchi pieces in an airtight container in a single layer, or in layers with a little flour between them, for up to 4 months. Cook the frozen gnocchi directly from the freezer (do not defrost before cooking).

RECIPE NOTES.

Peeling the sweet potatoes may seem strange, but it just works. They release a bit more moisture and then form a new skin! It's a nonna move, where you don't know 100% why it works, but it just does.

Fine flour is important! And if you're using freshly milled flour, like we do, you may need a little less, as it is more absorbent.

Because sweet potatoes can vary a little in moisture levels, this is a *feeling* recipe, so make sure you take note of what the dough is meant to *feel* like and adjust if necessary.

No souring or soaking is required in this recipe because it's all white flour, which we use sometimes (5% foods).

Double the quantities and freeze a batch for quick meals.

Cauliflower wraps.

Wraps are the best quick snacks and meals—fill them with whatever you have around the house. These wraps are full of flavour, quick, easy, gluten free, grain free and are super nourishing and satisfying to eat. We love that they are made from a vegetable and are full of flax and psyllium husk, which are great for our digestion. We often fill these with heaps of vegetables, mayonnaise (page 340) and pear, lemon and chilli jam (page 172), or with a fried egg and tomato sauce (page 123) for breakfast. The first time we made these, I was so happy that we could make gluten-free wraps at home that I think I said it about ten times in one day (sorry Matt). *–Lentil*

- 600 g cauliflower, cut into small chunks
- 100 g (1 cup) almond meal
- 100 g flaxmeal
- 2 tablespoons psyllium husk
- 1 egg, whisked
- 1 tablespoon natural yoghurt
- ½ teaspoon bicarbonate of soda
- a big pinch of unrefined salt
- a big pinch of freshly ground black pepper
- a handful of thyme, flat-leaf parsley or dill leaves, chopped (optional)

Blitz the cauliflower in a blender or food processor until similar to mashed potato or rice in texture. You may need to do this in batches.

Tip the cauliflower into a medium bowl with the remaining ingredients and bring together with your hands. It will come together to form a ball but will stick to your hands a little (it will be wetter than a standard bread recipe). Place the dough in the fridge for 30 minutes or so to cool and allow the flaxmeal and psyllium husk to fully absorb the liquid.

Preheat the oven to 180°C fan-forced.

Divide and shape the rested dough into six balls, about 6–7 cm in diameter. Place a ball between two pieces of baking paper and gently flatten with your hands, then roll with a rolling pin to flatten evenly. It should be about 5–6 mm thick and 18–20 cm in diameter. Pull off the top layer of baking paper (reuse this to roll out the next wrap), then transfer the wrap (on the baking paper) to a baking tray. You should fit at least three wraps on one large baking tray. Repeat until all the dough is rolled out. Bake for 12–15 minutes until golden brown on top and a little puffy.

Cool on the trays for a few minutes, then peel off the baking paper and transfer to cooling racks. Allow to fully cool before eating. Eat at room temperature or cold, filled with all the delicious things.

The wraps will keep in an airtight container in the fridge (don't fold them or they will break) for around 5 days.

RECIPE NOTES.

You can also keep the dough in the fridge in an airtight container and bake the wraps freshly as you need them throughout the week.

We've learnt to place fillings on the smooth side of the wrap for maximum strength!

Leftover-sourdough flatbreads.

THE QUICKEST WAY TO MAKE BREAD FROM A CULTURE AND THE BEST USE OF LEFTOVERS.

- extra-virgin olive oil
- 2 tablespoons warm water
- 2 teaspoons unrefined sugar (e.g. rapadura)
- 2 big pinches of unrefined salt
- 500 ml (2 cups) leftover sourdough culture (page 337)

OUR FAVOURITE ADDITION
(optional)

- ½ teaspoon fennel seeds
- 1 teaspoon nigella seeds

ALTERNATIVE ADDITIONS
(also optional—try one or two at a time)

- 1 garlic clove, crushed
- 1 teaspoon sesame seeds
- a few thyme sprigs, leaves stripped
- a few garlic or onion shoots, finely chopped
- a few rosemary sprigs, leaves stripped
- 2 big pinches of freshly ground black pepper

There was a point in Italy where I thought, 'If I ever have to see another panino in my life, I might cry.' Not really. But man, there are so many panini. There are even whole 'panino bars'. Everywhere. Where you get any form of alcohol you want, coffee, panini and water—and that's all they sell. I loved it, but sometimes I just wished there was a little more to it. More to the bread (sourdough!) and more stuff inside.

When you feed your sourdough culture every day, in preparation for baking bread, it becomes a part of your family. Something you feed each day and keep warm. It also gives you an excess of culture, as you're constantly refeeding and emptying out the leftovers. We used to feed the excess to the chickens. But since Italy, we use all our leftovers (sorry chickens) to make these awesomely textured flatbreads. They are by far the quickest way to make bread from a culture, and the best use of leftovers.

Seriously. We eat these a lot. They're delicious, versatile and awesome with everything. We love them with pickles (page 170), cheese, small plates and vegetables, on an antipasto plate, as pizza bases or as panini, filled with all the delicious things (pages 210 and 235). They can be gluten free, or not, depending on the culture and what you feed it. *–Lentil*

Preheat the oven to 180°C fan-forced.

Liberally coat two skillets (or two 20 cm round baking tins) with oil. If you're using any of the optional additions, sprinkle them into the skillets or tins.

Combine the water, sugar and salt in a medium bowl and stir until dissolved. Add the culture and stir until it is like a smooth, slightly thick pancake batter. This will depend on the ratio of flour to water you feed your culture. If the mixture is too thick, add a little water at a time until loosened. If it's too thin, add a little flour at a time until thickened.

Put the skillets in the oven for 5 minutes (or 2 minutes for tins) to get hot and toast any flavourings. Then pull them out of the oven and quickly pour in the batter, dividing it evenly between the skillets or tins. Bake for 15–18 minutes. When ready, the edges will be crisp and golden brown, and the top will be a light golden brown (or just turning golden, depending on your flour).

Cool a little in the skillets or tins, then loosen the flatbreads with a spatula and flip out onto a board. You should now have two very well formed and slightly airy flatbreads. If serving later, you can keep them warm between two tea towels, which will also soften them a little. Best eaten fresh, or you can store in an airtight container in the fridge (lying flat, don't fold) for up to 3 days. Reheat to eat.

RECIPE NOTES.

This recipe will be gluten free if you feed your sourdough culture with gluten-free flour.

See our guide to making your own sourdough culture on page 337.

MAKES 20-25 CRACKERS // TIME: 40-50 MINUTES + 4 HOURS SOURING (OPTIONAL)

Buttermilk, oat & lake salt crackers.

- 330 g medium-fine gluten-free oat flour (see note), plus extra for rolling
- 160 ml (⅔ cup) cultured buttermilk
- 2 tablespoons unprocessed honey
- ½ teaspoon pink lake salt
- 50 g unsalted butter, at room temperature, cut into chunks
- unrefined salt flakes, to sprinkle

These are crispy, lightly salted and just made for cheese and fruit. You can buy them in a packet, but you can also make them yourself. Ta-da! These are what we most often serve for dessert—these, fruit, cheese. Wine. Sweet wine. More wine. This recipe is designed to be made at the same time as baked plums, sage and warm cheese (page 325), as they go together so well! Great for share plates, for relaxing in the sunshine, or late nights with friends.

Combine the flour, buttermilk, honey and pink lake salt in a medium bowl. Bring together with your hands, but don't overwork! Your dough should be a little sticky and wet enough to form a ball. Place in an airtight container on the bench for about 4 hours to prepare and sour the flour. If you don't have time for this step, you can skip it and go straight to the next step.

When ready to bake, preheat the oven to 160°C fan-forced. Grease or line two large baking trays.

Add the butter to the dough and combine well with your hands.

Lightly flour the bench. Divide the dough into three pieces. Take one piece and coat both sides lightly in flour, then roll out on the bench until about 3–4 mm thick. Using a pastry cutter or the rim of a glass, cut into circles about 7 cm in diameter, then place on the prepared trays. Repeat with the remaining dough, rolling the scraps out again until all the dough is used.

Sprinkle the crackers lightly with salt flakes, then gently tap the salt into the dough. Prick the top of the crackers lightly with a fork and bake for 25–30 minutes, or until just turning golden brown. Remove from the oven and cool on the trays for 10 minutes, then transfer to a cooling rack.

Your crackers should be crisp, and snap when they break. They will keep in an airtight container or jar on the shelf for 5 days or more. Serve with baked plums and warm cheese (page 325), or mixed cheeses, fresh fruit (like pears, apples and stone fruits) and herbs (like basil and parsley).

RECIPE NOTE.

To make oat flour, blitz rolled oats in a blender until they form a medium-fine flour.

Sourdough rye friselli ('wet breads') & bagels.

- 100 g sourdough culture (page 337)
- 1 kg wholegrain rye flour, as freshly milled as possible
- 15 g unrefined salt
- milk of your choice, for brushing
- poppy seeds, to top (optional)

'Wet bread' is our name for friselli, Southern Italy's traditional response to a very hot and dry climate. Friselli are basically dried half-bagels that you bring back to life by soaking in water just before eating. Deliberately stale bread! They make the *best* bruschetta (page 221), and we have absolutely fallen in love with their sheer practicality—we feel like we always have spare bread at the ready now! This recipe makes fantastic fresh bagels too.

We made these with a man named Felice (Lucky). What a legend. A sturdy Northern Italian man transplanted into the South, who spoke enough English to fill in the gaps of our terrible Italian.

We'd only known Lucky for about two minutes when it was decided that he would teach us how to make friselli! We were relaxing at another new friend's house, but soon found ourselves instead zooming down narrow country lanes with Lucky, lanes with stone walls either side that leave little margin for error. Olive trees flew past overhead and stretched off in every direction as far as the eye could see. And then we arrived at Lucky's little farm, with all its fruit trees and dogs and ramshackle beauty. It was his paradise. His happy place, where he'd come and tinker all day before returning home to the village for dinner with his wife. He said he was poor, but he has the best food in the world, so he is happy.

To say thanks, we asked him to join us for dinner. He said that he couldn't eat because he had to go back and eat with his wife or she would think that he had eaten with another woman! This recipe is dedicated to Lucky, we hope you stay so for all your days.

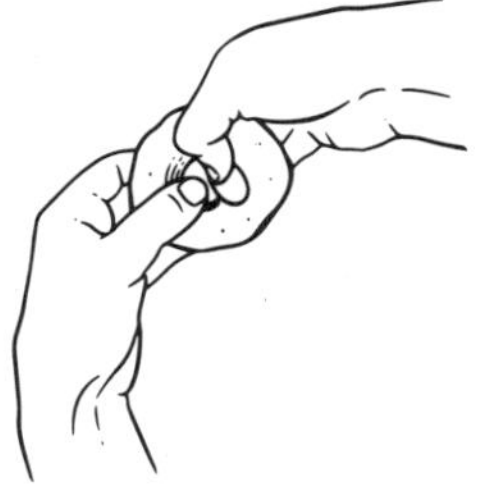

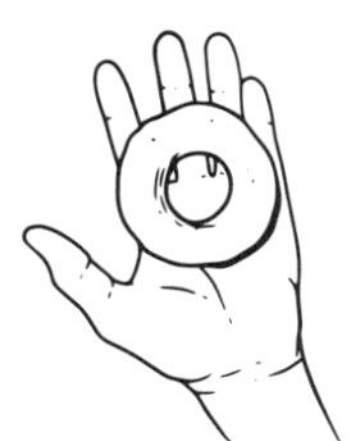

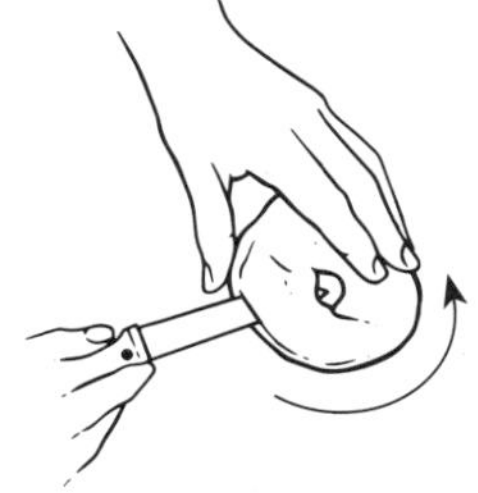

DAY 1

Make sure your sourdough culture is super happy and active. If you keep yours in the fridge, take it out, feed it with your choice of flour and place it in a warm place (we put ours on top of the coffee machine, so the culture sits around 38°C) for 12–24 hours. If your culture is already warm and pumping, head straight to day 2 instructions.

DAY 2

Combine the flour and salt in a large bowl and mix thoroughly with your hands to evenly distribute the salt. Add 700 ml of water and the culture to another large bowl and combine with your fingers. Add the dry ingredients to the wet and combine thoroughly with your hands, bringing the ingredients together in a circular motion with your fingertips. Continue with the circular motion, but begin to scoop the dough now with your whole hand. Eventually, grab the ball of dough and begin

Recipe continued over page →

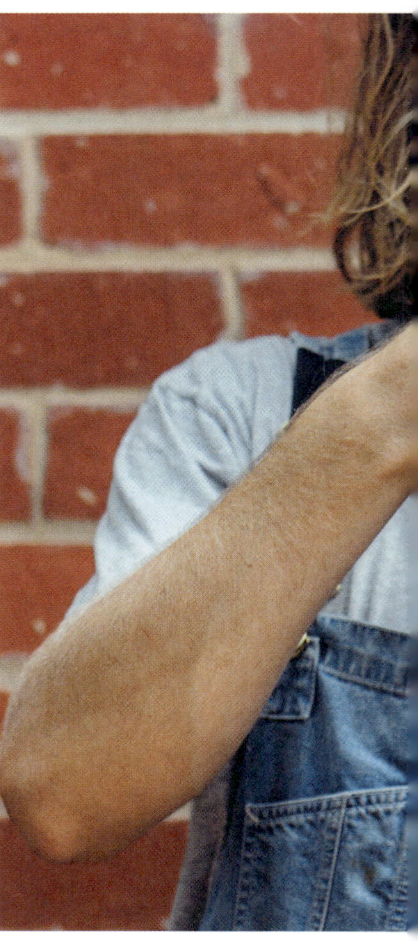

→ **Recipe continued from previous page**

to knead it in the bowl until you have a consistent, coherent ball. It will be a little sticky—this is the nature of whole-rye doughs, the bane of every baker's existence! If you wet your hands, it's much easier to work with.

The classic friselle shape is the same as a bagel. Wet your hands a little, then break off one tennis ball–sized piece at a time and form it into a rough sphere. Push your thumb through the centre to form an opening and work the dough into a smooth ring, then repeat until all the dough is formed (see top three diagrams, page 141). Place the rings in an appropriately sized container(s) with an airtight lid to ferment. You might want to place an oversized sheet of baking paper in the bottom and draw it up between each one as you go to stop them from merging into each other.

Seal the container and place in a really warm place (we put ours back on top of the coffee machine) and leave to ferment for 24 hours. You'll get best results when you keep the dough between 30–38°C. It's important to have a warm environment for the fermentation to work, so if it's a little cooler than the ideal range, leave for a bit longer, but it won't work if it's *too* cool.

DAY 3

Preheat the oven to 250°C fan-forced. Grease two large baking trays or line with baking paper.

Lay the dough rings out on the prepared trays, then brush with milk and sprinkle with poppy seeds (if using). Bake for 7 minutes.

Remove the trays from the oven. Reduce the temperature to 200°C and leave the door open. If making bagels, let them rest for a moment while the temperature drops. If making friselli, take the sharpest, most finely-bladed knife you have and wet it, then gently slice each friselle in half horizontally (see bottom diagram, page 141). Lucky uses a wire strung taut in a wooden frame.

When the temperature is down to 200°C (if you let it drop too much, just close the door and wait for it to come back up), return your bagels/friselli to the oven and bake for 30 minutes or so. Ovens can vary a bit, so keep an eye on them near the 30-minute mark. You are aiming at a lovely burnished milk chocolate tone (friselli will begin to look a little toasted). Friselli should be really quite firm and crisp, bagels also should have formed a crisp crust, but still be lovely and soft inside.

Once baked, set aside on a rack to cool. Both can be enjoyed immediately. Bagels will easily stay fresh at room temperature for a week. Friselli will keep at room temperature out on the bench for 1 month, or in an airtight container or jar for many months, and up to a year.

When you want to eat your friselli, soak them in a bowl of water for 6–10 minutes to rehydrate, then shake off any excess water. They will soak up the water and be soft (yet still crunchy) and delicious! See page 221 for our favourite toppings.

Fresh cheese.

2 litres full-cream cow's, goat's or sheep's milk

0.2 g mesophilic cheese starter culture (see field notes)

2–3 drops calf or vegetarian chymosin rennet (see field notes)

unrefined salt, finely ground

extra-virgin olive oil, to store

SPECIAL EQUIPMENT

thermometer

cheesecloth

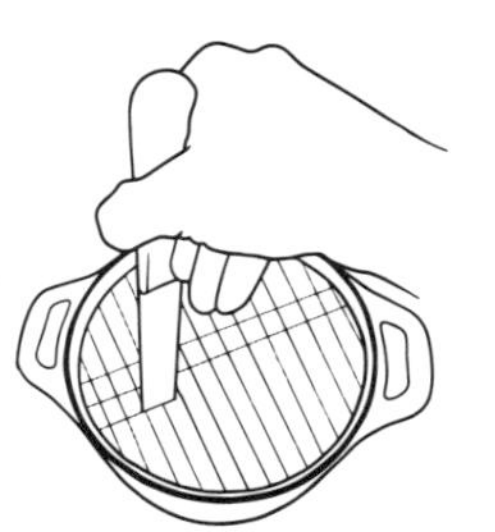

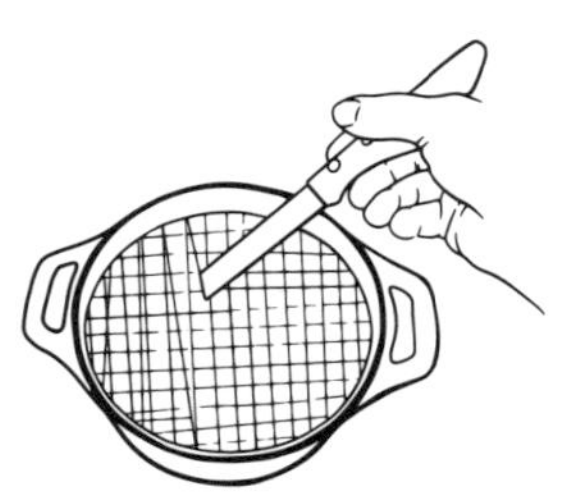

I've wanted to work out how to make a fresh cheese forever. And I finally took the time. We love this kind of spreadable cheese, especially when made from goat's milk, so it feels super special to be able to make our own. Making your own cheese is great value, takes hardly any time at all and is so rewarding!

This cheese is mild and fresh, and so perfectly acidic. We've been using it with everything lately—in sardine pasta sauce (page 303), on antipasti plates, with baked plums (page 325), and on top of cold polenta and grape slice (page 334). Amazing in both savoury dishes and desserts. *-Matt*

DAY 1, MORNING

Warm the milk to 25°C in a medium, heavy-based pot over medium heat. Add the starter culture and stir through, then cover and stand for 45 minutes.

After 45 minutes, mix the rennet with 80 ml (⅓ cup) of water and add to the pot. Stir through, cover and leave in a warm place (you want it to sit around 20–25°C the whole time) for 12 hours, completely undisturbed. It is set when you can gently press your finger on the top of the curd and it supports the pressure—that is, a solid suspended in liquid.

DAY 1, EVENING

After 12 hours, take a knife and cut the curd in a line down the centre of the pot all the way to the bottom and all the way across. Then cut parallel lines at 1 cm intervals across the curd. Do the same crossways, to form a checkerboard pattern. Finally, cut lines on a shallow angle in a few directions, so that you've created rough 1 cm cubes (see diagrams).

Gently strain the curds through a colander lined with two layers of cheesecloth, collecting the whey in a bowl underneath. Pour this initial collection of whey into an airtight container or jar and store in the fridge to use instead of water for baking bread or souring grains, or to feed to the chooks.

String up the cheesecloth, returning the bowl underneath, and drain for 12 hours in a cool room, below 20°C.

DAY 2, MORNING

After 12 hours, turn the cheese out into a bowl, sprinkle over 1 teaspoon of salt per 400 g yielded and mix through. Refrigerate with a layer of oil on top in an airtight container or jar. It should keep this way for up to 1 month, or it will keep for up to 2 weeks without the oil on top.

FIELD NOTES.

On cultures and rennet.

Cultures and rennet are the two key ingredients in cheesemaking. Fortunately these days, it's super easy to order both online, or alternatively, they can be bought at cheesemaking stores and even some health-food stores. The culture populates the milk with friendly bacteria (like the natural cultures in yoghurt) and the rennet separates the milk proteins from the whey so that you can capture the cheese solids from the milk.

Cacioricotta.

TWO CHEESES IN ONE RECIPE–A FRESH CHEESE AND A CURED GRATING CHEESE.

- 2 litres goat's milk (see notes)
- 1 teaspoon unrefined salt
- ¼ teaspoon calf or vegetarian chymosin rennet (see field notes, page 145)
- about 1 litre (4 cups) boiling water

SPECIAL EQUIPMENT

- thermometer
- 2 x 1 litre plastic bottles, filled with water and frozen solid
- 3–4 ricotta moulds, about 9–10 cm in diameter and 7–8 cm deep

We used to love keeping our cows, and it was a joy working so closely with an animal. The respect it required. The patience. The love. And it was a joy to witness this in tiny villages all over Italy—whole herds of sheep, goats and cows literally following their herders to the milking station while the herder talked to them, asking them about their day, telling them their stories.

We are so excited to bring you this cheese, because it is so good, yet so simple. Plus, it's actually two cheeses in one recipe—a fresh cheese *and* a cured grating cheese! This isn't traditional ricotta. It is a blend of a hard cheesemaking process and the ricotta-making process. But the result is as good as the best ricotta you've ever eaten. It is rich, delicious and addictive.

We learnt to make this cheese from Nonno Giuseppe—a sweet and stoic man that our friend Stellina introduced us to in Puglia. He usually makes it with goat's milk, but it works great with cow's milk too, and no doubt also with sheep's. This cheese feels truly life changing for us. We've been making small batches regularly and feeling completely spoilt to have access to such a fresh ricotta-style cheese that's so good, and so easy to make. Plus, it can be simply cured into a fantastic grating cheese! Giuseppe says that it is *just* for pasta, but we think it's great on *everything*!

Add the milk to a 3 litre (or larger), heavy-based pot and bring to a near boil (between 80–90°C) over medium heat, then turn off the heat. Stir in the salt, then lower in the ice bottles to rapidly cool to 38°C, which should take about 10–15 minutes. Remove the bottles at exactly 38°C. If you accidently cool the milk too much, that's fine, just gently warm it back up to exactly 38°C.

Once at temperature, in a small bowl, mix the rennet with 80 ml (⅓ cup) of water and add to the milk. Stir thoroughly (Giuseppe does exactly ten vigorous stirs), then set aside and leave completely undisturbed for 45 minutes to 1 hour, by which point the curd should be set (not *hard* set, but definitely set—see notes).

Stir the curds swiftly and thoroughly in one direction to completely disintegrate them, then add the boiling water, filling your 3 litre pot to about 1 cm from the top. The curds will set again and then sink. Place a ricotta mould on top of the liquid and let it sink in—this is your barrier to stop you from ladling out curd rather than pure whey. Begin to remove a ladleful of whey at a time from the inside of the mould into a container or bowl—keep this whey for baking bread or souring grains, or as Giuseppe does, feed it to the pigs!

Continue to ladle until most of the whey has gone and the liquid level is even with the curds. Place the remaining moulds on a rack over the sink (or a tray if you want to keep catching the whey) and use the mould in the pot to scoop the curds

out into the others, filling all the moulds to the top. You should fill about three moulds. Drain for 2 hours if making fresh cacioricotta. If you want to make cured cacioricotta, it holds its shape much better if you leave it in the moulds for 12 hours.

EATING IT FRESH

After 2 hours draining in the moulds, turn out the cheeses and place in an airtight container with a few tablespoons of whey. They will keep in the fridge for up to 1 week.

CURING IT FOR GRATING

After 12 hours draining in the moulds, turn out the cheeses and sprinkle a little salt on the top and bottom of each, then place on a slightly sloping board in an open, shaded and airy place (see Giuseppe's solution for this pictured on page 147) for 6–8 days (8 days maximum), flipping them every other day (see notes).

After 8 days, refrigerate the cured cheeses in an airtight container. If a little mould has formed on the outside during curing, that's fine, just wipe the cheese down with a clean cloth dipped in cool water before placing in the container. Your finished grating cheese will be firm, almost crumbly and quite salty—but fantastic grated over almost anything!

RECIPE NOTES.

You can also make this recipe using cow's milk. We've found that when you use cow's milk, however, it can take much longer than 2 hours for the curd to set (even up to 12 hours). That's okay, just wait until it has set before proceeding.

If you live in a particularly hot and humid climate you may have trouble curing the cacioricotta without mould becoming a problem, but it's worth a shot.

Whole cherry tomatoes in brine, page 172.

Preserves.

Fermented, bottled and cured goodness.

Leek jam.

When we first moved to our new village, the previous owners of our house had left us the loveliest gift—a stocked winter garden. It made us feel instantly at home. But our inherited patch also provided us with a very lovely dilemma—it was overflowing with leeks! And with spring upon us, the leeks wanted to shoot for the sky. The pressure was on. Well, we embraced the leek like we'd never embraced it before. We made leek soup, leek stew, leek fritters (page 222), leek cannelloni, roast leeks, grilled leeks...

But, even after weeks of leeking it up in a big way, we'd hardly made a dent! We gave leeks away to anyone who dared enter leek-land, then one day we gave a hefty bunch to our dear friend Gen. She left with a twinkle in her eye, and the very next week appeared with the loveliest little jar of leek jam—a thick, sweet, savoury jam that was amazing with cheese, on antipasti plates, sandwiches and with salads and meats. Brilliant. It inspired us to pull up all our remaining leeks that same afternoon. And this is what we made. *-Matt*

- 6 large leeks (about 1 kg in total), trimmed
- extra-virgin olive oil
- 1½ tablespoons yellow mustard seeds
- 4 dried bay leaves
- 180 ml (¾ cup) white wine vinegar
- 60 g (⅓ cup) unrefined sugar (e.g. rapadura)
- 1 heaped tablespoon unprocessed honey
- 1 heaped teaspoon unrefined salt

Cut leeks crossways into 5–6 cm long pieces, then halve each piece lengthways and continue slicing lengthways to make 4–5 mm wide strips (see note and diagrams).

Add a very generous splash of oil to a large, heavy-based saucepan over medium heat. Add the mustard seeds and bay leaves and fry for 1–2 minutes until fragrant. Beware, the mustard seeds may pop and splatter a little! Be careful not to burn them—we just want lightly toasted seeds.

Add the leek and stir to coat with the oil. Cover and cook for 10 minutes, stirring occasionally, until the leek has started to soften. Add the remaining ingredients and stir thoroughly to combine. Reduce the heat to low, cover and simmer for about 1 hour until the leek is really starting to fall apart.

After 1 hour, uncover and cook at the barest simmer for another hour, stirring occasionally to stop it from sticking, until it is darker and jammy and most of the liquid has evaporated.

Transfer into two clean 500 ml jars (or equivalent number of smaller jars) and seal as per the 'hot jar, hot liquid, hot lid' method (page 343). Store in a cool, dark place. Will keep for 1 year unopened. Once opened, store in the fridge for up to 1 month.

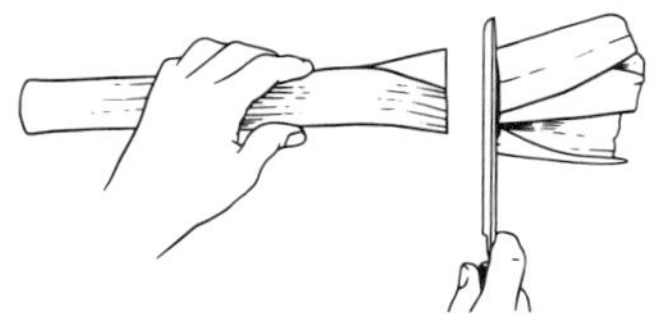

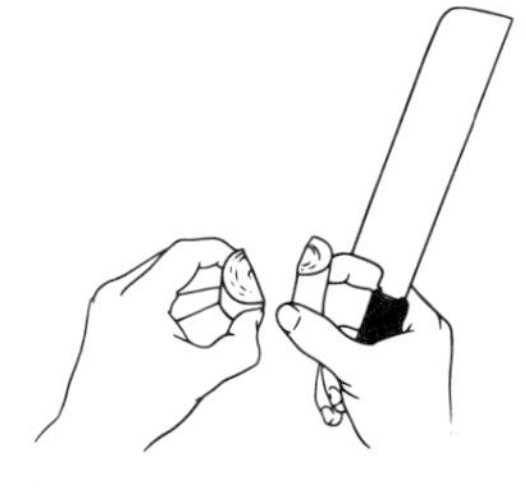

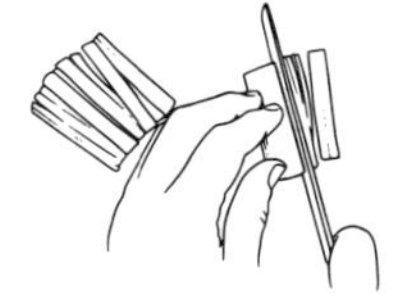

RECIPE NOTE.

We cut the leeks into strips lengthways, rather than crossways, so they don't collapse into a paste when cooked. This works because it maintains long strands of the natural fibres. You can use the same trick for making onion jam. Actually, we're sure you could use this recipe to make a fantastic onion jam too.

Italian kimchi.

- 1 kg wombok, coarsely chopped, with 1 large outer leaf reserved
- 300 g carrots, grated or very finely julienned
- 300 g cauliflower, stem finely sliced, florets finely chopped
- 150 g red onion, very finely sliced
- 160 g unrefined salt
- unchlorinated water (see notes)

PASTE

- 140 g unprocessed honey
- 65 g cured anchovy fillets (see field notes and notes)
- 60 g garlic cloves, crushed
- 30 g (3 tablespoons) hot chilli powder (less if you're not a chilli person)
- 10 g (½ packed cup) oregano leaves, finely chopped
- 5 g (¼ packed cup) thyme leaves, finely chopped
- 3 teaspoons unrefined salt

It's no secret that we are a kimchi household. Our friends have come to expect an enormous jar of it front and centre every time they open the fridge. And they help themselves. To bowlfuls! But although we think traditional kimchi goes with absolutely everything savoury, for some time we have wanted to integrate the greatness of kimchi with the Mediterranean ingredients that we grow and love so dearly. We hoped to create a condiment that even *more* perfectly accompanied our everyday dishes. And we think we have. To our knowledge, there is no Italian equivalent to kimchi, so we just called it 'kimchi'. Maybe this will be the start of something special.

DAY 1

Add the vegetables and salt to a very large bowl (or food-grade bucket) and mix thoroughly with your hands. It should look like a colourful Italian slaw. Add enough water to just cover, then place a plate on top so the vegetables are submerged (a few floating on the surface is fine). Cover and leave overnight at room temperature to brine the vegetables.

DAY 2

Drain the vegetables and submerge in fresh water. Drain, taste and repeat. When ready, the wombok shouldn't taste at all bitter and be just saltier than seems normal. If too salty or at all bitter, wash, drain and taste again. If not salty enough, add more salt until you hit the spot.

Using a mortar and pestle or high-powered blender, thoroughly grind or blitz all the paste ingredients until smooth.

Add the paste to a large bowl with the vegetables and massage thoroughly with your hands. You may want to wear gloves—it's spicy! Stuff the mix into a clean 1.5 litre jar (or equivalent number of smaller jars), pushing the vegetables down super firmly to extract the liquid—this is very important (see field notes). If you're not extracting enough liquid to submerge everything, leave for 5 minutes for the salt to do its thing, then try again, pressing even harder! If you *still* don't have enough liquid, top it up with a little unchlorinated water. Stuff the reserved wombok leaf into the jar, tucking the leaf under the shoulder of the jar to keep everything submerged. Place a small, damp cloth over the top of the jar, then push the lid down over the cloth (don't seal—it's just to hold everything in place).

Sit the jar on a plate (liquid will likely spill over the lip during fermentation) and leave to ferment for 5–7 days at room temperature. Check on it daily, moistening the cloth and topping up the liquid level as needed to keep everything fully submerged.

Recipe continued over page →

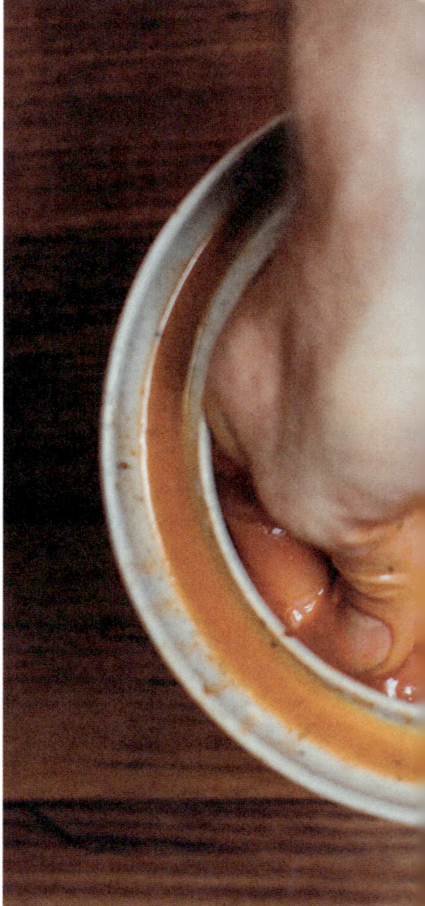

→ **Recipe continued from previous page**

DAY 7

Remove the top wombok leaf and taste the vegetables underneath. When ready, the kimchi will be sharply acidic and smell very pungent, but it shouldn't smell 'off' at all, and the vegetables should be crunchy.

If it isn't sharp enough yet, ferment for another couple of days. If your submerged vegetables have turned soft, or black or colourful moulds have developed on them, something has gone wrong, and the batch should be discarded. But if a little mould has developed on the surface, just discard and enjoy the vegetables underneath.

Once ready, discard the top leaf, seal with the lid and store in the fridge. The kimchi will keep for at least a year in the fridge, but realistically much longer.

RECIPE NOTES.

Tank water or spring water are ideal for this, but most town water should be fine unless yours tastes obviously chlorinated. Heavily chlorinated water will likely negatively affect the good bacteria required for successful fermentation.

For a vegetarian version of this recipe, replace the anchovy fillets with 2 tablespoons of soy sauce or tamari.

This recipe is based on summer and early autumn fermentation. Fermentation takes longer when it's colder (shorter if you're in the tropics).

See the appendix (page 342) for more information on lacto-fermentation.

FIELD NOTES.

On fermenting anchovies. When we first decided to add anchovies to this mix, we were tentative. Is it really safe to ferment anchovies? Actually, though, fermented anchovies have formed the base of traditional fish sauces for at least as long as anyone has thought to record such things. Generations of testing, check. Play it safe by using only cured anchovies (salted anchovies preserved under oil, as most of us know them) because they have already been properly prepared for the job.

On keeping everything submerged. Making your own kimchi for the first time can be quite daunting. But we promise it's super easy to get right and super difficult to stuff up. The key to a successful ferment is creating the right environment for anaerobic fermentation (without the presence of oxygen), rather than aerobic fermentation (with oxygen), which will just grow mould. A better word than anaerobic is 'submerged', because that's literally all you need to do to ensure a successful ferment. This is why we use some sacrificial leaves on top to hold everything else under, while the leaves get attacked. Everything should be submerged right from the beginning of fermentation, so check your ferment daily, topping up the liquid level as needed at any time with unchlorinated water. Finally, if anything does get exposed to the air and turns mouldy, just discard that bit. Everything properly submerged underneath will still be perfect and delicious. Happy fermenting!

Fermented vine leaves.

- 3 teaspoons unrefined salt
- unchlorinated water (see notes, page 159)
- 1 teaspoon black peppercorns
- 1 garlic clove (unpeeled is fine, if clean), crushed under the heel of your hand
- 30–35 freshly picked young vine leaves of good size (fresh, young growth is key, not thick, mature growth—they will be too chewy)
- 4–5 fennel flowers

Vine leaves are the best things to wrap so many fun treats in. We all know dolmades (page 228), but that's just one option. If you grow a grapevine, or have access to one grown well, making these is a no-brainer. And when you pickle your own vine leaves, it makes you want to experiment with them. We've started to wrap all kinds of vegetables, herbs, grains, nuts, seeds, spices, cheeses and meats in them for quick snacks and easy share plates.

Add the salt and 800 ml of water to a clean 1 litre jar. Seal with the lid and shake to dissolve the salt. Add the peppercorns and garlic, then roll the vine leaves up together and add them too. Place the fennel flowers on top, tucking them under the shoulder of the jar to keep the leaves submerged (see field notes, page 159).

Place a small, damp cloth over the top of the jar, then push the lid down over the cloth (just to hold it in place—don't seal). Sit the jar on a plate (liquid will likely spill over the lip during fermentation) and leave to ferment for 5–7 days at room temperature. Check on it daily, moistening the cloth and topping up the liquid level as needed to keep everything fully submerged.

DAY 5

Remove the fennel flowers (they may look a little strange if they got exposed to the air—that's normal) and try a vine leaf underneath. When ready, the leaves will have turned a deep olive green, be tender and taste sharply acidic and delicious. If they are soft, or black or colourful moulds have developed, something has gone wrong, and the batch should be discarded. But if a little mould has developed on the surface, which is normal if the flowers were exposed, just discard them and enjoy the leaves underneath. If a white film has formed on the surface of your brine, that's just penicillin—scrape it away and discard, it's completely harmless. If the leaves are still a little chewy, ferment for another 2–3 days and check again.

Once ready, discard the fennel flowers, seal with the lid and store in the fridge. The vine leaves will last for at least a year in the fridge, but usually much longer.

RECIPE NOTES.

This simple lacto-fermenting technique can also be used to ferment other vegetables too. Replace the vine leaves with any fresh, crisp vegetable and mix up the herbs and spices!

This recipe is based on summer and early autumn fermentation. Fermentation takes longer when it's colder (shorter if you're in the tropics).

See the appendix (page 342) and field notes (page 159) for more information on lacto-fermentation.

Burnt capsicums under oil.

These capsicum strips are just so fresh and delicious—naturally sweet and perfectly acidic with that lovely overtone of char. Great with antipasti, as a sandwich filler or a side. Blitzed, they also make instantly tasty sauces, bringing a complexity of flavour that seems so much more developed than the simple thing they are. And, when you finish the jar, the wonderfully perfumed leftover oil can be used to bring all manner of salad dressings and dishes to life. This is a truly handy preserve, and a fun one to make. *-Matt*

- 700-800 g perfectly ripe red, yellow or orange capsicums, cored and cut into 3-4 cm wide strips
- 250 ml (1 cup) red wine vinegar
- 1 teaspoon unrefined salt
- extra-virgin olive oil

DAY 1

Turn the oven grill on as hot as it goes.

Arrange the capsicum, skin-side up, on a baking tray. Grill 15–20 cm below the element for about 10 minutes, or until there are many blackened and blistered patches, then remove from the oven.

Add the vinegar, salt and 250 ml (1 cup) of water to a medium saucepan and bring to the boil. Add half the capsicum strips (you will only be able to fit half at once), ensuring they are covered in liquid. Once the water returns to the boil, reduce the heat and simmer for 2 minutes, then remove the strips with tongs, shaking any excess liquid back into the pan. Repeat with the remaining capsicum. Set the leftover vinegar aside to cool—use it throughout the week in salad dressings.

Place a tea towel on a rack (for air circulation) and lay out the strips to cure overnight.

DAY 2

Pour 1 cm of oil into a clean 500 ml jar (or equivalent number of smaller jars). Add the capsicum strips one by one, adding a little oil occasionally and pressing down gently with a clean spoon as you go. When all the strips are in, press down so that the capsicum is no higher than 2 cm from the jar lip. If it is higher, remove a few pieces and enjoy. Fill with oil to 1 cm from the lip so that all the capsicum is submerged. Leave for a minute in case the oil level drops, then top up if necessary.

Secure the lid and seal using the 'classic water bath' method (page 343). Remove the jar after the 20 minutes and check that the oil level is still above the capsicum. If it has dropped, immediately heat some oil in a small saucepan to 72–80°C, then top up to cover the strips, to within 1 cm of the lip. Seal again immediately. The lid should suck down as it cools.

Store in a cool, dark place. As long as the oil remains at least 1 cm above the capsicum, they will keep for at least 1 year on the shelf, even after opening. Remove with a clean fork to avoid contamination.

'Quick-pickled' broad beans.

- 250 g freshly shelled broad beans
- 2 garlic cloves (unpeeled is fine, if clean), halved
- 3 flat-leaf parsley sprigs, finely chopped, stalks and all
- 125 ml (½ cup) white wine vinegar
- 1 tablespoon unprocessed honey
- ½ teaspoon unrefined salt
- ½ teaspoon freshly ground black pepper

We told her we'd had a massive lunch and didn't need much dinner. She replied, 'Yeah, no problem.' Out came eight sides with crackers and bread—olives, pickled artichokes, pickled peppers, cardoons, sweet pickled carrot, pickled broad beans, cannellini beans, cheese. Then pasta with red sauce, followed by three meat dishes—wild deer, wild boar, veal (luckily, I managed to tell her we didn't want donkey!). Then dessert—lemon sorbet, limoncello, orangecello and almond cookies. There is no such thing as a small meal in Italy. And there is no such thing as takeaway. You eat it all. She was warm and loving, and we called her 'Mumma'.

Until then, we'd never thought to pickle broad beans. But they're such a perfect pickling candidate, given their short season. We call this a 'quick' pickle because they are so delicious that even during broad bean season we serve them this way. In these times, we don't bother with the jarring. We simply place the just-cooked beans and liquid in a bowl in the fridge overnight and then, the next day, we strain them (the pickling liquid is a great base for a salad dressing) and toss in a little olive oil. *–Matt*

Place a 500 ml jar (or equivalent number of smaller jars) and lid in a saucepan half full of water and bring to a rollicking boil to sterilise (see the 'hot jar, hot liquid, hot lid' method, page 343). Omit this step if you want to eat them soon rather than preserve them.

Meanwhile, add all the ingredients to a small saucepan with 125 ml (½ cup) of water. Cover and bring to the boil over medium heat, then reduce the heat and cook at a bare simmer for 2 minutes.

Using tongs, remove the jar from the water and shake dry. Using a clean spoon, fill the jar with the broad bean mix, then pour in the liquid. Wipe the lip of the jar with a clean, dry cloth.

Using tongs, remove the lid and shake dry, then seal the jar tightly, without overtightening—it's not how tight you screw on the lid, but the vacuum created as the jar cools that forms the seal. Leave to cool. The lid should suck down. If it doesn't, reseal with a new lid as per the 'classic water bath' method (page 343).

Store in a cool, dark place. Will keep for at least 1 year unopened. Once opened, store in the fridge and eat within 2 weeks.

RECIPE NOTE.

This recipe works well with other crisp vegetables like carrots, sliced onions, green beans or cauliflower too. Just cut to 'pickling size' and substitute for the broad beans.

Sardines under oil.

unrefined salt
1.6 kg whole sardines, filleted and washed in fresh, cool water (see diagrams over page), or 1 kg clean sardine fillets (bought pre-filleted)
extra-virgin olive oil
1 teaspoon black peppercorns (optional)
1 teaspoon dried chilli flakes (optional)
3 dried bay leaves

When we learnt to preserve tuna under oil, we were staggered by how much better it tasted compared to canned tuna. But it's taken us a few more years to explore the medium of fish and oil any further. We're happy to say that this latest foray has been just as intuitive, successful and delicious as the first. These jarred sardines are just so much fishier (in the best way) and tastier all round than normal canned sardines. Potently so. They are a little saltier, for sure, so take that into account when using in recipes. But they're just so good, and so quick and easy to make. Always use only the freshest sardines that have clear, black eyes—learn when sardines run past your closest coastline and preserve them!

Sprinkle some salt on a large chopping board, then lay the sardine fillets, flesh-side down, on top of the salt—it's okay if the sardines overlap a little to fit. Sprinkle a generous layer of salt over the top of the fillets, then place the board on a slight angle over the sink or a large bowl to catch the water that runs off as the sardines cure. Leave to cure for 2–3 hours.

After 2–3 hours, pile the fillets into a large, clean bowl and gently toss to mix the salt through a little more evenly. Lay them back out on the board as before, sprinkling over any salt left in the bowl. Set the board back on an angle over the sink or large bowl and cure for a further 2–3 hours.

Once cured, take the fillets one by one and thoroughly brush off any salt, then place in a large, clean bowl. When all the fillets are brushed clean and piled up in the bowl, cover with a generous splash of oil and sprinkle over the peppercorns and chilli (if using). Gently toss until the fillets are completely coated in oil.

Add 1 cm of oil to the bottom of three clean 450 ml jars (or equivalent number of smaller jars), then place a bay leaf in each. Fill with the sardine fillets to within 2 cm of the rims, pressing down gently to fit as many as possible. After the last fillet is in, evenly distribute any remaining oil, peppercorns and chilli, then fill with oil to 1 cm from the top. Leave for a minute, in case the oil level drops, then top up if necessary. Secure the lids and seal using the 'classic water bath' method (page 343), except cook for 1 hour, rather than the 15–20 minutes the method states.

After 1 hour, remove the jars from the water and check that the oil is still above the sardines. If it has dropped in any of the jars, immediately heat some oil in a small saucepan to 72–80°C and top up above the fillets, to within 1 cm of the lip. Seal again immediately. The lids will suck down as they cool. If they don't, reseal with a new lid as per the 'classic water bath' method (page 343).

Recipe continued over page →

→ **Recipe continued from previous page**

Store the sardines in a cool, dark place. While it is said sardines preserved this way can keep for up to a year on the shelf, we prefer them between 1 and 3 months. After 3 months, we refrigerate them to hold that perfect freshness, where they easily keep for the remainder of the year. Once opened, store in the fridge and eat within a month.

RECIPE NOTE.

We feed the scales and innards to the chickens and make stock with all the other discarded bits (just wash everything well for a nice clean stock), but they would also make a very welcome addition to your compost, or dig directly into your garden. The ancient Aztecs are said to have buried a piece of fish offcut under every corn seedling. Smart.

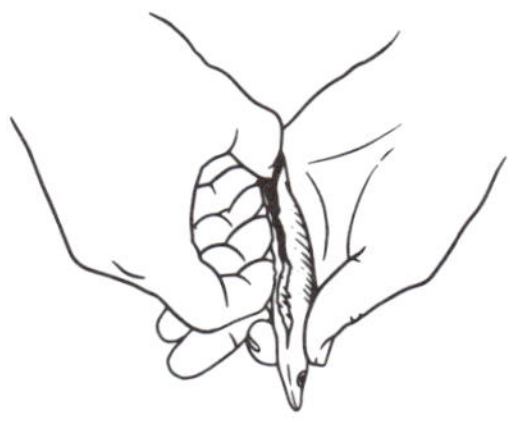

1. Make an incision along the whole length of the sardine's belly with your thumbnail.

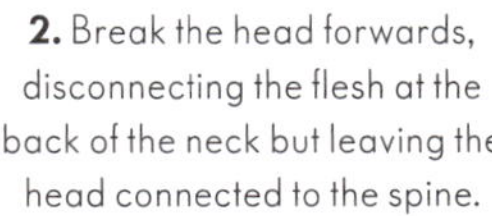

2. Break the head forwards, disconnecting the flesh at the back of the neck but leaving the head connected to the spine.

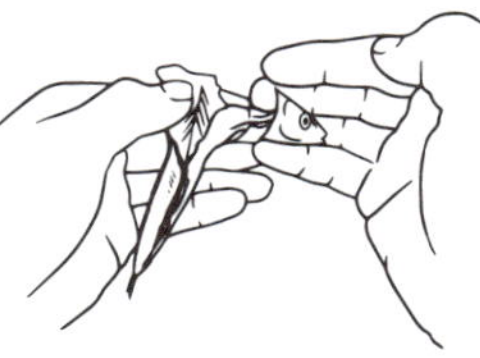

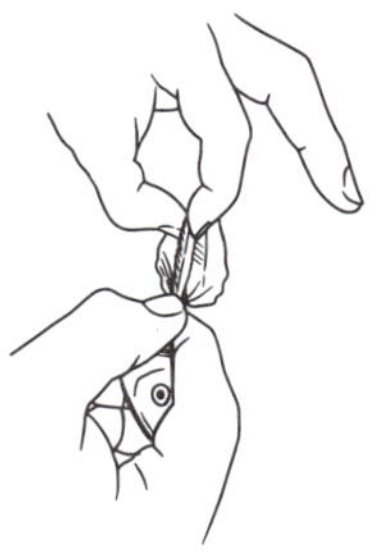

3. Slide your fingers down the spine towards the tail, disconnecting the fillet from the spine, head and guts as you do.

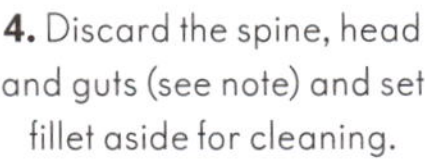

4. Discard the spine, head and guts (see note) and set fillet aside for cleaning.

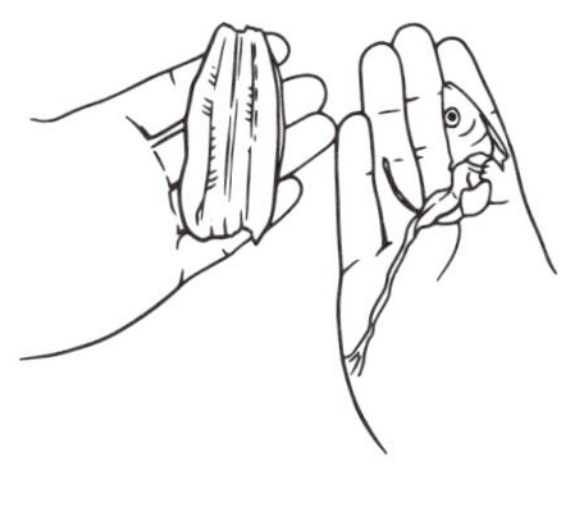

Zucchini pickles.

- 800 g zucchini/summer squash, finely sliced on a mandoline
- 100 g onion, finely sliced on a mandoline
- 1 tablespoon unrefined salt
- 1 tablespoon mustard seeds
- ¾ teaspoon celery seeds
- 160 ml (⅔ cup) white wine vinegar
- 110 g (½ cup) raw sugar (see field notes)
- 1¼ teaspoons ground turmeric

SPECIAL EQUIPMENT

- thermometer

The first vegetable garden I ever planted was a zucchini garden. 200 plants! And ever since that first year growing zucchinis, the need to do something with the abundant harvest has been starkly apparent. On hot days, you can almost watch zucchinis grow on the plant. And it only takes a few plants in a home garden before you'll be swimming in the beautiful, glossy fruits and scratching your head wondering what to do with them all.

In response, we have spent years perfecting this delicious zucchini pickle. Our friends who visit have come to expect and request this as a part of any meal. They have a wonderful flavour—a little sweet, a little mustardy—and the perfect amount of crunch. These pickles have been making their way around our village for years, so we thought it was time they made their way around yours. *–Matt*

DAY 1

Thoroughly combine the zucchini/squash, onion and salt in a large bowl. Refrigerate for at least 6 hours, or preferably overnight.

DAY 2

Rinse the zucchini/squash and onion in cold water, then drain well. Add to a large bowl with the mustard and celery seeds and combine well, then gently stuff into a clean 1 litre jar (or equivalent number of smaller jars).

Add the vinegar, sugar and turmeric to a small saucepan and heat gently while stirring until the sugar dissolves.

Pour the liquid into the jar, filling to 1 cm below the lip. If you have extra pickling liquid, mix it with some olive oil for a delicious dressing. If you fall a little short, top up with vinegar. Secure the lid on your jar and seal using the 'classic water bath' method (page 343), except cook for 40 minutes, rather than the 15–20 minutes the method states.

Store in a cool, dark place. These pickles will keep for at least 2 years unopened. We find that they're best eaten after 3 months. Once opened, store in the fridge.

RECIPE NOTE.

We never make just one jar of these at a time because it takes as long to make one jar as it does to make seven or eight—however many jars fit in your biggest pot! You can use this recipe to pickle as many zucchinis/squash as you have. Just adjust the ingredient quantities based on the zucchini/squash weight.

FIELD NOTES.

On using raw sugar.

We use raw sugar—rather than unrefined sugars (like rapadura)—in recipes such as this that have the most stunning natural colours. Unrefined sugars make an equally tasty (slightly nuttier tasting) pickle, that is for sure a little healthier, but it turns out a little on the brown side. Sometimes you've got to break your own rules for a higher cause!

Pear, lemon & chilli jam.

MAKES 1 x 500 ML JAR
TIME: 40–50 MINUTES

A clean-tasting, sweet and sticky chilli jam with minimum sugar. We make it in huge batches because we eat it on so many things (double or triple the batch, depending on how many pears you have and how much *you* love chilli jam!). We love it for breakfast with a fried egg, on panini (page 210), on a cheese board, or as an awesome addition to any leftovers.

500 g pears, cored and roughly chopped

160 ml (⅔ cup) lemon juice (juice of about 4 large lemons)

1 teaspoon unrefined salt

160 g raw sugar or unrefined sugar (e.g. rapadura)

1 tablespoon hot chilli flakes (or about 8 hot chillies, finely chopped—adjust to taste, as chillies vary greatly in spice)

1 tablespoon lemon zest

Place a small plate in the freezer.

Add the pear, lemon juice and salt to a blender and puree.

Add the puree to a small, heavy-based saucepan over medium heat and bring to a simmer. Add the remaining ingredients and stir until the sugar has dissolved. Reduce the heat and simmer, uncovered, for about 30 minutes until the mixture has thickened and looks sticky and glossy (it should have reduced by about a third). Try not to stir at all, which can delay the setting point, except to prevent it from sticking.

Take the plate out of the freezer and place a drop of jam on it. If it sets, your jam is ready to jar. If not, simmer with the lid off for another 10 minutes or so and test again.

When your jam is ready, place a clean 500 ml jar (or equivalent number of smaller jars) and lid in a pot of boiling water and follow the 'hot jar, hot liquid, hot lid' method (page 343) to jar it. Store in a cool, dark place. Will keep for at least 2 years unopened. Once opened, store in the fridge.

Whole cherry tomatoes in brine.

MAKES 1 x 500 ML JAR
TIME: 25 MINUTES

Who knew you could preserve whole cherry tomatoes in just a simple brine? Stellina did, a beautiful Italian woman who popped open her brined tomatoes, threw them in a pan with some of the water, cooked them and served them with some pasta, fresh cheese and basil. Brilliant. All these years growing and harvesting overwhelming abundances of them and we had *never* thought to do this. We should have. We knew tomatoes were acidic enough to preserve safely, and that a simple salt brine would be a tasty pickling liquid to keep them company. We just never put two and two together. This is *such* a quick and easy way to preserve tomatoes for winter. It could never replace passata, of course, but it's nice to have another super simple tomato preserving option on hand. Plus, these guys have their own special power that passata doesn't—you can simply turn them out into a bowl, add just a splash of extra-virgin olive oil and you've *instant* antipasto gratification.

250 g cherry tomatoes

1 heaped teaspoon unrefined salt

Add the tomatoes and salt to a clean 500 ml jar. Fill to within 1 cm from the lip with water and seal using the 'classic water bath' method (page 343).

Store in a cool, dark place. Will keep well into the following season. Once opened, store in the fridge.

RECIPE NOTES.

You can scale this recipe up as much as you like. The key is to add 2–3% salt-to-water by weight. For example, if it takes 1 litre (1000 g) of water to fill a jar of tomatoes to the lip, you'll need 20–30 g of salt for the preservation to be a success.

See the appendix (page 343) for more information on hot-bottling. Note that this recipe requires neither vinegar nor sugar because the tomatoes themselves are acidic enough.

Dry-salted olives.

Olives preserved this way are like a whole new fruit. They are denser and meatier in texture and more intense in flavour. The majority of olives are prepared using a brining technique (see our first book), whereas these are dry-cured, which transforms them in a totally different way. This technique works best for olives picked later in the season, when the olives are black and ripe but still firm.

- 1 kg firm ripe black olives (ideally, shaken from the tree so they're naturally a little bruised)
- 200 g unrefined salt
- 5 dried oregano sprigs
- 4 dried chillies
- 1 teaspoon fennel seeds
- extra-virgin olive oil

SPECIAL EQUIPMENT

- 2 x 1.5 litre (or larger) containers, one with drainage holes in the bottom
- a stack of heavy plates or weights (approximately 3–4 kg) that will fit inside the containers

DAY 1

Place the olives in the container without holes and cover with salt, mixing well with your hands. Place the weights on top of the olives and set aside. Leave the container somewhere that you walk past daily, and agitate the olives every day as you walk past. Leave to cure for 5 days or so.

DAY 5

Transfer the olives to the container with the drainage holes, then place the weights on top again. Stand over another container or the sink and allow to drain for 7–10 days until the olives taste sweet and not bitter—if they are still bitter, leave for a few more days until their sweetness develops.

DAY 12–15

Once your olives are sweet to taste, briefly wash them in fresh water and then pat dry with a tea towel. Lay the olives out in a single layer on a baking tray. Dry the olives in the sun for a few hours, or place them in the oven at 50°C for about 15 minutes or so, agitating occasionally, until dry.

Fill a 1 litre jar (or equivalent number of smaller jars) with the olives, oregano, chillies and fennel seeds (distribute evenly if using more than one jar). Half fill the jar with oil and place on the shelf.

Your olives are ready to enjoy, however their flavour will improve greatly over time as the herbs and spices infuse. Agitate the olives occasionally when you walk past them to make sure they're always coated in oil. We usually leave ours for at least a month before eating the first of them. Will keep for years on the shelf provided they remain coated in oil this way, however we always tend to eat them all before the next season's batch is ready!

RECIPE NOTE.

Of course, adjust the recipe for how many olives you pick. We usually make at least 20 kg at a time.

MAKES 1 x 400 ML JAR // TIME: 1 HOUR 30 MINUTES

Rhubarb, orange & mint cordial.

- 700 g trimmed rhubarb, roughly chopped
- 500 ml (2 cups) fresh orange juice (juice of about 4 large oranges)
- 40 g mint leaves (about 40 sprigs, leaves stripped)
- 300 g unrefined sugar (e.g. rapadura) (or unprocessed honey)

For us, cordial has to be made with something we have in total abundance, because it cooks down to so little. Mint and rhubarb are always something we have too much of—rhubarb, because even one plant is too much for our house, and mint, because ours grows seriously wild. And oranges are *always* abundant for us because one tree is half a tree too many for most households, and we have access to a whole orchard! So this solves many problems. This is great as a cordial on hot summer days—it's fresh, sticky, minty and has a deep sweet syrupiness from the rhubarb. But it's also an awesome syrup for desserts like broken cake (page 320) or as an accompaniment to something as simple as natural yoghurt or cream.

Add all the ingredients to a medium, heavy-based saucepan. Cover and bring to the boil over high heat. Stir to dissolve the sugar, then reduce to a simmer. Cover and simmer for about 1 hour—don't stir, as the rhubarb will break down and make it difficult to strain.

After 1 hour, the rhubarb should be super soft but still just hold its shape—again, don't stir. Place a fine mesh strainer over a bowl (try to find a bowl that fits your strainer, so you don't have to hold it). Pour the syrup into the strainer and leave for a few minutes to strain fully. You will be left with a delicious fibrous rhubarb mix in the strainer. Store this in an airtight container in the fridge and eat on everything—yoghurt, muesli, cake!

Pour the syrup back into the pan and simmer with the lid off for about 15 minutes to reduce it a little. When ready, it will be a deep red-brown colour and be thin like honey. Once cool, the cordial will thicken greatly!

When your cordial is ready, place a clean 400 ml bottle (or equivalent number of smaller bottles) and lid in a pot of boiling water and follow the 'hot jar, hot liquid, hot lid' method (page 343) to bottle it. Store in a cool, dark place. Will keep on the shelf for 1 ½–2 years unopened. Once opened, store in the fridge. Enjoy!

FIELD NOTES.

On rhubarb plants. Okay, we know what you're about to ask us. Your stalks are green, right? Assuming the plant is otherwise thriving (leaves are lush, robust and deep green), the most likely explanation is simply that your rhubarb cultivar is green stemmed! There *is* such a thing as green rhubarb (they're extremely common, actually). This is just how they are. Not all rhubarb is red. If this is the case for you, it is very edible, even though it is green. So when your rhubarb stalks are as thick as your thumb, pick them and enjoy, no matter what the colour!

Grapefruit, orange & fennel marmalade.

- 1.2 kg sweet grapefruits (such as oro blanco, pink or pomelo)
- 800 g oranges
- 1 large lemon
- 1 tablespoon dried fennel seeds (and fennel flowers, if you have them) (or 3–4 tablespoons fresh fennel seeds)
- 400 g unrefined sugar (e.g. rapadura) (or unprocessed honey)

SPECIAL EQUIPMENT

- muslin bag
- kitchen twine

At home, we call this 'marma-jam', a soft set, jam-like marmalade. That's how we like it. I feel marmalade may have somewhat gone out of fashion, but we seriously love it—maybe even more than jam. It's amazing on toast, rye bagels (page 141) or 'stale' cake (page 204) with whipped butter and olive oil (page 120), fresh cacioricotta (page 148) or ricotta. This is just a classic that speaks of an abundance at home and in the wild—it makes me think of wild fennel and overloaded grapefruit and orange trees, and sunshiny days. And I love that this speaks to those in dry climates, the tropics and everywhere in between. A preserve for everyone's home. *-Lentil*

DAY 1

To state the obvious, it is important to use organic fruit and wash them well, as you are eating their skins! Using a vegetable peeler, peel the grapefruits and oranges. Slice the peel as finely as you can into strips about 2 cm long, then add them to a medium, heavy-based saucepan. The easiest way we've found to do this is to take a pile of the skins at a time and cut them crossways. (Be patient, this might take a few minutes—call it your daily meditation!)

Halve the grapefruits, oranges and lemon and remove any pips. Place the pips in a muslin bag—you should have at least 25 pips.

Juice the lemon and add the juice to the pan. Add the remaining lemon pulp and the juiced lemon halves to the muslin bag.

Juice half the grapefruits and oranges and add the juice to the pan. Add the juiced grapefruit and orange halves and their pulp to the bag.

Cut the pithy skins off the remaining grapefruit and orange halves and add to the bag. Tie the bag up with kitchen twine and add to the pan. Roughly chop the remaining grapefruit and orange flesh and add to the pan.

Add 1 litre of water to the pan. Push down to ensure the bag and the peel are covered with liquid, cover, then bring to the boil. Turn off the heat and stand for 12 hours. (The addition of water and the brief boiling is to soften the peel and release the pectin.)

Recipe continued over page →

→ **Recipe continued from previous page**

DAY 2

Place a small plate in the freezer.

Remove the muslin bag and squeeze out all the juices. Empty the bag, except for the pips, tie again and return to the pan. Or, if you're like us, just throw the pips straight into the marmalade, as we don't mind them being there.

Place the pan back on the stove and add the fennel seeds (and flowers, if you have any). Cover and gently simmer for 2 hours. The orange and grapefruit will really start to break down over this time.

After 2 hours, uncover and bring to the boil. Add the sugar and stir until dissolved. Boil for 10–15 minutes until it reaches the setting point. To test, place a drop of the marmalade on the frozen plate. When ready, it should set a little, like a soft-set jam, and should not be sticky like toffee. We find the colour to be a good indicator—it should be a deep orange and translucent. If you like your marmalade super sticky (although not the 'done' thing), you can continue to boil for longer until it becomes a richer amber colour and stickier.

When your marmalade is ready, place two clean 500 ml jars (or equivalent number of smaller jars) and lids in a pot of boiling water and follow the 'hot jar, hot liquid, hot lid' method (page 343) to jar it. Store in a cool, dark place. The marmalade will keep for at least 2 years unopened. Once opened, store in the fridge.

FIELD NOTES.

On keeping pips for pectin. It's the little things that make a home. Our friends Todd and Siv have this little dish on their kitchen bench that they collect citrus pips in. Every time we go over, I find myself peering into the dish to check how many are in there. It's fun to watch the collection grow and then all of a sudden they've all been used up for something, and it's time to start again! The same cycle is now happening in our home constantly. As you eat your citrus through the year, keep *your* pips in a little dish. They will keep indefinitely, and you can add them to your jams to help them set because they have lots of pectin in them (pectin is the very rare and special complex sugar that sets jams). *-Lentil*

Egg surprise for every season, page 194.

Breakfasts.

Small things to eat
together to start
the day.

GF | DF | VG

MAKES 1 LARGE SMOOTHIE // TIME: 5-10 MINUTES

All year

Everyone's smoothie chart.

ROUGHLY CHOP EVERYTHING, PLACE IN A BLENDER AND BLITZ UNTIL SMOOTH.

Matt's cousin Kynan and his family are just awesome really. They once had this tiny smoothie chart on their wall, which I am now told, 'Oh, it was just a handwritten thing, so I threw it out'! So we made this. For their *new* kitchen wall! The secret to a good smoothie is to always include something frozen to make it a bit thicker. Experiment and use what you've got! *-Lentil*

Fruits.	Vegetables.	Nuts/seeds.	Liquids.	Extras.	Frozen.
1–2 portions of these.	**1 portion of these.**	**1–2 portions of these.**	**160 ml (⅔ cup) of these.**	**1–4 portions of these.**	**1 portion of these.**
½ cup berries (any) ½ banana, chopped ½ cup chopped rockmelon* 2 tablespoons lemon juice* ½ cup chopped pear ½ cup chopped peach ½ cup chopped apricot ½ cup chopped nectarine ½ cup chopped apple ¼ cup pitted cherries ½ cup peeled kiwifruit*	Handful of kale/ collard greens Handful of spinach ¼ avocado Stick of celery, diced* ¼ cup grated zucchini/summer squash	1 tablespoon flaxmeal 1 tablespoon chia, sunflower or pumpkin seeds 1 tablespoon nut butter (any) 1 tablespoon gluten-free rolled oats 1 tablespoon tahini Handful of almonds or hazelnuts	Coconut milk Soy milk Almond milk Oat milk Natural yoghurt Water Coconut water Rice milk Kombucha (page 118)* Fresh orange or grapefruit juice* Cow's milk	½ teaspoon vanilla extract Big pinch of ground cinnamon 1 teaspoon wheatgrass 1 teaspoon psyllium husk 1 teaspoon honey 1 teaspoon cacao nibs 2 cm piece of fresh ginger or turmeric, grated, or ½ teaspoon ground 2 teaspoons raw cacao powder 2 teaspoons bee pollen 2-3 dates/dried persimmons Small handful of mint or basil leaves*	½ avocado ½ banana, chopped ½ cup ice ½ cup berries (any) ½ cup chopped nectarine ½ cup chopped peach ½ cup chopped apricot ½ cup grated zucchini/summer squash ½ cup chopped pear ½ cup chopped apple ½ cup pitted cherries

Notes.

Ingredients marked with an asterisk are best combined without dairy products. They're also great combined together.

If your smoothie is too thick, add a little liquid. If too thin, add another portion of something frozen—ice is always good!

If you're in the tropics, you can also use pawpaw, mango and pineapple.

Coffee and a cookie.

In Sardinia, in one of the longest-living villages in the world, it took about two weeks for us to work out why we were always the only ones walking around eating or even drinking water. The answer: they don't eat or drink *and* walk—what's the rush?

Every morning, they start their day with a coffee and a sweet—whether it be a pastry or a cookie. If they're not home, they sit or stand at the bar to drink their coffee and eat their sweet. There is no such thing as takeaway.

We love a coffee (or tea!) and a cookie for breakfast—it's something small, quick and easily shared, and it's a delicious start to the day. And it's not just the Sardinians who practise this ritual, but something that's commonly practised by many of the longest-living populations of the world. Time and again, our culture tells us it's important to have a big breakfast, but who says there is just one way?

Our theory is that this village approach gives your body a bit of a rest, starting the day with minimal food and allowing your body's digestive system to do its thing.

Whatever it is, we're into it.

MAKES 20-25 BISCOTTI // TIME: 45 MINUTES - 1 HOUR 5 MINUTES + COOLING

Marmalade & honey biscotti.

FOR UNEXPECTED VISITORS: BISCOTTI HAVE TO BE THE HEART OF A HOME.

- 150 g (1½ cups) almond meal
- 30 g (3 tablespoons) tapioca (cassava) flour
- 3 tablespoons unprocessed honey
- 1 tablespoon marmalade (page 180)
- 3 tablespoons almonds, roughly chopped and toasted
- ¼ teaspoon unrefined salt
- ½ teaspoon bicarbonate of soda
- a squeeze of lemon juice

'What *is* this delicious biscuit?' Ru is probably on top of the list of unexpected visitors in our house, and his *favourite* thing is sweets. When he stays for long periods, we often make a big batch of cookies for him and him alone. And it's like all of his dreams have come true. It's always a good exchange. Because with Ru comes tales of ridiculous antics, decisions and theories.

Biscotti are just made for the 'pop in', always sitting on the shelf at the ready. They've got your back. This recipe isn't super sweet, is sweetened mostly with honey, has a toasty flavour from the nuts and a bit of saltiness. Plus, bonus, these biscotti are not throw-it-at-the-wall-and-it-won't-break hard.

Preheat the oven to 150°C fan-forced. Grease or line a large baking tray.

Add the almond meal, tapioca flour, honey, marmalade, almonds and salt to a medium bowl and bring together with your hands, massaging until well combined. Add the bicarbonate of soda and squeeze the lemon juice on top (which will activate it and make it bubble), then massage to combine. You should now have a firm, smooth ball of dough.

Shape the dough into two logs about 2 cm wide and 3 cm high and lay on the prepared tray, accounting for spreading—they will at least double in width as they bake. Bake for 30–35 minutes, or until golden brown—the goldenness is essential for crispness! They will have spread and be around 2.5 cm high. Don't touch and allow to fully cool (this will take about 1 hour).

Once fully cooled and hardened, use a sharp knife or breadknife to cut the logs into 5–10 mm slices. Now you should have biscotti that are half crispy and half chewy. If this is how you like them, stop here and store them in an airtight container or jar for 3–5 days on the shelf (after this they will begin to soften). But, if you want them crisp and to last for a long time, take the next step.

SECOND BAKE

Preheat the oven to 140°C fan-forced.

Place the biscotti back on the baking tray and bake for 15–20 minutes, which will dry them out and crisp them up. Again, take them to maximum goldenness for ultimate crispness. Allow to fully cool on the tray.

Store the biscotti in an airtight container or jar on the shelf for 1 month or more.

RECIPE NOTE.

Make a double batch if you get lots of visitors—twice baked they last a long time on the shelf.

The naked rye cookie.

CRUNCHY ON THE OUTSIDE, A LITTLE SALTY, A LITTLE SWEET.

- 150 g unsalted butter, at room temperature
- 100 g unrefined sugar (e.g. rapadura)
- 2 tablespoons extra-virgin olive oil
- 2 squeezes of lemon juice
- ¼ teaspoon unrefined salt
- 1 egg
- 200 g (2 cups) wholegrain rye flour

This is rye's moment. Rye is an all too often forgotten grain when it comes to anything but bread. And these are just so good—could eat them every day good. These cookies are crunchy on the outside, a little salty, a little sweet. All the things you want in a cookie. Plus, they have minimal ingredients, keeping it simple. There's no topping for these, because we tried them all, and they're just the best as they are, naked.

DAY 1

Using an electric beater, cream the butter, sugar, oil, lemon juice and salt in a medium bowl until the sugar is fully combined (this is key to avoiding big chunks of melted sugar in your cookies). Once super creamy and pale, crack the egg into the bowl, then continue to beat until the mixture is well combined and glossy.

While continuing to beat, slowly add the flour. When it's mostly combined, gently stir with a wooden spoon to combine fully. You should now have an airy, wet ball of dough.

Wrap the dough in baking paper or a beeswax wrap and roll into a log (sometimes ours turns into a square/rectangle, which is fine too) 5–6 cm in diameter—this makes it easy to cut later! Refrigerate for 12–24 hours to prepare the flour and cool the dough.

DAY 2

Preheat the oven to 170°C fan-forced. Grease or line two large baking trays.

Cut the dough into slices about 8 mm thick. Place on the prepared trays and bake for 12–16 minutes, or until golden brown on top and a little browned on the edges—the goldenness is key to crispness! Allow to cool on the trays until firm, then transfer to a cooling rack to cool completely.

Serve as is, or make them into peach and cream slabs (page 316). These will keep on the shelf in an airtight container or jar for 5 days or more.

RECIPE NOTE.

Unrefined sugar is key to the flavour of these, so use as unrefined as you can get.

FIELD NOTES.

On traditional mills and flour.

It seems that some people have become white flour fascists. These people even go as far as saying their pastries and breads are *traditional* when made this way. But it isn't the traditional way at all. Actually, there were once village mills. Places to go to mill whatever wholegrain you liked. Largely, these mills exist no more and it was crazy to see the reality of this in Italy—to see the shutdown mills and the lack of wholegrains in baking—but when we got to the traditional south, we breathed a sigh of relief to see that wholegrains remained the popular choice. They were *still* making traditional breads, cookies and pastries with a mix of freshly milled wholegrain, nut and seed flours, the way it has *always* been done. And those breads, pastries and sweets all tasted *so* much better. They tasted real and nourishing (no surprise there) and it confirmed our drive to keep these traditions alive!

SERVES 2, OR 4 IF SERVING ON TOAST // TIME: 30 MINUTES

All year

Egg surprise for every season.

- extra-virgin olive oil
- 1 small onion, finely chopped
- 1 garlic clove, crushed
- a few sprigs of hard herbs (see below), leaves stripped
- ¼ teaspoon ground turmeric
- ¼ teaspoon unrefined salt
- a big pinch of freshly ground black pepper
- 500 g vegetables (see below), cut as desired
- 100 g greens (see below), cut as desired
- 250 ml (1 cup) passata
- 4 eggs
- a few drops of hot sauce (or 2 teaspoons pear, lemon and chilli jam, page 172) (optional)
- a handful of soft herbs (see below), roughly chopped
- toast (gluten free if preferred), sourdough flatbreads (page 134) or bagels/friselli (page 141), to serve (optional)

This is a breakfast born of the road. When we were road tripping up and down the east coast of Australia and through Tasmania in our van, we only had some simple cooking gear and a little icebox to keep things cool. We'd brought along a few spices and bottles of preserves, like passata, but largely we were just eating fresh produce we found along the way at farm gates and roadside stalls. Whenever we found fresh eggs, we would always make this, and our friend Mel (who joined us on the road for a while) would call them 'egg surprises', as she loved the surprise of finding out what was underneath.

Eggs, of course, make the perfect breakfast, and pairing them with fresh vegetables is even more perfect. This is really more about the idea, or the style of the dish, than it is about being super specific about the ingredients. So, use the vegetable/greens/herb combinations as a guide—have a search through the garden and fridge, and make this your own!

Add a generous splash of oil to a heavy-based frying pan over medium heat. Add the onion and sauté for 3–4 minutes until beginning to soften. Add the garlic, hard herbs, turmeric, salt and pepper and sauté for a minute or so until the garlic is just turning golden.

Add the vegetables and greens and cook for a couple of minutes until the greens are starting to wilt. Add the passata and a splash of water and stir through. Cover, reduce the heat a little and simmer for about 10 minutes, or until all the vegetables are soft (this will vary a little based on the produce you are using). You may need to add a splash of water every now and again if things get a little sticky.

When everything has softened and come together, crack the eggs on top of the vegetable mixture, sprinkle the hot sauce/chilli jam on top (if using) and cover again. Cook until the eggs are to your liking—about 3 minutes for still-soft yolks. Finish with a drizzle of oil and the soft herbs. Serve over your choice of bread, or as we preferred on the road, on its own, in all its glory.

SUMMER / AUTUMN SUGGESTIONS

Vegetables: zucchini/summer squash, tomatoes (if you have enough fresh tomatoes you can add an extra 500 g to replace the passata too), capsicum

Greens: chard

Fresh hard herbs: oregano

Fresh soft herbs: basil

WINTER SUGGESTIONS

Vegetables: celery, carrot, sweet potato

Greens: kale

Fresh hard herbs: thyme

Fresh soft herbs: flat-leaf parsley

SPRING SUGGESTIONS

Vegetables: peas, broad beans, garlic shoots

Greens: upland cress

Fresh hard herbs: rosemary

Fresh soft herbs: mint

MAKES 12-15 MUFFINS // TIME: 30-40 MINUTES + 12 HOURS SOURING (OPTIONAL)

Oat, fruit & vegetable breakfast muffins.

FULL OF ALL THE GOOD THINGS.

DAY 1

- 350 g grated fruit and veg (any mix of zucchini/summer squash, carrot, apple, pear and/or pumpkin—see notes)
- 150 g gluten-free medium-fine oat flour (see notes)
- 150 g buckwheat flour
- 1½ tablespoons psyllium husk
- 120 g (½ cup) natural yoghurt
- 100 g (⅓ cup) unprocessed honey
- 80 ml (⅓ cup) extra-virgin olive oil
- 1 tablespoon ground cinnamon

DAY 2

- 4 eggs, whisked
- 2 teaspoons bicarbonate of soda
- a squeeze of lemon juice
- 100 g fresh or frozen berries (blueberries, raspberries, blackberries, quartered strawberries)
- ½ cup roughly chopped nuts (walnuts, almonds, brazil nuts, hazelnuts)

TOPPING

- 1 tablespoon unprocessed honey
- 1 tablespoon warm water
- 50 g (½ cup) gluten-free rolled oats
- 2 tablespoons pumpkin seeds and/or sunflower seeds

These are big, delicious, wholesome and filling I-just-had-breakfast muffins. Everyone gets one as they walk out the door, and you feel satisfied that everyone is well fed and ready for their day—I am a secret nonna.

These are super easy, but just have a deceivingly longish ingredient list, because they are full of *all* the good things. They are delicious, moist, airy, wholegrain, vegetable-and-fruit-filled muffins with a crunchy and sweet top! My dream breakfast muffin, right here. *-Lentil*

DAY 1

Add all the day 1 ingredients to a medium bowl and bring together with your hands until they form a wet dough. Place the dough in an airtight container and refrigerate overnight for about 12 hours to prepare and sour the flours. If you don't have the time, skip souring and go straight to the day 2 instructions.

DAY 2

Preheat the oven to 180°C fan-forced. Grease (well!) or line a standard 12-hole muffin tray (you may need two trays for this).

Place the dough and egg in a medium bowl and stir with a fork and/or your hands to massage together until well combined. Add the bicarbonate of soda and squeeze the lemon juice on top to activate it (it will bubble). Stir to combine, then add the berries and nuts and combine again. Your mixture should be a well-combined, thick and wet batter, like thick porridge.

Spoon the muffin mixture into the prepared tray(s), filling each to the top.

For the topping, mix the honey and water in a small bowl until dissolved, then add the remaining ingredients and combine.

Sprinkle the topping mixture evenly over each muffin, then bake for 20–25 minutes. Once ready, a skewer inserted into a muffin should come out clean, the topping ingredients should have browned, and the muffins should have doubled, or almost doubled, in size. Cool the muffins in the tray(s), then gently loosen with your hands and transfer to a cooling rack.

Your muffins should be fluffy in texture and crunchy on top. These are best served warm with butter or whipped butter and olive oil (page 120).

Store in an airtight container in the fridge, or freeze for easy breakfasts and snacks.

RECIPE NOTES.

To make oat flour, blitz rolled oats in a blender until they form a medium-fine flour.

Use what's in season. Your muffins will change in flavour depending on what fruit or vegetables you choose. For a sweeter muffin, just use apple and pear, or if they just aren't sweet enough for you, add a little unrefined sugar.

Spiced apricots with fresh cheese & honey.

As a kid, my mum would make me stewed apricots, and we would have them with cheese and honey on toast. We were pretty weird. Then I met Matt, and he told me about this magical breakfast he had of stewed apricots and cheese in Iran. And he said he could eat it daily, and that it was one of the best breakfasts ever. And then we made it at home one day and realised we were talking about the same dish! And it all made sense.

This is such a simple and perfectly balanced breakfast. The sweetness of the honey, the savoury depth of the ricotta, the warmth of the spiced apricots. It's as gentle as it is bold. Awesome with a garden sage tea. *-Lentil*

- 1 tablespoon unsalted butter
- 1 teaspoon ground cinnamon
- ¼ teaspoon ground nutmeg
- 1 teaspoon anise seeds
- 1 sage sprig
- 1½ tablespoons unrefined sugar (e.g. rapadura)
- 6 large ripe apricots (about 400 g in total), halved and pitted
- ½ teaspoon unrefined salt
- juice of ½ lemon

TO SERVE
(quantities are per person)

- 1 tablespoon coarsely chopped almonds
- a pinch of unrefined sugar (e.g. rapadura)
- a pinch of unrefined salt
- 100 g fresh cacioricotta (page 148), fresh cheese (page 144) or ricotta
- unprocessed honey
- 1 plain sourdough flatbread (page 134) or similar

Melt the butter in a small saucepan over low–medium heat. Once the foam subsides, add the spices and sage and fry gently until fragrant. Add the sugar and stir until melted, taking care not to burn the sugar. Add the apricots and salt and gently stir until coated. Cover and simmer for 5 minutes.

Meanwhile, gently toast the almonds with the sugar and salt in a small frying pan over medium heat, then set aside.

After 5 minutes, uncover the apricots, reduce the heat a little and simmer for another 5 minutes. Don't stir, as the apricots are very fragile at this stage and will break apart if you do. If the mixture is too dry to simmer uncovered (some apricots have more liquid, some less), add a touch of water. The mix should look like apricots swimming in a thick, sticky sauce. Once ready, remove from the heat, add the lemon juice and gently stir through.

To serve, place the cheese in bowls and top with the apricots. Finish with a sprinkle of almonds, a drizzle of honey and a flatbread on the side. Forget the cutlery—scoop with your flatbread for the full experience!

RECIPE NOTES.

The spiced apricots taste even better the next day. We often make a double batch so that we'll have plenty left over and can eat the whole dish cold the next morning. Double joy.

Also great as a dessert–try these with yoghurt or ice cream instead of cheese.

via
vincenzo monti

All the nonnas' 'stale' cake.

The every-nonna cake, in every nonna's house. And now the nonna cake of our house. Firstly, this cake isn't really stale. It's moist, like a dense sponge, and tastes almost like a doughnut. And yes, after a while, like any cake, it goes stale. But it actually lasts for about two weeks in the fridge, and it's still delicious. Really, this is designed for people who don't like baking, but love cake!

We call it stale cake because we joke that in Italy, everything is stale. Matt says that when he first went to Italy, what stood out was that everything was stale—stale bread, stale cake and then you would just add jam or salami to 'unstale' it. And since, in our visits to Italy together, in every nonna's house there has always been a stale-ish cake, with a similar sponge-ish texture and corn-ish flavours, and you always fill it with jam and sometimes cream, and generally have it for breakfast.

So stale cake is a food memory, and despite how it sounds, it's super delicious and should, in our opinion, be a part of every home.

Story continued over page →

Our nonna 'stale' cake.

- 200 g unsalted butter (cut into chunks if cold)
- 200 ml full-cream milk
- 100 g (⅓ cup) unprocessed honey
- 50 g unrefined sugar (e.g. rapadura)
- 1 teaspoon vanilla extract
- 2 teaspoons lemon zest
- 2 eggs, whisked
- 4 egg yolks, whisked
- 190 g fine wholegrain cornflour (see notes)
- 120 g fine brown rice flour
- 1 teaspoon bicarbonate of soda
- a pinch of unrefined salt

FILLING/TOPPING
(any of your choice)

- jam or marmalade (page 180)
- double cream or whipped cream
- a triple batch of buttercream (page 317) to cover the whole cake
- seasonal fresh fruit: berries (mulberries, strawberries, raspberries, cherries, blueberries, blackberries), sliced figs, sliced apricots, sliced peaches, sliced plums

Stale cake is a great celebration cake. It's what I request for my birthday every year, always filled with berries and whipped cream. *–Lentil*

Preheat the oven to 180°C fan-forced. Grease or line a 20 cm round cake tin.

Add the butter, milk, honey, sugar, vanilla and lemon zest to a medium saucepan over low heat and whisk until the butter and sugar have melted and everything is combined—do not boil! Turn off the heat and slowly pour in the eggs and yolks while whisking continuously. The mixture will thicken a little and everything should be well combined.

Sieve all the dry ingredients into a medium bowl. Make a well in the centre and slowly pour in the wet ingredients from the pan while whisking. Whisk until a thick, smooth batter forms.

Place the prepared tin into the oven for a few minutes, then pull it out and pour the cake batter into the hot tin (this gives the cake crispy edges). Bake for about 20 minutes, or until set, golden brown and a skewer inserted into the cake comes out clean. The cake should have risen by at least half and be super spongy! Cool in the tin, then flip out onto a cooling rack. Fully cool before serving. We love this cake best cold!

When ready to serve, slice the cake in half crossways to create a two-tiered cake, then layer as you choose. We like to put jam or marmalade in the middle, then top it with fresh cream and fruit. This way you can simply place the jam or marmalade in the middle, store it in the fridge and then add fresh cream and fruit when served, as we often store it in the fridge and eat throughout the week. Or, if you want something more elaborate, add jam and buttercream in the middle of the cake and then fully cover (top and sides) with more buttercream.

Store in an airtight container in the fridge. From our experience, it lasts this way (without the layered cream) for up to 2 weeks.

RECIPE NOTES.

It is super important that you get the right flour. It needs to be fine wholegrain cornflour. It should look yellow and fine like a flour, not like cornmeal, and is made from actual corn, not wheat. In Australia and New Zealand you can now readily buy it at health-food stores and in the health-food section of many supermarkets.

If you just want a little cake, you can bake a half batch in a 14–15 cm cake tin.

Breakfast bowls.

Breakfast bowls are so good for easy breakfasts, to feed heaps of people and to get through leftover goodness in the fridge. These are only examples. We want to inspire you to create your own breakfast bowls full of all your seasonal abundances. Adjust the quantities for however many mouths you are feeding.

#1—Lentil's summer/autumn breakfast bowl.

- 1 piece of sourdough bread (gluten free, if preferred) or rye bagels (page 141)
- butter (or extra-virgin olive oil for a dairy-free version)
- 40 g bacon (or salami), chopped
- a small handful of fennel fronds and flowers, roughly chopped
- a big pinch of freshly ground black pepper
- 2 tablespoons passata
- a handful of heirloom beans, cut in half
- 1–2 eggs
- a splash of milk of your choice
- 1–2 heirloom tomatoes, diced
- ½ small carrot, julienned
- a handful of microgreens
- extra-virgin olive oil, for drizzling
- ½ lemon
- unrefined salt

I love breakfast bowls. They are healthy and just down-home delicious! This is one of my favourites. This is how I do breakfast eggs (almost every time), and I love the buttery-ness of the beans and the fresh flavours and crunchiness of all the other elements. *–Lentil*

Roughly tear the bread into a bowl.

Melt 1 teaspoon of butter in a small frying pan over medium heat. Add the bacon, fennel and pepper and fry for about 2 minutes until fragrant and just starting to brown. Add the passata, beans and a splash of water, cover and simmer for about 5 minutes until sauce is thick and the beans are just tender. Pour over the bread in the bowl.

Return the pan to the heat, adding more butter or a splash of oil if needed. In a small bowl, whisk the egg(s) and milk until well combined, then pour into the pan. Cover and cook over medium heat for 1 minute, but don't stir! Reduce the heat to low and continue to cook for another minute or so (again, no stirring!) until the egg is just starting to set. Break apart gently with a wooden spoon, then cover again and continue to cook (without stirring!) for another minute until the egg is fully cooked. The egg will be halfway between an omelette and a scramble.

Add the egg to the bowl, then follow with the tomato, carrot and microgreens. Drizzle over some oil, squeeze over some lemon and season to taste.

Continued over page for bowl #2 →

#2—Matt's winter/spring breakfast bowl.

All winter and spring, I am all about brassica shoots—the flower buds of broccoli, cabbage, cauliflower, mustard greens, radish, turnip, kohlrabi and brussels sprouts. They are so diversely colourful and flavourful, and are so easy to cook (and are often found growing wild). They just tick all the boxes for me for fun garden food. Upland cress (see field notes, page 275) is also right up there with brassica shoots. It's the most nutrient-dense green per calorie, plus it protects our brassicas from white cabbage butterfly grubs (see page 91), so we always plant them together. This is my perfect breakfast bowl for these seasons, utilising what's thriving in the garden, what's readily abundant in the fridge and some tasty pickles to sharpen it all into focus. Make it yours. *-Matt*

- 2 eggs
- extra-virgin olive oil
- a pinch of poppy seeds
- a pinch of chilli flakes
- a handful of brassica shoots
- a handful of upland cress
- a pinch of unrefined salt
- 1 cup leftover cooked gluten-free grains (brown rice, quinoa, millet etc.) (see note)
- ½ avocado, sliced
- a spoonful of Italian kimchi (page 156)
- a spoonful of pickled broad beans (page 164)
- 1 radish, finely sliced
- a small handful of sprouts (page 340)
- a pinch of black sesame seeds

Bring a small saucepan of water to the boil. Using a spoon, gently lower the eggs right to the bottom of the pan (to avoid cracking) and gently boil for exactly 6 minutes. Remove from the pan immediately, refresh under cold water, then peel and halve. The eggs should be perfectly soft-set. Set aside.

Meanwhile, add a very generous (I mean *very* generous) splash of oil to a medium, heavy-based frying pan over medium heat. Add the poppy seeds and chilli and fry for 1 minute, taking care not to burn them. Add the brassica shoots, cress and salt (beware of spitting—you might want to cover the pan for a moment) and fry for 1–2 minutes until just softened and the colour has brightened nicely. Transfer to a bowl and set aside.

Add the grains to the pan and stir to soak up all the oil. Cover, turn off the heat and leave for a minute to warm through just from the heat of the pan, then transfer to a serving bowl.

Add eggs, greens and remaining ingredients to the bowl any way you like and feast!

RECIPE NOTE.

If you don't have any leftover grains, place 1 cup of white rice and 1½ cups of water in a small-medium saucepan, cover and bring to the boil. Reduce to a simmer and cook for 15 minutes.

Breakfast panini.

SERVES 1
TIME: 10 MINUTES

Sure, lunchtime might be the *correct* time for panini, but who cares. These little sandwiches as the first thing to light up your tastebuds in the morning will really make you feel like it's going to be a good day. Make them your own.

#1 GF, All year

FRIED EGG & BACON WITH ZUCCHINI PICKLES, CHILLI JAM & CHEESE.

sourdough flatbreads (page 134), quartered

eggs, fried

bacon or ham, fried (optional)

tasty, asiago or pecorino cheese, grated

zucchini pickles (page 170)

pear, lemon and chilli jam (page 172)

#2 GF | V, All year

MUSHROOMS, MELTED CHEESE, GREEN SAUCE & LEEK JAM.

sourdough flatbreads (page 134), quartered

mushrooms, sautéed in butter

melting cheese (cheddar, mozzarella, asiago), sliced and melted

all the herbs green sauce (page 124)

leek jam (page 155)

Prepare the ingredients and sandwich between two quarters of flatbread. Toast in a sandwich press or frying pan with a little butter, if you like.

Sit. Eat. Go do the day.

Small plates.

Small bits and pieces,
best for sharing.

Joe's burnt baba ganoush.

'It's like my friends have a sixth sense when it comes to knowing when I'm making my baba ganoush. Almost every time I'm making it, I hear this knock, knock, knock at the door.' The spirit of Joe and Monty is palpable—you couldn't hold it down if you tried. It's big, vivacious, truthful and gentle all at the same time. Their home is always full of people. It's open, and it's there to care for people and the world.

Joe says you can make this in 10 minutes—that's his personal best. It takes me 20. But see how you go. This recipe is all about the smoky and fresh flavours (all at the same time). And as Joe says, 'Put it on everything forever—it's soooooo delicious! Happy baba time!' *-Lentil*

- 4 large eggplants (about 1.5 kg)
- 2 garlic cloves, chopped
- 3 tablespoons extra-virgin olive oil
- ½ teaspoon unrefined salt
- 100 ml lemon juice (juice of about 2 large lemons)
- 3 tablespoons hulled tahini
- 1 teaspoon ground cumin

TO SERVE

- sumac
- a big handful of mint leaves, torn or roughly chopped
- extra-virgin olive oil
- sourdough flatbreads (page 134) or carrot sticks

Firstly, as Joe says, 'Char those mighty eggplants.' With both of the below methods, don't be scared to burn them (see image, page 217). They should be collapsed and the flesh almost translucent. Actually, severely burning them is the whole point. If not, your eggplant won't be as caramelised and delicious as it needs to be.

METHOD 1. OPEN FLAME, GAS STOVE OR BARBECUE

Get your open flame cranking. Place the whole eggplants on the barbecue or open flames of the stovetop, using all four burners. Turn the eggplants occasionally, cooking for about 10 minutes, or until charred, super collapsed and oozing juices.

METHOD 2. OVEN

Turn the oven up as hot as it goes, usually about 250°C fan-forced.

Place the whole eggplants on a large baking tray and cook until super collapsed and charred, about 40 minutes.

THE REST

Meanwhile, using a mortar and pestle, pound the garlic, oil and salt until well combined, then pour into a medium bowl. Add the lemon juice, tahini and cumin and stir to combine.

Cool the eggplant for about 5 minutes, or until cool enough to handle (or do as Joe does, and use an oven mitt while they're hot). Using a spoon, remove the flesh from the skin and add to the bowl. Discard the skin. Mash with a fork until well combined but still chunky. Tahini and eggplants can vary in moisture levels, so if the baba is not wet enough, add a little more tahini and oil. Don't use a food processor, as it will ruin the texture.

Spoon the baba into a bowl, top with a sprinkle of sumac, the mint and a splash of oil. Serve with flatbreads and carrot sticks. Well, it's good with anything really!

BLUES

Anytime chickpea pancakes.

PANCAKES

- 200 g chickpea flour (besan)
- 500 ml (2 cups) warm water
- 3 tablespoons dry white wine
- 2 tablespoons extra-virgin olive oil
- ½ teaspoon unrefined salt

SAVOURY TOPPING OPTIONS
(one or more—optional)

- a big pinch of unrefined salt and/or freshly ground black pepper
- a sprig or two of rosemary or thyme, leaves stripped
- a handful of roughly chopped olives

SERVING IDEAS
(our favourites—optional)

- whipped butter and olive oil (page 120)
- salami
- ricotta or goat's cheese
- baked plums (page 325)
- spiced apricots (page 201)
- fish soup (page 277)
- creamy mushrooms (page 263)

These are inspired by our time in Italy, where local wine is always paired with antipasti, and olives are a given—they just want to feed you. The people are generous, life is full of colour and it always feels abundant. These pancakes are featured in many regions. In each region they are a little different and are given a different name. And we make them differently again. These are one of our favourite antipasti additions—alongside carrot sticks in a jar, some local salumi, an end-of-the-day glass of wine and anything else left over from the day before. They are also fantastic as part of a savoury breakfast, with dessert or a simple salad or soup, with stewed or roasted fruit or just as a simple snack—all on their own.

DAY 1

Add the batter ingredients to a medium bowl and whisk until a smooth and very thin batter forms. Pour the batter into an airtight container or bowl, cover and set aside on the bench at room temperature for 12–24 hours. This will allow the mixture to come together and also prepare and sour the flour.

DAY 2

Preheat the oven to 200°C fan-forced. Liberally coat two 20 cm skillets (or two 20 cm round baking tins) with oil and set aside.

Stir the batter to make sure it's smooth and fully combined.

Put the skillets in the oven for 5 minutes (or 2 minutes for baking tins) to get hot. Then pull them out of the oven and quickly pour in the batter, dividing the mixture evenly (it should be about 8 mm–1 cm thick). If you are adding any extra toppings, sprinkle them on top now.

Cook the pancakes for 10–15 minutes (or 20–25 minutes for baking tins) until set, just turning golden brown on top and crisp at the edges. Make sure not to overcook the pancakes, as they will become less custard-like and dryer in texture if you do. Cool in the skillets for 5 minutes, then flip out onto a board to serve.

Cut the pancakes into slices and serve warm and fresh with some olive oil, salt and pepper, or pair with any of the above serving suggestions! We have served them here with an adapted version of our baked plums, using mixed fruit.

RECIPE NOTE.

Liberally coating the skillets or baking tins with oil and quickly pouring in the batter is essential. It will stop the pancakes from sticking and ensure they get nice and crispy.

Friselle bruschetta.

We are obsessed with friselli (page 141). We've been eating friselli with leftover stew (pages 294 and 306); with pasta sauce (page 312); with fresh tomatoes and fresh cheese (page 144); with dill pickles, cured cacioricotta (page 148) and olive tapenade. One of my favourite lunches in recent memory was with Lentil and our dear photographer brother/cousin Shantanu after a market visit in Southern Italy. It was simply friselli piled high with fresh tomatoes, olives and olive oil, so many cheeses, freshly roasted porchetta and sundried tomato spread! We'd just picked it all up from the local market that morning and it was the ultimate messy, fun, oil-dripping, laugh-out-loud meal. The best. These are two of our favourite friselle bruschetti. The ultimate light-up-your-face treats, while you sit, share, laugh and drink. Create your own. *-Matt*

#1 WF | DF | VG, Su | A

LUCKY'S CLASSIC.

From the baron of friselli himself (page 138), a truly simple but phenomenally satisfying bruschetta. The first thing Lucky did after showing us how to make friselli was grab a cold beer and make this to share. He said, 'This is how it is and must be done.' Legend.

- 1 friselle (page 141)
- 1 garlic clove, halved
- sun-warmed tomatoes from the garden, thickly sliced
- air-dried oregano (dry your own by hanging a fresh bunch in an airy place—you'll never buy it from a store again)
- unrefined salt
- extra-virgin olive oil

Hydrate the friselle in a bowl of water for 6–10 minutes until perfectly crunchable, then shake dry. Rub the cut side of the garlic all over the top of the bread, then top with tomato slices. Sprinkle over some oregano and salt and drizzle all over with oil. Take a deep breath. Eat.

#2 WF | V, All year

CREAMY MUSHROOMS.

These mushrooms were *made* to live on friselli. I really have nothing else to say. But if I had to say something, it would be to double the creamy mushroom recipe when you make it. Because you can never make enough.

- 1 friselle (page 141)
- creamy mushrooms (page 263)

Hydrate the friselle in a bowl of water for 6–10 minutes until perfectly crunchable, then shake dry. Pile on the mushrooms. You know the drill.

Nonna's leek & spinach fritters.

PERFECT FOR PICNICS, EASY WEEKLY MEALS AND LEFTOVERS.

BATTER PART ONE

- extra-virgin olive oil or unsalted butter
- 4 leeks (about 500 g in total), trimmed and cut into 1 cm slices (see field notes)
- 1 onion, diced
- 100 g (2 packed cups) spinach, roughly chopped (see notes)
- 1 garlic clove, crushed
- ¼ cup oregano leaves, finely chopped
- ½ teaspoon unrefined salt
- a big pinch of freshly ground black pepper

BATTER PART TWO

- 2 eggs, separated
- a squeeze of lemon juice
- 150 g (¾ cup) cottage cheese (or ricotta)
- 125 ml (½ cup) milk of your choice
- 120 g chickpea flour (besan)
- 2 teaspoons apple cider vinegar
- 1 teaspoon bicarbonate of soda
- 1 teaspoon unprocessed honey

DIPPING SAUCE

- 250 g (1 cup) natural yoghurt
- 2 tablespoons extra-virgin olive oil
- juice of 1 lemon
- ½ garlic clove, crushed (optional)
- a pinch of unrefined salt

We are at Nonna's house in a tiny Sardinian mountain village, 'Mangia, mangia, mangia!' She isn't a blood-related nonna, but she feels like she could be in this moment. It's as if every night she feeds you and tucks you into bed with a hot water bottle.

We arrive after a long day of driving—so exhausted. It's not always all rainbows and pretty views on the road. We have never met her before, yet she anticipates our needs. She hands us a plate of leftovers—fritters, sliced cheese and thickly sliced, oily baked eggplant from the day before, and a pot of herbal tea. With a bite of the fritters I am taken back to my childhood. And I instantly feel better. I tell her she is a beautiful woman and a magnificent cook, and she just tells me, 'No, *you* are a beautiful woman' and walks away. She is so humble, and thinks nothing of what she does. But she has one of the most important jobs there is, and makes a difference to lives in the most important way—with love.

There were bright-pink synthetic sheets, and the house had that old smell. You know the one. Yet nothing could have been more perfect. And we slept so well. *-Lentil*

BATTER PART ONE

Add a generous splash of oil or knob of butter to a large frying pan over medium heat. Add the leek and onion and sauté until beginning to soften. Add a splash of water to the pan, cover and cook for 12–15 minutes until just starting to brown. Throw the spinach in to wilt for the last 2 minutes of cooking.

Transfer the leek mixture to a bowl with the garlic, oregano, salt and pepper and combine, then place in the fridge to cool. Set the pan aside until you are ready to cook your fritters.

BATTER PART TWO

Meanwhile, beat the eggwhites and lemon juice in a medium bowl to form stiff peaks. Set aside.

Add the remaining part two ingredients to a large bowl and whisk until well combined. The mixture should be really thick and slightly bubbly, like a thick pancake batter but with a few lumps from the cheese. Add the leek mixture you made earlier (which should be cool) to the batter and combine. Finally, fold in the eggwhites very gently.

Recipe continued over page →

→ **Recipe continued from previous page**

Heat a generous splash of oil or knob of butter in the pan over medium–high heat (note: if it's too hot, the fritters will burn before they cook through). Spoon the mixture into the pan to form fritters—1 tablespoon should make one fritter about 5–7 cm in diameter. Cover and fry for a few minutes on each side until just brown and crisp. If they're cooking too quickly, just reduce the heat and make sure you keep the lid on. Cook in batches, covering the cooked fritters with a tea towel as you go, or placing them in a low oven to keep warm.

When ready to serve, add the dipping sauce ingredients to a jar and shake to combine.

Serve the fritters warm or cold with the dipping sauce on the side. Add a salad and a fried egg to make it a meal, or simply eat as a healthy snack! The fritters will keep in an airtight container in the fridge for up to 5 days.

RECIPE NOTES.

Instead of spinach, we often use wild mallow.

You could also add herbs and spices, such as chilli, parsley and coriander to this recipe.

FIELD NOTES.

On preparing leeks. I remember, when I first started cooking, being totally confused about which part of a leek to use. Can I use the top green part? If not, how far can I go? Is this safe? Well, the reality is that you can absolutely eat all of a leek, including the roots, but for sure the best bit is the white stalk and the first (lighter) green bit.

Trim off the root and a couple of millimetres of the base, then peel back any dry layers from the outside to reveal a perfect, clean stalk. Then, start cutting into slices from the base and just work your way up the stalk right into the green where it's beginning to sprout leaves. Cut to within 5 mm of the first leaf, then remove the remainder of that leaf layer, wipe the stalk clean of any dirt and continue to work up to 5 mm from the next leaf. Repeat until you're down to about a finger-thick stalk—the remaining top can go to the chickens. *-Lentil*

Milanese sardines.

SERVES 2
TIME: 10 MINUTES

So little needs to be said about this dish beyond that it is *the* perfect two-person snack with your end-of-the-day wine. It's so quick and easy and uses super-simple ingredients. If you're prepared, the salad can be made ahead of time, or the whole thing can be whipped up before you're halfway through your first glass of wine on a Friday evening. Savour with someone you love.

- extra-virgin olive oil (ideally from the sardine can/jar)
- a handful of pine nuts
- a handful of sultanas
- a small handful of very finely sliced red or brown onion
- 1 packed cup flat-leaf parsley leaves, roughly chopped
- 1 orange, peeled, segmented and deseeded
- ½ grapefruit, peeled, segmented and deseeded
- juice of 1 lemon
- ¼ teaspoon unrefined salt (omit if using home-preserved sardines)
- 100 g can sardines in oil (or sardines under oil, page 166), drained, oil reserved

Add a generous splash of oil to a medium, heavy-based frying pan over medium heat. Add the pine nuts and sultanas and sauté for 2 minutes. Turn off the heat, then add the onion and sauté in just the heat of the pan for 1–2 minutes, which will soften the onion a little. Tip out into a medium bowl.

Add the parsley, orange, grapefruit, lemon juice, salt (if required) and 2 teaspoons of oil to the bowl and toss to thoroughly combine. Set aside for at least 5 minutes. It's also nice if you chill the salad for half an hour or so before serving.

To serve, arrange the sardines on a small serving dish and top with the salad. Serve immediately with a nice glass of wine.

Dolmades.

- extra-virgin olive oil
- ½ onion, diced
- ¼ bunch (30 g) flat-leaf parsley, leaves separated from stalks, both finely chopped
- ¼ bunch (20 g) dill, fronds separated from stalks, both finely chopped
- 1 teaspoon lemon zest
- ¼ teaspoon fennel seeds (and a handful of the fronds and flowers, if you have them)
- a big pinch of freshly ground black pepper
- 1 tablespoon pine nuts
- 1 large garlic clove, crushed
- 110 g (½ cup) medium grain brown rice, soaked for 12–24 hours in water with a dash of apple cider vinegar, then drained (page 338)
- 200 ml unseasoned chicken stock (page 341)
- unrefined salt
- juice of ½ large lemon
- 15 fermented vine leaves (page 160) (see note)

DIPPING SAUCE
(optional—omit for a dairy-free version)

- 3 tablespoons natural yoghurt
- extra-virgin olive oil, to taste
- 1 teaspoon lemon zest
- unrefined salt
- freshly ground black pepper
- a squeeze of lemon juice

These are one of my favourite things. Fermented vine leaves (page 160) filled with delicious, lemony brown rice. In Malta, they love them. So, naturally, I love them too. They're an awesome snack or appetiser, with a delicious flavour from the fermented vine leaves, acidic in a bright lemony/fermented way, super herby and fresh tasting—great served with feta cheese, side salads and some good bread. If you have a big group, double the mix. *–Lentil*

Add a generous splash of oil to a deep saucepan over medium heat. Add the onion, herb stalks, lemon zest, fennel seeds and pepper and sauté for about 5 minutes until the onion has softened and is translucent. Add the pine nuts and garlic and fry for a few minutes until the pine nuts are a little toasted. Add the rice and fry for a few more minutes. Add the stock and herb leaves and cover. Bring to the boil, then reduce the heat and simmer for 30–40 minutes, or until the rice is cooked but still holding its shape and all the liquid is absorbed. If it gets too dry before the rice is fully cooked, add a splash of water and continue to cook until it's ready.

Fry for a minute or so with the lid off to fully dry. Turn off the heat and stand until it's cool enough to touch, then season to taste and stir through the lemon juice.

It's time to roll your dolmades. First, make sure your vine leaves are soft enough to eat. Taste one! If it is a bit firm, they may not be fully fermented. If so, you can just blanch them quickly in boiling salted water to soften. Place about 1 tablespoon of rice mixture per leaf, depending on the size of the leaf, then roll them up tightly (see diagrams).

When ready to serve, combine the dipping sauce ingredients (if making) and serve alongside the dolmades.

Store the dolmades in an airtight container in the fridge, coated with a little oil. They will keep for at least 1 week.

RECIPE NOTE.

If you don't have any fermented vines leaves, blanch fresh, young vine leaves for about 10–15 minutes in salty water until super soft but still holding together. Taste to check if they are soft enough to eat! You can also buy a brined version, if you prefer.

Mumma Michelle's egg & bread muffins.

THE FIRST THING I EVER LEARNT TO COOK!

This may seem to be the simplest recipe ever, but it is so deeply held in my heart. It was the first thing I ever learnt to cook, my first memory of cooking on my own and feeding my family, and I felt so proud. I remember my mum patiently teaching me to roll the bread and crack the eggs. Granted, as a small child, mine were much simpler—bread, an egg and cheese on top. As I have grown older, this is what they have become—a little more grown up!

These easy-to-make egg, vegetable and cheese-filled muffins are so comforting and wholesome and are awesome for quick meals, breakfasts, lunch boxes and picnics. Add fresh sides, like tomato, avocado and rocket, to make them into a bigger meal.

I hope this recipe is the first, of many things, that lots of kids learn to cook—they can, like me, always start with just the bread, egg and cheese. *-Lentil*

- 50 g amaranth greens (or spinach), finely chopped
- unrefined salt
- 6 eggs
- a splash of milk of your choice
- 5 large slices of sourdough bread (gluten free, if preferred), crusts cut off (see note)
- 80 g pumpkin, shaved into strips with a vegetable peeler
- 80 g fresh cacioricotta (page 148) (or ricotta)
- 2 large spring onions (or onion or garlic shoots and flowers, if you have them), finely chopped
- 10 slices of mozzarella (or cheddar)
- freshly ground black pepper
- a handful of poppy seeds

TO SERVE (optional—if in season)

- a big handful of basil leaves, torn
- 1 avocado, sliced
- quick tomato sauce (page 123)

Preheat the oven to 180°C fan-forced. Grease (well!) or line a standard 12-hole muffin tray.

Add the amaranth greens, a splash of water and a pinch of salt to a small frying pan over medium heat. Cover and cook for about 3 minutes until the greens have totally wilted, then remove from the heat and set aside.

Whisk the eggs and milk in a medium bowl until well combined.

Roll the bread out with a rolling pin until about 2–3 mm thick.

To assemble the muffins, fit a slice of bread into a muffin hole, working from one edge of the bread. Cut off the remainder of the bread, which should be about half a slice, to make the next muffin. Repeat for all the slices. They will look a bit rustic and imperfect—perfect! From your five slices, you should get ten muffins.

Layer the muffins, dividing the ingredients evenly between them. Start with a few pumpkin slices, a teaspoon of cacioricotta, some amaranth and a sprinkle of spring onion, then pour in enough egg to fill and top with a slice of mozzarella. Season with salt and pepper and finish with some poppy seeds. Bake for about 20 minutes, or until the bread is crisp and the filling fully cooked and golden on top.

Serve warm with some fresh basil, avocado and our quick tomato sauce, if you like.

RECIPE NOTE.

With any leftover crusts, you can make breadcrumbs. Just put them in the oven to toast and then blitz in a food processor or blender.

Panino city.

Florence is so different to the rest of Italy. It was there that I was reminded how different each small region of Italy is, and how differently they all see themselves. In so many ways, it's like heaps of tiny countries rolled into one. You can't simply say you are eating Tuscan food—it's specific. The way they do things is specific. In each area, they have a way.

Here they have an attitude about them. They hate you half the time. And love you the other half. I kind of love it.

Florence is modern. The rest of Italy is not. Well that's an exaggeration, but put it this way, it's easy to stay away from the 'modern' in many parts of Italy. And yet, there is another element here that I love so much—they are so real. They eat the scrappiest parts of the meat. They eat offal. They were poor. Once. They seem to understand what it's like to have nothing. Even though that's not how it is now.

In Florence, you can literally have a proper farm 10 minutes from the city, and a store in the city selling its produce. So, it's a special place. Like a small village in its quality of food and produce, small stores and traditional dishes, but a modern and thriving city.

Story continued over page →

Quick panino.

While we are visiting Florence, a friend Emiko (a lovely fellow author!) takes us to this man's teeny-tiny panino shop. He is so cool. I mean he has to be about 60, but he is a dude. A dude with a tiny store and a blackboard, with his daily offering written on it. This is like speaking to my dreams. I tell him I can't have the bread, and he just smiles and makes me a salad of all the ingredients of my chosen panino. And then apologises profusely. I love Italy. I love it.

Of course, we wouldn't say we do panini like them. This is simply inspired by them. It's not *the* way. It's our version. Food that we love, inspired by our experiences, and made our own—in this case, by using our leftover-sourdough flatbreads. Here's today's blackboard. *-Lentil*

#1 GF, All year

YESTERDAY'S STEW WITH PARSLEY SALAD & PARMESAN.

- ½ packed cup flat-leaf parsley leaves
- a few pieces of finely sliced red onion
- 1 teaspoon extra-virgin olive oil
- ¼ teaspoon red or white wine vinegar
- ¼ teaspoon unrefined salt
- 1 sourdough flatbread (page 134)
- leftover freestyle stew (page 306)
- grated parmesan

Add the parsley, onion, oil, vinegar and salt to a bowl and toss firmly with your hands to extract the goodness. Set aside for at least 5 minutes.

Quarter the flatbread and pile some stew on two of the quarters. Top with cheese and parsley salad and cover with the remaining quarters. Now feast!

#2 GF | DF, All year

ANCHOVIES, BITTER GREENS, ORANGE & CHILLI.

- 120 g bitter greens (witlof, radicchio, chicory), finely chopped
- 1 navel orange, segmented and deseeded
- 10 anchovy fillets, halved
- 2 teaspoons oil from the anchovy jar
- ¼ teaspoon chilli flakes
- 1 sourdough flatbread (page 134)

Add all the ingredients except the flatbread to a bowl and toss firmly with your hands to extract the goodness. Set aside for at least 5 minutes.

Quarter the flatbread and pile the salad on two of the quarters. Cover with the remaining quarters. Take a deep breath. And devour.

#3 GF, Su | A

BACON WITH COLD RED SAUCE.

- a few rashers of smoked pasture-raised bacon
- 1 sourdough flatbread (page 134)
- leftover simplest red sauce (page 312)

Fry the bacon in its own lard in a heavy-based frying pan over medium heat.

Quarter the flatbread and lay the bacon on two of the quarters. Top with cold red sauce and cover with the remaining quarters. Take a seat. And savour.

Zucchini rolls.

- 2 large zucchinis (500–600 g in total), cut into 12 slices about 1 cm thick
- ½ sweet potato (150–200 g), julienned
- extra-virgin olive oil
- unrefined salt
- freshly ground black pepper
- 2 apricots, sliced
- 50 basil leaves
- 1 carrot, julienned
- 1 small cucumber, deseeded and julienned

DIPPING SAUCE (see note)

- 1 tablespoon extra-virgin olive oil
- 2 teaspoons apple cider vinegar
- 2 teaspoons unrefined sugar (e.g. rapadura) (or unprocessed honey)
- 2 teaspoons lemon juice
- 1 garlic clove, crushed
- 1 teaspoon hot chilli flakes (or 2 hot chillies, finely chopped)
- a pinch of unrefined salt

'You know, food is just *the* everything—it's nourishment, it's love, it's community, it's ... [makes the biggest circular motion with hands].' Hermione, Joe and their three children are just those people that you meet and you know that you are meant to know each other, you're meant to be in each other's village. We have the best memories, simple ones, of just sitting together eating these, as we sweated in the intense heat of summer, and the chaos of their three children surrounded us. And the memory makes me smile.

When it's hot, I just want to eat these, they are super-fresh rolls that are a bit chunky, a bit sweet and a bit spicy from the sauce. The combination of the filling and the abundant basil leaves is key—you have to have it all. We make these all-veg, no-carb rolls in place of sushi or rice paper rolls, and although they are in the share section, we often eat these for dinner (for two) on a hot summer's day. If you are somewhere tropical, replace the apricot with mango.
-Lentil

Preheat the oven to 180°C fan-forced.

Arrange the zucchini and sweet potato on two separate baking trays. Lightly rub the vegetables with oil and season with salt and pepper. Bake for 8–10 minutes until the zucchini is just turning translucent and softening. Set the zucchini aside for about 5 minutes, or until cool to touch. If the sweet potato hasn't softened, bake for a few more minutes until it's fully cooked through.

Take a slice of zucchini and then layer up a few pieces of sweet potato, a slice or two of apricot, some basil leaves and a small handful each of carrot and cucumber. Fold the ends of the zucchini over the top to form a wrap and secure with a toothpick. Repeat for all the rolls.

Add the dipping sauce ingredients to a small jar, screw the lid on and shake well.

To serve, place the rolls on a share plate with the dipping sauce on the side. Or do as Joe does, and pour the sauce on top of the rolls. Share!

RECIPE NOTE.

If you have some pear, lemon and chilli jam (page 172), simply use 1 tablespoon of the jam, 1 tablespoon of extra-virgin olive oil and 2 teaspoons of apple cider vinegar for the dipping sauce.

Baked eggplant & pear slices.

Okay, admittedly this might sound strange. But it's super delicious. Also, there is a crossover when the pears and eggplants start to ripen in season, so they are destined to go together—I am just the only one who knows about it! The eggplant soaks up all the flavour and acts as the base for a delicious pear and cheese match on top. *-Lentil*

- extra-virgin olive oil
- 2 eggplants (about 500 g in total), cut into 2.5 cm thick rounds
- unrefined salt
- freshly ground black pepper
- balsamic vinegar
- 250 ml (1 cup) passata
- 1 garlic clove, roughly chopped
- a handful of basil leaves
- ¼ teaspoon sweet paprika
- 1 pear, cored and sliced
- a big handful of grated pecorino or parmesan

Preheat the oven to 180°C fan-forced. Liberally oil a large baking tray.

Lay the eggplant slices out on the prepared tray and season with salt and pepper. Liberally splash with oil and vinegar and bake for 10 minutes.

Meanwhile, add the passata, garlic, basil, paprika and a generous splash of oil to a blender and pulse until chunky and just combined. You can also use a mortar and pestle for this, but just grind the basil and garlic before adding the other ingredients.

After 10 minutes, pull the eggplant from the oven and flip the slices with a spatula. Top with the tomato mixture (you should have more than enough to top each slice) and continue to bake for 15 minutes.

After 15 minutes, top each piece of eggplant with a slice or two of pear and liberally sprinkle with cheese. Bake for about 5 minutes until the eggplant is falling apart and looking delicious! Cool a little and serve as a side with salads, sourdough flatbreads (page 134), or on its own as an appetiser with a glass of red.

PRODOTTO
PEPERONI
PREZZO
€ 4.00
AL KG.
CATEGORIA
EXTRA

Vegetables.

Heaps of them.
As a side or as a main.

Everyone's salad chart.

Vegetables. The foundation. Add at least one.

Steamed, boiled, sautéed or fried.

300–500 g of one or a mix.

- Amaranth
- Asparagus
- Beetroot tops
- Broad beans (& tips)
- Broccoli/broccolini
- Brassica shoots
- Chard/silverbeet
- Collard greens
- 'Green' beans
- Kale
- Kohlrabi
- Mushrooms
- Mustard greens
- Potato
- Spinach
- Sugar snap, snow and shelling peas
- Sweet corn
- Sweet potato
- Turnip
- Turnip tops
- Upland cress
- Warrigal greens
- Wild greens (mallow, stinging nettle, fat hen, wild dandelion, wild radish)

Roasted or baked.

500 g of one or a mix.

- Beetroot
- Brussels sprouts
- Capsicum
- Carrot
- Cauliflower
- Eggplant
- Fennel
- Garlic
- Jerusalem artichoke
- Mushrooms
- Onion/French shallots
- Parsnip
- Potato
- Pumpkin
- Sweet potato
- Zucchini/summer squash

With herbs/spices.

- Black pepper
- Chilli flakes
- Fennel seeds
- Marjoram
- Mustard seeds
- Rosemary
- Thyme

Raw (finely sliced, grated, julienned or chopped).

300 g of one or a mix.

- Asparagus
- Beans
- Beetroot
- Bitter greens (chicory, witlof, radicchio)
- Broccoli
- Cabbage
- Capsicum
- Carrot
- Cauliflower
- Celery
- Cucumber
- Fennel
- Garlic or onion shoots
- Japanese turnip
- Kohlrabi
- Onion or red onion
- Radish
- Sugar snap, snow and shelling peas
- Tatsoi
- Tomato
- Wombok
- Zucchini/summer squash

Salad-makers. The framework. Add one of each.

Dressing basics.

It's not a salad without a dressing!

A combination of.

- Extra-virgin olive oil
- Garlic, crushed
- Honey/sugar
- Horseradish, freshly grated
- Lemon or lime juice
- Mayonnaise (page 340)
- Mustard
- Natural yoghurt
- Pickling liquid
- Red or white wine vinegar or balsamic
- Tahini

Or premade.

- All the herbs green sauce (page 124)
- Family salad dressing (page 244)
- Pesto (page 124)
- Yoghurt dressing (page 258)

Must have.

A big pinch or so of unrefined salt

Some extra flavour.

One or two to brighten everything up.

A big pinch of spice seeds, toasted.

- Chilli
- Nigella
- Sichuan pepper

A big handful of leafy herbs, finely chopped.

- Basil
- Chervil
- Chives
- Coriander
- Dill
- Garlic chives
- Lemon verbena
- Marjoram (only fresh new growth)
- Mint
- Oregano (only fresh new growth)
- Parsley
- Summer savory
- Summer tarragon

Other.

Red onion, diced or finely sliced

My friend Sarah is the real-life superwoman. Her house always smells so good; her ability to genuinely smile, all the time, is unreal; and she manages to feed her kids only healthy things. But, at the beginning of the week she plans out all of her meals, then buys all of the *exact* ingredients (which just breaks my mind). So, this chart is for her—and everyone like her—to inspire you all to ad-lib a little, use what you've got in the fridge/garden and make some salads! *-Lentil*

	Taking it next-level. The WOW. Add one or more for something *really* special.			
Something fresh/green. 300 g of one or a mix.	**Fruits—grilled or raw (halved or sliced).** 300 g of one or a mix.	**Nuts/seeds, raw or toasted, for crunch.** 1–2 big handfuls of one or a mix.	**An acid for balance.** ½ cup, diced, of one or a mix.	**Make it a meal.** 1–2 x 150–200 g portions of one or a mix.
Bitter greens (chicory, witlof, radicchio)	Apple	Almonds, roughly chopped	Capsicum under oil (page 163)	Bacon/ham
Endive/escarole	Apricot	Chestnuts, boiled and peeled	Dill pickles	Broken friselle (page 141) or torn bread
Kale	Avocado	Dukkah (page 120)	Lacto-fermented jalapeños	Cooked grains (quinoa, millet, rice, buckwheat etc.—see preparation notes, page 338)
Lettuce	Berries	Flax seeds	Lacto-fermented vegetables (green beans, brussels sprouts, radish seed pods)	Cooked pulses/legumes (cannellini and borlotti beans, chickpeas, lentils)
Mibuna/mizuna	Cape gooseberry	Hazelnuts, roughly chopped	Leek jam (page 155)	Feta
Mustard greens	Citrus (grapefruit, orange)	Pecans, roughly chopped	Olives (page 177)	Fresh cheese (page 144)
Nasturtium leaves	Fig	Pine nuts	Pickled capers, garlic, mushrooms or globe artichokes	Fried paneer/haloumi
Rocket	Kiwifruit	Pistachios	Preserved lemons	Leftover roast meats
Spinach	Nectarine	Poppy seeds	Quick-pickled broad beans (page 164)	Mozzarella
Sprouts	Peach	Pumpkin seeds	Zucchini pickles (page 170)	Preserved anchovies
Winter purslane	Pear	Sesame seeds		Preserved tuna
Wood sorrel	Plum	Sunflower seeds		Prosciutto
	Pomegranate seeds	Walnuts, roughly chopped		Ricotta/cacioricotta (page 148)
	Tomatillo			Sardines under oil (page 166)
				Shaved parmesan, aged pecorino or cured cacioricotta (page 148)

Notes.

Your salad should be coated in a dressing, if not add a little olive oil.

If you are in the tropics, use local ingredients also, like mango, pineapple, lime, coconut and macadamia nuts.

Weights and measures are just an approximate guide. Play around and make it yours!

Family salad dressing.

MAKES ABOUT 170 ML
TIME: 5 MINUTES

This is *the* salad dressing. It has been passed down through generations. In my aunty's house as children, it went on *everything*—quiche, salad, pizza—and we used to joke that she could bottle it and make a million dollars! And now, in our house, it dresses so many vegetables to make them into what we formally call a salad. I actually don't know my aunty's recipe, but this is my version of it. Make a big batch to keep in the fridge and dress *your* vegetables to formally make them salads too. *-Lentil*

2 teaspoons unrefined sugar (e.g. rapadura)

1 teaspoon apple cider vinegar

a splash of boiling water

3 tablespoons extra-virgin olive oil

2 tablespoons mayonnaise (page 340)

2 small garlic cloves, crushed

1 teaspoon wholegrain mustard

juice of ½ lemon

a pinch of unrefined salt

Add the sugar, vinegar and boiling water to a small jar, seal and shake to dissolve the sugar. Add the remaining ingredients and shake super well. Use to dress everything.

RECIPE NOTES.

If using fresh mayonnaise, the dressing will keep in the fridge for at least 1 week, but much longer if using store-bought mayonnaise.

Double the quantities to make easy meals and salads throughout the week (see our salad chart on page 242).

To thin it out, or if it's been sitting in the fridge, put a *tiny* splash of water in the jar and shake to get the remaining dressing out. It makes a slightly thinner dressing, but it's just as good!

This dressing is really good with potatoes to make a quick potato salad.

Husk-baked cheesy corn.

SERVES 4-8 AS A SIDE OR SNACK
TIME: 40 MINUTES

There is no simpler way to prepare corn than baking it in the husk. And there is no better thing to serve it with than this rich, garlicky, herby—purple!—cheese sauce. This recipe is pure summer—simple, unpretentious, deliciously fun food to share with friends and family. *-Matt*

4 ripe corn cobs, with full husks

extra-virgin olive oil

2 garlic cloves, finely chopped

1 rosemary sprig, leaves stripped and finely chopped

½ teaspoon freshly ground black pepper

2 tablespoons wholegrain purple maize flour (or wholegrain yellow cornflour—see notes, page 204)

180 ml (⅔ cup) full-cream milk

100 g parmesan, grated

sweet paprika, to serve (optional)

Preheat the oven to 250°C fan-forced.

Bake the corn cobs, still in their husks, on an oven shelf for 30 minutes.

Meanwhile, add a generous splash of oil to a small, heavy-based saucepan over medium heat. Add the garlic, rosemary and pepper and sauté for 1–2 minutes until the garlic is just beginning to turn golden. Add the flour and fry for a minute, then pour in the milk and stir or whisk to combine, breaking up any lumps. Bring to a simmer and cook, stirring occasionally, for 2–3 minutes until the sauce thickens. Remove from the heat, add the cheese and stir through. Stand for a minute while the cheese melts, then stir again so you have a silky, smooth sauce.

When the corn is ready, remove the husks (hold the cobs with a tea towel so you don't burn yourself). Cut the cobs in half and place on a serving dish, then cover with the cheese sauce. Lentil likes to sprinkle over some paprika for added colour, flavour and fun. Serve steaming hot.

Tomato, garlic & barley salad.

- 3 cups cooked pot barley (as per preparation guide, page 338) (see note below, and field notes, page 260)
- 1 cup cooked white beans (as per preparation guide, page 339)
- 500 g cherry tomatoes, halved
- 3 celery stalks, diced (if in season)
- 1½ cups flat-leaf parsley leaves, coarsely chopped
- 1 cup basil leaves, coarsely chopped
- 1 tablespoon finely diced red onion

DRESSING

- 80 ml (⅓ cup) extra-virgin olive oil
- 4 garlic cloves, finely chopped
- 2½ tablespoons balsamic vinegar
- 3 teaspoons unrefined sugar (e.g. rapadura)
- 1 teaspoon unrefined salt
- ½ teaspoon freshly ground black pepper

RECIPE NOTE.

You can also use pearl barley for this recipe. In that case, forgo the soaking step in the traditional preparation guide on page 338 referred to above.

She looked at us so disappointed. We just couldn't finish it. We tried and tried. But there was no getting around it. Half of the food was still sitting on our plates, and we were only at primi—the first course!

The antipasti that had come before was epic. There was a plate of local cheese (including the best burrata we have ever tasted), a plate of local salami (from the neck of the pig), baked eggplant with passata and melted cheese (see our version on page 239), mashed potato with pancetta and cheese on top, stewed beef, omelette squares, bread. Even by that point, we were so full.

Then we had our primi of pasta—still just a warm-up to the main course! But there was no way we could finish it, let alone eat *more* food.

She finally surrendered and cleared our plates ... and immediately brought out complimentary sorbetto! At first it confused me—we had said we were full! But then I realised this is just how it's done. And actually it was so light and refreshing. As if our stomachs were full of marbles and this was the liquid to fill the gaps. *Now* the jar of marbles was full.

Then, she asked us if we wanted a digestive! Well, it wasn't really a question, it was more a statement. So we finished with a fennel digestive. Now the jar was *really* full. The marbles, and all the spaces were filled. *So* filled. And somehow, that fennel digestive really did start to dissolve all the marbles.

Out of everything that night, for some reason, this salad stood out. It was so garlicky and so simple. There were plates and plates of the most incredible looking food being brought out to us, an abundance of colours and intriguing shapes and ingredients. And this pale barley salad. Sitting there so unimpressively. But when we tried it, it was the most delicious thing there!

What looked like a simple plate of barley, was *dripping* with amazing flavour! We've made it ours with a whole lot of fresh goodness from the garden, but still every time we make it we are back at that restaurant, in that moment. *-Matt*

Add all the salad ingredients to a large bowl and gently combine with your hands.

For the dressing, add the oil to a heavy-based frying pan over medium heat. Add the garlic and sauté, taking care, as you want the garlic to only *just* start to turn golden. If it burns, it will add a slight bitterness to the dressing. When the garlic is *just* beginning to turn golden, pour the oil and garlic over the salad.

Add the remaining dressing ingredients to a jar, seal with the lid and shake well to combine. Pour the dressing over the salad, toss gently with your hands to combine well and serve.

Pickled nectarine & prawn salad.

300 g prawns (see field notes), cooked and peeled (150 g peeled) (see notes)

250 g nectarines, thickly sliced

MARINADE

160 ml (⅔ cup) extra-virgin olive oil

80 ml (⅓ cup) red wine vinegar

½ red onion, diced

½ red capsicum (or 4 tomatillos), diced

80 ml (⅓ cup) orange juice (juice of about 1 orange)

3 tablespoons lemon juice (juice of about 1 large lemon)

2 teaspoons orange zest

1 teaspoon lemon zest

2 teaspoons capers

2 teaspoons unrefined sugar (e.g. rapadura) (or unprocessed honey)

1 teaspoon wholegrain mustard

unrefined salt

a pinch of freshly ground black pepper

TO SERVE

200–250 g rocket leaves and/or mixed salad leaves

½ bunch (60 g) of basil, leaves stripped

sourdough bread (gluten free if preferred) with butter or whipped butter and olive oil (page 120)

For me, this just says Christmas. And lots of people, and chaos and all the love. And summer. And white wine. The marinated prawns and nectarines, in all the citrusy juices, are just so good. I eat it and it takes me years back, when a lovely lady named Denise made something similar. And ever since, it's been a favourite for me. We make it with both prawns and nectarines, but you can just make it with one or the other—whichever way you like it! *-Lentil*

DAY 1

Add the marinade ingredients to a large (about 1 litre) jar, seal with the lid and shake well to combine. Alternatively, if you'd like everyone to have individual jars, combine the marinade ingredients and divide equally between four to six small jars. Add the prawns and nectarine to the jar(s) and shake some more! Refrigerate for 24 hours to marinate.

DAY 2

Add the leaves and basil to a medium salad bowl, or individual bowls, and pour the jar(s) over the top, then season to taste. Serve with bread to dip into the leftover dressing in the bottom of the bowls.

RECIPE NOTES.

For a vegetarian version of this recipe, just replace the prawns with about 150–200 g more nectarine.

If nectarines are out of season, you can use more prawns in their place.

FIELD NOTES.

On sustainable prawns. Prawns are so good for you. They are packed with iron, selenium, zinc and magnesium, and are an excellent source of protein, plus they contain omega-3 fatty acids and good cholesterol. But eating prawns isn't always so healthy for the planet. The world's oceans are under serious strain from our growing population, and so it's more important than ever to know which fish and shellfish species are sustainable options, and which should be avoided. It will differ depending on where you live, but the information is readily available. Take the time to seek it out. In Australia, our sustainable prawn species at the time of writing are wild-caught Queensland greasyback prawns, wild-caught Spencer Gulf king prawns, and small-scale, locally farmed prawns of all species. Support these options and encourage sustainable fisheries.

Shaved zucchini & apricot salad.

SERVES 6 AS A SIDE
TIME: 15 MINUTES

They like to party hard here. Out of all of Italy, Puglia is where they look like they live the lives of movie stars. They live in white sandstone houses, have large lavish pools overlooking the hills, have big family lunches, cook on the fire and drink copious amounts of wine and digestives. But they are down to earth. Normal people. Who are not rich. It's simply the lifestyle. It's fun. It's elaborate. They are dramatic and speak with their hands. And we love it. And we fit right in.

After not knowing us for very long, a beautiful Pugliese couple invite us over on a hot summer's day for lunch with friends. They make frittata, have bowls of fresh fruit and this salad—well, something similar! It's so simple, so fresh and just brings with it happiness. Thanks for your big smiles, elaborate personalities and warmth, Antonio and Annalise.

Serve this the Pugliese way, with some good bread, salami, fresh cheeses and great friends.

- 4 zucchinis/summer squash (500–600 g in total)
- 8 small apricots (250 g in total), thickly sliced
- a big handful of mint leaves, torn
- 1 hot chilli, finely chopped
- 3 tablespoons extra-virgin olive oil
- 2 teaspoons lemon juice
- unrefined salt

Using a vegetable peeler, shave long slices of zucchini/squash into a medium bowl. If the zucchinis/squash are mature, there might be a seedy/floury middle, which should be discarded.

Add the remaining ingredients to the bowl and gently massage and toss with your hands to combine. Season to taste. You have a salad!

Millet & beetroot (tops, stems & roots) pilaf.

- 1 kg beetroots, bulbs/roots cut into large chunks, stems cut into 10 cm lengths, leaves coarsely chopped (see note)
- extra-virgin olive oil
- unrefined salt
- 1 onion, finely diced
- 3 garlic cloves, crushed
- a handful of pistachios, coarsely chopped
- a handful of sultanas
- 1 small bunch (40 g) of flat-leaf parsley, leaves separated from stalks, both finely chopped
- ¾ teaspoon freshly ground black pepper
- 3 cups cooked millet (as per preparation guide, page 338) (see field notes, page 260)

This dish is super simple and all about using the whole beetroot, not just the roots, but the greens and stems too, which are the most under-celebrated parts! Beets are an amazingly versatile vegetable, and it's so satisfying to pick a small bunch of them and be able to create a complete meal with just a few other basic ingredients. This dish partners excellently with our pear, lemon and chilli jam (page 172) and can be enjoyed as a meal in itself or as part of a larger spread.

Millet is such a wonderful wholegrain to use in salads because of its lightness. When prepared properly, it behaves just like classic couscous, but it is so much better for you and so much tastier. And partnered with these crispy baked stems, sweet roots and silky greens, it makes a fantastic dish.

Preheat the oven to 180°C fan-forced.

Place the beetroot chunks and stems on a large baking tray and rub all over with oil and a pinch of salt. Roast for about 50 minutes, mixing everything around halfway through cooking, until the roots are tender and the stems are crispy.

When the beetroot has about 10 minutes to go, add a splash of oil to a large, heavy-based frying pan over medium heat. Add the onion and sauté for a couple of minutes until beginning to soften. Add the garlic, pistachios, sultanas, parsley stalks, pepper and ¾ teaspoon of salt and sauté for 1–2 minutes until the garlic is beginning to turn golden. Add the beetroot tops and parsley leaves and stir through. Add a splash of water, cover and steam-fry for about 5 minutes until the greens have completely softened and the liquid has evaporated. Add a splash of oil, then the millet and fry for a minute, stirring constantly.

Tip the greens and millet mixture onto a serving platter. Top with the beetroot, then add the crispy stems and finish with a drizzle of oil.

RECIPE NOTE.

If you can't get whole beets, replace the stems and leaves with chard stems and leaves.

FIELD NOTES.

On buying the best beets.

If we don't have beets in the garden, we always try to buy *whole* beets at the farmers' market. This is because the freshness of the tops is the best indicator of the freshness of the roots. If the beet stems are firm and crisp, and the greens glossy and upright, you can be sure they are super fresh. If the stems are floppy and the greens limp, not so much. If your only option is roots only, always look for firm, hard ones that are not soft in any way.

Baked butternut pumpkin & cherry tomatoes.

While wandering the streets of a tiny village in Italy, we passed an enormous pizza shop (i.e. the *pizzas* were enormous—the shop was tiny!), and one particular pizza was singing out to us. It was all bright red and purple on top and the topping was just so thick and juicy. On closer inspection, we could see it was smothered in baked cherry tomatoes, caramelised red onion and black olives. It was so dark and visceral. Immediately, we knew it was the pizza for us. Here's our version, trading a pizza base for pumpkin. This is an incredibly beautiful dish to place on the table and is loaded with deep nuttiness from the pumpkin, tangy sweetness from the cherry tomatoes and an umami punch from the olives, capers and onion. *-Matt*

- ½ butternut pumpkin (about 700 g), cut lengthways (see notes)
- extra-virgin olive oil
- unrefined salt
- freshly ground black pepper
- 400 g ripe cherry tomatoes
- 2 large red onions, coarsely chopped
- 3 garlic cloves, finely chopped
- 1 large rosemary sprig, leaves stripped and finely chopped
- ½ cup pitted black olives
- 1 heaped tablespoon capers
- parmesan cheese, to serve (optional) (see notes)

Preheat the oven to 180°C fan-forced.

Rub the pumpkin all over with oil and a pinch of salt and pepper and place, cut-side up, in the centre of a medium, deep baking tray.

Add the remaining ingredients, except the parmesan, to a medium bowl with ½ teaspoon each of salt and pepper and a generous glug of oil. Combine gently with your hands until everything is glistening with oil.

Distribute the mixture around the pumpkin on the baking tray and bake for about 1 hour and 10 minutes. Once ready, the pumpkin should be completely soft when poked with a fork, blistering brown and golden all over and beginning to crisp up at the edges. Don't worry if your tomatoes, olives and onions get a bit crispy too.

Arrange on a serving dish the same as it was in the baking tray, or as we often do, serve in the baking tray! Generously grate some parmesan over the top (if using) and serve.

RECIPE NOTES.

Butternuts are so great for this recipe because of their shape, but an equivalently thick slice of another variety of pumpkin would be just as tasty!

For a dairy-free and vegan version of this recipe, simply omit the parmesan cheese.

123

Wild Sardinia.

We stayed for two weeks in a tiny village in Sardinia where the local drink is made from the fruit and leaves of a wild local plant. Its name translates to 'iron wire'. They told us that they make everything into alcohol—but these days it is a bit illegal, hence the iron wire. When the government started cracking down on this kind of thing, people didn't *stop* making it, they just started burying it! And all that would be exposed was an iron wire so they knew where it was! They tell us how there are rules, but the people don't follow them. It's so great.

They call Matt 'Hey-zeus' (Jesus) and me Mary Poppins. I like their humour. And they feed us until we explode. If we tell them we had a big lunch, so only need a small dinner, it's still four courses. When we have them all over for dinner, Matt makes this dish from all the wild greens around our little hut. They've never seen anything like it. It's an amazing thing, because these wild greens are in fact so traditional and they surround us, they are abundant. It seems as though they have lost these skills and this part of the tradition—they loved it though, so maybe we taught them something too.

Story continued over page →

SERVES 2-4 AS A SIDE // TIME: 20 MINUTES

Wild greens with fresh dukkah & yoghurt.

- extra-virgin olive oil
- ½ red onion, diced
- 4 garlic cloves, finely chopped
- 2 bunches (about 600 g) of wild greens, chard or kale (we used amaranth, mallow and chard), coarsely chopped
- ¼ teaspoon unrefined salt
- 1 tablespoon fresh dukkah (page 120)

YOGHURT DRESSING

- 3 tablespoons natural yoghurt
- 2 tablespoons extra-virgin olive oil
- 2 tablespoons fresh dukkah (page 120)
- a pinch of unrefined salt
- a pinch of freshly ground black pepper

This recipe is, for sure, far and away the best thing we've ever thought to do with wild greens. It is so rich and satisfying, and so multi-dimensional that it's almost a meal in itself (and sometimes we even eat it that way), but it is also the most fantastic side dish. The cooking technique for the greens is simple enough and really makes them the hero. But it's the dukkah and yoghurt dressing that elevates it to the next level. Together, it's earthy and tangy and crunchy and salty and silky all at once. And it's as good with any of the wild greens, like mallow, wild radish, fat hen or nettles, as it is with chard or kale from the garden. How good are greens? *-Lentil*

Add a generous splash of oil to a large, heavy-based frying pan over medium heat. Add the onion and sauté for 3–4 minutes until beginning to soften. Add the garlic and sauté for 1–2 minutes until it starts to turn golden.

Add the greens and salt and stir thoroughly to combine. Add a splash of water, cover and reduce the heat a little. Steam-fry for 5–10 minutes until the greens have completely softened. Some greens will take a little longer, some less, some will need a little more water to soften, some less. Work with what you have.

Meanwhile, place all the dressing ingredients in a small bowl and stir to loosely combine. You don't need everything to come together perfectly—it's nice to still be able to see the oil and yoghurt separately, swirled together.

When the greens are ready, lay them out on a serving dish, top with the dressing and sprinkle with dukkah. An extra drizzle of oil never hurts either. Serve hot.

Honey onion, buckwheat & lentil salad.

- extra-virgin olive oil
- 2 onions, diced
- 2 teaspoons unprocessed honey
- 3 garlic cloves, finely chopped
- a handful of almonds, coarsely chopped
- 2 teaspoons cumin seeds
- ¼ teaspoon freshly ground black pepper
- 1 cup cooked buckwheat (as per preparation guide, page 338) (see field notes)
- 1 cup cooked puy lentils (as per preparation guide, page 339) (see field notes)
- unrefined salt

HERB DRESSING

- 1 packed cup basil leaves (or if not in season, replace with other soft herbs, like parsley, mint or dill)
- ½ packed cup marjoram leaves
- 1 garlic clove, crushed
- 125 g (½ cup) natural yoghurt
- 80 ml (⅓ cup) extra-virgin olive oil
- ¼ teaspoon unrefined salt
- ¼ teaspoon freshly ground black pepper

This salad is a celebration of the humble onion. All too often they're considered just a base ingredient, rather than the real feature, so here we've really tried to up the onion ante. While it may *look* like a simple plate of buckwheat and lentils, they are just the carrier for sweet, oniony goodness. The honey and olive oil kick off some serious caramelisation at the beginning of the cooking process and that sweet, umami flavour-bomb permeates everything in the finished dish. A brilliant partner to simple roast veggies or a spread of share plates, this salad is a sure way to impress next time you need to feed many mouths. *-Matt*

Add a very generous splash of oil to a large, heavy-based frying pan over medium heat. Add the onion and sauté for a couple of minutes until beginning to soften. Add the honey, reduce the heat a little and sauté for about 8 minutes. As it cooks, reduce the heat if necessary to ensure the onion doesn't burn.

Meanwhile, add the dressing ingredients to a blender and blend well.

When the onion is golden and blistered, increase the heat to medium and add the garlic, almonds, cumin and pepper. Sauté for about 2 minutes until the garlic is fragrant and beginning to turn golden. Add another splash of oil, then the buckwheat and lentils. Fry for another 2 minutes, stirring constantly, then season to taste.

Tip the salad onto a serving platter and pour over the dressing. Or, as we often do, serve the salad in individual bowls with their own little serve of dressing on the side—because it's so much fun dipping your spoon between the two!

FIELD NOTES.

On cooking the perfect salad grains. Using grains (and pulses/legumes) in salads is a wonderful way to elevate them from side dish to main event. But if they aren't prepared properly for the role, the result can be a gluggy mess. It's all about getting the grains to behave like individuals. That way they disperse evenly through the salad and carry the flavours. Our trick for perfect salad grains is super simple. Use the basic preparation techniques (page 338 for grains, or page 339 for pulses). Leave the cooked grains in the pan until they're cool enough to touch, then empty into a large bowl. Add a splash of olive oil and a pinch of salt, then ever so gently collect a double-handful at a time and gently rub to separate the grains. Repeat until you've achieved a light pile of individual grains. They will now be very lightly seasoned and coated in oil and will remain separated like that until you are ready to use them.

Creamy mushrooms.

Autumn is wild mushroom season, but in Australia our wild mushroom varieties are limited (as they aren't native). So seeing wild mushrooms in their native landscape in Italy was a joy. In Calabria, in the deep south, we were told there are just so, so many porcini and *tartufi* (truffles) during this time that they don't know what to do with them. They grate tartufi over everything and eat porcini every day. They say they eat so many porcini and *tartufi* that they are completely sick of them for the rest of the year! Life should be so abundant.

This dish is inspired by a dish we had in one such area. It was so rich, had a wonderful slippery texture from the porcini and was deeply umami-meets-earthy in flavour. We've since discovered that it's just as amazing with regular white or brown Swiss mushrooms, or make it with all the wonderful saffron milk caps, slippery jacks or crab brittle gills available to us during wild mushroom season. Our version is extra rich and garlicky. An incredibly simple and easy but super-rewarding dish to celebrate the wonderful, abundant mushroom. And it makes a great pasta sauce (try serving it with our sweet potato gnocchi, page 128) or fantastic bruschetta (page 221).

- extra-virgin olive oil
- 3 garlic cloves, crushed
- 1 packed teaspoon thyme leaves, finely chopped
- 1 rosemary sprig, leaves stripped and finely chopped
- ½ teaspoon freshly ground black pepper
- 350 g mushrooms of your choice, cut into 5 mm slices
- 250 ml (1 cup) chicken stock (page 341)
- ¼ teaspoon unrefined salt
- 2 heaped teaspoons double cream
- 2 tablespoons dry white wine

Add a generous splash of oil to a large, heavy-based frying pan over medium heat. Add the garlic, herbs and pepper and sauté for 1–2 minutes until the garlic is beginning to turn golden.

Add the mushrooms and more oil (the mushrooms love to soak it all up), stir through and cook for 4–5 minutes, stirring occasionally, until the mushrooms collapse and turn dark and glossy. Add the stock and salt, stir through and simmer, uncovered, for 6–7 minutes until the liquid has reduced by half.

Once reduced, lower the heat and add the cream and wine, stirring until well combined. Then increase the heat and simmer, uncovered, for 7–8 minutes, agitating the pan occasionally, until the liquid has come together as a thick, oily sauce that coats the mushrooms. Serve hot.

Sweet potato steaks with leeks & wine.

- 1 kg large sweet potatoes, cut lengthways into 1 cm slices
- extra-virgin olive oil
- unrefined salt
- freshly ground black pepper
- 5 garlic cloves, crushed
- 2 large leeks, trimmed and cut into 5 mm slices (see field notes, page 225)
- a big handful of sultanas
- 250 ml (1 cup) dry white wine (plus a glass for you)
- juice of 1 lemon
- 2 tablespoons white wine vinegar
- 2 teaspoons unprocessed honey
- 2 tablespoons pine nuts, lightly toasted

This dish is inspired by the most amazing little deli in Milan. It had everything! All the cheeses and smallgoods stacked and hanging about, and so many different vegetable sides all laid out next to each other on big round trays. We were on our way to the train station, carrying all our bags, but upon seeing the deli we dropped everything and were captivated. The owner was such a sweetheart, had the biggest smile and gave us extra things to taste just because—this in itself made us feel so loved. We took little paper containers of so many things away that day and had the biggest feast on the train (which is totally normal in Italy). There were the most amazing creamy mushrooms, freshly pickled anchovies, bright saffron Milanese risotto, eggy fritters, delicate fish cakes, pink beetroot gnocchi and this beautiful little dish—except the sweet potato was salmon (also highly recommended)!

When we had an overabundance of leeks in the garden last spring, we ate this every week. But leeks and sweet potatoes are readily available all year, so enjoy this anytime.

Preheat the oven to 180°C fan-forced.

Rub each sweet potato steak liberally with oil, season with a good pinch of salt and pepper and lay on baking trays. Bake for 30–35 minutes until completely soft on the inside and turning crisp and golden on the outside.

Meanwhile, heat a large, deep frying pan over medium heat. Add a generous splash of oil and sauté the garlic for 1–2 minutes until just beginning to turn golden. Add the leek, sultanas and a generous pinch each of salt and pepper, then sauté for a couple of minutes more. Once the leek has softened a little and the sultanas are glossy with oil, add the wine and simmer, uncovered, for a few minutes until the alcohol has evaporated. Cover the pan, reduce the heat a little and simmer for about 10 minutes until the leek has really broken down and the liquid has almost totally evaporated.

Once cooked, remove the pan from the heat and add a final generous splash of oil (the Milanese *love* their olive oil), the lemon juice, vinegar and honey and stir through. Your leek mixture should be glossy with oil, saucy from the wine and vinegar, tangy and a little sweet.

When the sweet potato steaks are ready, lay them out on a serving dish and cover with the leek mixture. Top with the pine nuts and serve.

Creamy carrot and parsnip soup, page 270.

Soups.

Bowlfuls of comfort, year round.

Tomato & brown rice soup.

- extra-virgin olive oil
- ½ large onion, diced
- ½ small bunch (40 g) of flat-leaf parsley, leaves and stalks separated, both finely chopped
- 1 large rosemary sprig
- ½ teaspoon sweet paprika
- a big pinch of freshly ground black pepper
- 1.25 kg super-ripe heirloom tomatoes (see field notes)
- 2 large garlic cloves, crushed
- 1 teaspoon unrefined sugar (e.g. rapadura)
- 110 g (½ cup) medium grain brown rice, soaked for 12-24 hours in water with a splash of vinegar, then drained (page 338)
- 1.5 litres vegetable stock (page 341) or water (or a combination)
- juice of 1 large lemon
- unrefined salt
- freshly grated parmesan, to serve (optional) (see notes)

'I'm sorry the meal isn't anything amazing, we've had visitors for the past 31 days straight and have run out of money [laughs], so I hope this meal is okay.' -Eugene (it was amazing).

Eugene has seven children. And they are all beautiful people, with kind hearts, different religious beliefs and a love for music. And here everyone is accepted, fed and loved. All seven children were brought up in this tiny house—I have no idea how they all fit—but Eugene just tells me he can't see why we all need anything beyond food, shelter, music and love.

When I think about my Maltese-Australian uncle and my cousins, it's like getting a warm hug. And this is a recipe inspired by them. It's something they would make for me, or I would make for them (doubling the mix!)—something simple, comforting and good for you, to feed all the mouths. It's thick, comforting, bright, refreshing and naturally sweet. *-Lentil*

Add a generous splash of oil to a large, heavy-based saucepan over medium heat. Add the onion, parsley stalks, rosemary, paprika and pepper and sauté for about 5 minutes until the onion has softened.

Break the tomatoes into the pan, tearing them apart roughly. Add the garlic and sugar and increase the heat to high. Cook for 5 minutes, trying not to stir, until the tomatoes stick to the base of the pan a little. Reduce to a simmer and add the rice, stock or water and 2 tablespoons of oil. Cover and simmer for about 2 hours.

After 2 hours, the rice should be super soft but still hold its shape. The soup should be sticky and thick, look oily and delicious, and some tomato chunks should remain. Turn off the heat and stir in the lemon juice, then season to taste.

Serve in bowls topped with parmesan (if using), parsley leaves and a drizzle of oil.

RECIPE NOTES.

You can also experiment, adding oregano and bay leaves to the soup.

For a dairy-free and vegan version of this recipe, simply omit the parmesan.

FIELD NOTES.

On heirloom tomatoes. In summer, we just have so many tomatoes. So many. This is so good for using them all up (especially the split or damaged ones). We only grow heirloom varieties, sun ripened, and the taste is just unreal! So just a note to use good, heirloom, super-ripe tomatoes to achieve the full, naturally sweet and delicious flavour. It makes all the difference.

Creamy carrot & parsnip soup.

- extra-virgin olive oil
- 1 onion, diced
- 3 large dried bay leaves
- 1–2 large rosemary sprigs, leaves stripped
- a big pinch of freshly ground black pepper
- 6 carrots (about 450 g in total), roughly chopped
- 2 parsnips (about 400 g in total), roughly chopped
- 2 large garlic cloves, crushed
- 1.25 litres chicken stock (or turkey stock) (page 341)
- ½ teaspoon unrefined salt (if the stock is seasoned, adjust with salt to taste)
- 2 tablespoons cream
- juice of ½ large lemon

TO SERVE

- extra-virgin olive oil
- cream
- lemon
- flat-leaf parsley leaves, finely chopped

A thick, creamy, slightly sweet, beautifully coloured and fresh-tasting soup. Eat your entire vegetable quota for the day in one sitting. Great cold or hot, works for any time of the year.

Add a generous splash of oil to a large, heavy-based saucepan over medium heat. Add the onion, bay leaves, rosemary and pepper and sauté for 3–4 minutes until the onion begins to soften.

Add the carrot, parsnip and garlic and sauté for a few minutes until the garlic is fragrant. Add the stock and salt, cover and bring to the boil, then turn down the heat and simmer for 1–1½ hours.

Once cooked, turn off the heat and remove the bay leaves. Blend the soup with a handheld blender until smooth. You should now have a thick, creamy, fresh-tasting and very orange soup. Stir through the cream and lemon juice.

Serve hot or cold with a splash of oil, a drizzle of cream, a squeeze of lemon and a sprinkling of parsley.

Wild fennel & bread soup.

- 150 g stale bread, (gluten free if preferred; we use rye friselli/ bagels, page 141), torn or cut into 2-3 cm pieces (see note)
- extra-virgin olive oil
- ½ large fennel bulb (about 250 g) (young wild fennel, if possible—look for the ferns in spring), bulb sliced, fronds chopped
- ½ teaspoon unrefined salt
- 1 white or brown onion, diced
- ½ bunch (60 g) of flat-leaf parsley, leaves and stalks separated, both finely chopped
- ¼ teaspoon freshly ground black pepper
- 2 large garlic cloves, crushed
- 3 tablespoons grated pecorino or parmesan, plus extra for grating
- a thick piece of parmesan or pecorino rind
- lemon, to serve

'Waste not, want not' rings in my ears when I make this dish. There is nothing fancy about this soup, it's just down to earth and simple. Often, I am amazed when something so simple tastes so good—a sticky, thick soup that is almost creamy from the fennel and bread mixture, with a clean and classic flavour. This is born from a dry climate, where wild fennel grows abundantly, so if you can make it with young wild fennel in spring, do—it just adds that next level of flavour. *-Lentil*

Preheat the oven to 200°C fan-forced.

Add the bread to a 37 cm x 22 cm (6.5 litre) deep casserole dish (or equivalent) and coat liberally with oil. Bake for 8–10 minutes until crunchy and just browned, then set the dish aside.

Add 500 ml (2 cups) of water, the sliced fennel and salt to a medium saucepan, cover and bring to the boil. Gently simmer for about 5 minutes until the fennel has begun to soften, then turn the heat off.

Meanwhile, add a generous splash of oil to a medium saucepan over medium heat. Add the onion, fennel fronds, parsley stalks and pepper and sauté for about 5 minutes until the onion has softened. Add the garlic and fry for a minute or so until fragrant. Transfer the fennel and its cooking water to the pan and turn off the heat.

Pour the fennel mixture over the bread in the dish. Add the cheese, parsley leaves, cheese rind and 1.5 litres of water and stir. Grate some extra cheese over the top and bake, uncovered, for about 50–60 minutes.

It's ready when it's super bubbly, has reduced a little (by at least 1 cm) and has a slight crust on top with an almost caramel colour. You should have a thick broth, with melted fennel and an oily top. Allow to cool a little in the dish (it will be super hot!) before serving. Season to taste and serve with a squeeze of lemon.

RECIPE NOTE.

The thickness and acidity of the soup will vary based on the kind of bread used (for example, whether it is sourdough and what type of flour it's made from). We like to use rye bread, which makes for a delicious and sticky soup, but experiment to see what works for you.

Spring broth with peas, greens & egg.

This is a comforting broth. To me, broth is always just that. Putting egg and greens in a broth may seem unusual, but it's delicious and makes sense in spring. The watercress is a particularly special addition, as it's so full of vitamins and minerals—and it's often found growing wild (for us, in the creek near our house). This soup has an awesome mix of flavours—it's sweet from the peas, earthy from the asparagus, and the egg is like a surprise! It's kind of like a chicken and egg sandwich, but heaps better. *-Lentil*

- extra-virgin olive oil
- 2 garlic cloves, crushed (or 2 garlic shoots, finely chopped)
- a piece of parmesan or pecorino rind (see notes)
- zest and juice of 1 large lemon
- ½ teaspoon chilli flakes (or 1–2 teaspoons pear, lemon and chilli jam, page 172)
- 2 big pinches of freshly ground black pepper
- 2 litres chicken stock (page 341)
- 200 g peas, shelled or frozen (or snow peas)
- 200 g asparagus, cut into 3 cm lengths
- 2 packed cups watercress leaves (see field notes)
- ½ teaspoon unrefined salt
- 4 eggs, whisked
- a few handfuls of mizuna or baby cos leaves

Add a splash of oil to a large, heavy-based saucepan over medium heat. Add the garlic, cheese rind, lemon zest, chilli and pepper and sauté for a few minutes until fragrant. Add the chicken stock, cover and gently boil for about 10 minutes.

Add the peas, asparagus, watercress, lemon juice and salt, then gently simmer for 3–4 minutes. When ready, the vegetables should be bright green and just cooked. Turn the heat off, then stir the egg into the broth, which will cook in 10 seconds!

Serve the broth hot, adding a sprinkle of fresh leaves (they should wilt a little in the heat of the broth) and a splash of oil to each bowl. Serve as is, or for a heavier meal serve with sourdough flatbreads (page 134), friselli (page 141) or rice.

RECIPE NOTES.

Spring greens and herbs are super fun, so feel free to adapt the recipe to add a few different green things (like parsley or spinach) that come from your spring garden.

For a dairy-free version of this recipe, simply omit the parmesan or pecorino rind.

FIELD NOTES.

On growing and gathering cress. Watercress has become a super-common wild green in certain parts of our state, and can be prolific along creek edges during springtime throughout temperate areas of the world. Look out for its lush, deep green, broad-lobed foliage and little white flowers when wandering creeks and streams next spring. Fortunately, those of you not living near such creeks are in luck too, because watercress's garden cousin, upland cress, is super-easy and fun to grow, tastes exactly the same and is just as good for you! Upland cress seeds are readily available online and are grown just like rocket. For more information on when to plant, see page 91.

Fish soup.

THIS SOUP FEELS LIKE IT COULD CURE ANYTHING.

He is straightforward, direct and well-meaning. You select a fish. His wife guts and cleans it. He wraps it in paper, and you take it home. He is only found if you are in a town near the sea, and only has local fish—the fishmonger.

I like to think he alone is responsible for so many versions of this homely and super-traditional Italian soup. Throughout Italy, if you are anywhere near the sea, you will find a version of this soup on a nonna's table or in a local deli, the best quick meal to go. It's always a little bit different, but always super refreshing, super grounding and so addictive. Plus, it's loaded with nutrients! If you're looking for a more sustainable approach to eating seafood, this technique really helps one fish go a long way. And it works for pretty much any fish you can get. *-Lentil*

- extra-virgin olive oil
- 1 large red onion, diced
- 5 garlic cloves, crushed
- 1 teaspoon freshly ground black pepper
- 3 potatoes, cut into sixths
- 1 small bunch (40 g) of flat-leaf parsley, stalks separated from leaves, both finely chopped, with some leaves reserved for garnish
- ½ large hot fresh or dried chilli, finely sliced
- 500 ml (2 cups) dry white wine
- 1 x 700 g responsibly sourced whole fish (we used dusky flathead), cleaned and filleted (carcass reserved), fillets deboned if necessary and cut into chunks
- 700 ml passata
- unrefined salt
- 150 g (1 cup) fresh or frozen peas
- juice of 1 lemon

SPECIAL EQUIPMENT

- muslin bag (or cheesecloth and kitchen twine)

Add a very generous splash of oil to a large, heavy-based saucepan over medium heat. Add the onion and sauté for a couple of minutes until beginning to soften. Add the garlic and pepper and sauté for a minute or so until the garlic is beginning to turn golden. Add the potato, parsley stalks and chilli and stir through. Add the wine and boil for about 5 minutes.

Meanwhile, place the fish carcass in a muslin bag or wrap it in a piece of cheesecloth and fasten with cooking twine. This step saves you having to fish out (no pun intended!) all the tiny bones from the soup after the skeleton falls apart during cooking.

Add the passata to the pan. Rinse the passata bottle with 125 ml (½ cup) of water and add that too. Stir well, then add the fish carcass, making sure it's completely submerged. Cover, reduce to a bare simmer and cook for 2 hours.

After 2 hours, remove the bag and set aside in a bowl to cool. Season the soup to taste, then add the chunks of fish fillet, peas, chopped parsley leaves and lemon juice. Stir through and simmer for 5 minutes.

Once the fish carcass has cooled enough to handle, squeeze out any excess liquid and pick any large pieces of flesh from the bones. Return the liquid and any flesh to the pan and stir through.

Serve the soup hot with a drizzle of oil and the reserved parsley leaves. This is great served with chickpea pancakes (page 218).

Potato, asparagus & parsley soup.

- extra-virgin olive oil
- 1 onion, diced
- 1 leek, trimmed and sliced
- 1 bunch (120 g) of flat-leaf parsley, leaves and stalks separated, both finely chopped
- a few big pinches of freshly ground pepper
- 800 g potatoes, roughly chopped
- 350 g asparagus (about 2 bunches), cut into 3 cm lengths
- 4 garlic cloves (wild garlic if you have it!), crushed
- 150 ml dry white wine
- unrefined salt
- 1.5 litres vegetable stock (page 341) or water (or a combination) (see note)
- 2 tablespoons double cream

TO SERVE

- extra-virgin olive oil
- lemon
- all the herbs green sauce (page 124) or pesto (page 124) (optional)

My Aunty Terri is like my second mum, who very much took on the role of mum after mine passed away when I was little. I always admired how she managed to feed everyone and be so very nonchalant about 20 people turning up to dinner instead of ten. I want to write that she 'fed everyone effortlessly', but that's not totally true. As she cooked, she generally stumbled over four things, lost her glass of wine or drank yours, and always managed to burn something. (And not always the food—once she put her rubber shoes on our wood-burning stove to 'dry'.) I think maybe that's why I can never exactly replicate her recipes, because there is always something in there that is just a little bit burnt. But these are the flavours of my childhood, of chaos, of feeding 20 people and everyone having had a little too much wine.

She always made some version of potato soup, similar to this in many ways. This one is inspired by spring, so it mirrors the garden and the wild with its abundance of parsley, greens and asparagus. It has lots of garlic, a little cream and is thick—just how my aunty likes it. *-Lentil*

Add a generous splash of oil to a large, heavy-based saucepan over medium heat. Add the onion, leek, parsley stalks and pepper and sauté for 3–4 minutes until the onion begins to soften.

Add the potato, asparagus and garlic and sauté for about 5 minutes. Just as the mixture begins to stick to the base of the pan, add a splash of wine and stir. Repeat two to three times over the 5 minutes. Add ½ teaspoon of salt and the stock, cover and bring to the boil. Turn down the heat and simmer for 1–1½ hours.

Once cooked, turn the heat off and stir through the parsley leaves. Blend the soup with a handheld blender until smooth. Turn the heat back on to low–medium and reduce with the lid off for 10–20 minutes until the soup is at your desired thickness. As you reduce it, the potato will become more delicious and sticky and the soup will thicken. Once at the desired thickness, stir in the cream and season to taste.

Serve with a drizzle of oil, a big squeeze of lemon and a swirl of green sauce or pesto, if desired. This is great hot or cold!

RECIPE NOTE.

If your stock is already salted, wait to add salt to the soup until the end, then season to taste.

FIELD NOTES.

On the spring famine. There's a time in spring where the garden often has a 'famine'— your winter crops are harvested, and your spring crops aren't *quite* ready. And we have always referred to it as the 'spring famine'. But being in Italy and watching what they ate over springtime was an amazing reminder of the traditional diet. To use what you have, in as many ways as you can. To nurture yourself and others, and to create variety in your diet using whatever you have, however limited that may be. There may have only been potatoes, parsley, wild greens and garlic, but there was an *abundance* of them all. Even in the wild, we could see wild garlic covering the hills. And to not use it all, in as many ways as possible, would be crazy. –*Lentil*

Sunday chickpea soup, Greek-island style.

THE EASIEST OF SOUPS.

- 220 g (1 cup) dried chickpeas, soaked for 8 hours in water with a pinch of unrefined salt (see field notes)
- 2 large red onions, diced
- 4 garlic cloves, peeled and crushed with the heel of your hand
- ⅓ packed cup dried oregano leaves
- ½ teaspoon dried thyme leaves
- 3 large dried bay leaves
- 2 teaspoons unrefined salt
- 1 teaspoon freshly ground black pepper
- 80 ml (⅓ cup) extra-virgin olive oil

TO SERVE

- extra-virgin olive oil
- lemon

We think this is one of the most incredible dishes. It is so bold to present chickpeas so nakedly. And yet it is mind-blowingly delicious. We learnt this super-traditional dish while visiting a tiny village on an equally tiny Greek island. It was so hot and dry there that it's amazing anyone had bothered to inhabit the island in the first place! But thousands of years ago they had. And they stayed. And they carved out a food tradition full of only the simplest, hardiest food plants to accompany the abundant seafood.

Traditionally, this is a Sunday soup. You fire the wood oven on Saturday, bake bread and roast meat and cook whatever else you feel like. Then, when all that is done, you place all the ingredients for this soup in a clay pot and put the pot in the oven in the early evening. By lunchtime the next day, the oven has slowly cooled, the chickpeas have softened so perfectly, and the flavours have developed so beautifully that you really can't believe how much these simple ingredients have transformed. It *was* a Sunday when we first ate this dish. We sat in the shade of a simple grape vine arbour with Greek grappa and a table full of crisp, simply dressed cucumbers, olives and seasoned feta, while the land around us from whence these ingredients had somehow grown literally glowed in the fierce sunlight. It was marvellous.

Drain and rinse the chickpeas, then place all the ingredients in a large, heavy-based saucepan with 1.4 litres of water. Cover and gently bring to the boil, then reduce to the barest simmer and cook for 8–12 hours.

Serve in bowls finished with a drizzle of oil and a squeeze of lemon.

RECIPE NOTE.

You can of course make this recipe the traditional way—in the oven (especially efficient if you have a wood-fired oven like us that you are burning for warmth anyway!). Preheat your oven to 150°C, place all the ingredients and 1.4 litres of water in an ovenproof pot with lid, cover and place in the oven. Reduce the temperature to 100°C and leave to cook for 8-12 hours as per the recipe.

FIELD NOTES.

On properly cooking chickpeas. The time it takes to properly cook chickpeas is almost always underestimated. They are a truly incredible plant food and a nutritional powerhouse, but if not cooked for long enough, you are only able to digest a fraction of that nutrition, and the most likely result is going to be bloating and discomfort from very hard to digest carbohydrates called oligosaccharides. Chickpeas need *at least* 4 hours cooking. But this is a best-case scenario when the chickpeas are fresh, and everything goes just right. Cooking any pulse is really a matter of feel, and often it's going to take a lot longer to reach the butter-soft holy grail than you might think. This dish is the perfect example. The traditional recipe calls for a very slow stewing for 19 hours! 19! Our ancestors understood the value of taking the time to extract the most from their pulses. In any case, never eat pulses unless they are *completely* butter-soft all the way through. And you might find that properly cooked pulses are no longer a sure path to unwanted gas and might become a new household favourite. For more information on preparing and cooking pulses, see the appendix (page 339).

Mains.

Always shared.

SERVES 6 // TIME: 1 HOUR

Fish & chip pie.

I love the idea of fish and chips on a Friday or Saturday night, as a weekly routine, where you all sit together and just hang out. But the reality of it, all of the oil and grease, makes me feel sick for a good 24 hours after. So this is my solution—a one-tin wonder that is super comforting and delicious, but still healthy. And you can serve it with whatever else you have left over to feed many!

Use whatever fish you have local to you—we often use preserved tuna (we preserve one a year) or trout (because there are lots in the streams near us). I love it warm. Matt loves it cold. You do you. *-Lentil*

- 1 potato (about 200 g), cut into 1 cm cubes
- ¼ head cauliflower (about 250 g), cut into 1 cm florets, stem diced
- extra-virgin olive oil
- 2 onions, diced
- ½ bunch (60 g) of flat-leaf parsley, leaves and stalks separated, both finely chopped
- ¼ bunch (30 g) of dill, fronds separated from stalks, both finely chopped (see note)
- a big pinch of freshly ground black pepper
- 3 garlic cloves, crushed
- 7 eggs
- 80 ml (⅓ cup) cream or sour cream
- 3 tablespoons oil from the preserved fish (or extra-virgin olive oil if using fresh fish)
- 50 g (⅓ cup) wholemeal spelt flour
- ½ teaspoon bicarbonate of soda
- ¼ teaspoon unrefined salt
- 200 g drained preserved tuna (or fresh fish fillets, cut into chunks)
- 1 large lemon, peeled, sliced and deseeded

Preheat the oven to 180°C fan-forced. Grease or line a 20 cm round springform cake tin.

Parboil the potato and cauliflower in salted water for 4–5 minutes. Drain, refresh under cold water, then set aside to cool.

Meanwhile, add a splash of olive oil to a small frying pan over low–medium heat. Add the onion, herb stalks and pepper and sauté for about 5 minutes until the onion has softened. Add the garlic, turn the heat off and set aside.

Add the eggs and cream to a medium bowl and whisk well. Add the oil from the fish, the flour, bicarbonate of soda and salt, then whisk until a smooth batter forms. Add the onion mixture and herb leaves and stir to combine.

Pour about half the batter into the prepared tin. Evenly layer the potato, cauliflower and fish on top of the batter and cover with the remaining batter. Shake the tin gently to settle all the ingredients, making sure the vegetables and fish are covered.

Top with the lemon, then bake for 45 minutes. When ready, the pie should be golden brown, the lemon a little burnt and a skewer inserted into the centre should come out clean. Leave to cool in the tin for 10–15 minutes before serving (it will be super hot!).

Serve the pie warm or cold, with a few side salads and tomato sauce (page 123).

RECIPE NOTE.

Sometimes fresh dill can be hard to find. You can replace it with a big pinch of dill seeds, just sauté them with the onion.

Lach's brown rice risotto.

- extra-virgin olive oil
- 2 onions, diced
- 100 g smoked bacon (see notes), diced
- 4 garlic cloves, crushed
- 180 g mushrooms (see notes), diced
- 2 carrots, finely diced
- ¼ bunch (30 g) of flat-leaf parsley, leaves and stalks separated, both finely chopped
- 1 packed teaspoon thyme leaves, finely chopped
- 400 g zucchini/summer squash, asparagus or broccoli (whatever is in season), finely diced
- 250 ml (1 cup) white or red wine
- 440 g (2 cups) medium grain brown rice, soaked for 12-24 hours in water with a splash of vinegar, then drained (page 338)
- 750 ml (3 cups) stock of your choice (page 341)
- 4 baby spring onions, finely sliced
- 3 heaped tablespoons parmesan cheese (add more if you like it extra cheesy!)

TO SERVE

- extra-virgin olive oil
- parsley leaves
- lemon wedges
- something fermented, like pickled veg

Lachy is a big part of what makes up our 'family'. When we go to his place for dinner, he almost always makes a version of 'risotto'—always different, but kind of the same. There is always wine, mismatched plates and his hair is never brushed, his nails always dirty with soil. And we love him. He's like a brother.

Getting Lachy to give you even a semblance of a recipe, for one of his many versions of risotto, is like asking a cow to talk. Never going to happen. But I think we have nailed a replica of it, and we've tried to add his voice to the recipe, so you get the full experience. Hope it makes sense! Enjoy the experience—it's one we love. *-Lentil*

Add a big splash of oil to a big, heavy saucepan over medium heat. Add the onion and sauté for 5-ish minutes until softened. Add the bacon, garlic, mushrooms, carrot, parsley stalks and thyme—get it all in there—and sauté for 4–5 minutes.

Add the zuke/squash, asparagus or broccoli and cook for 4–5 minutes until the liquid from the vegetables has all floated away. Deglaze with half the wine, and stir for a minute to boil off the alcohol. Add the rice, stir thoroughly and fry for 2–3 minutes, letting it get all sizzle-y and sticky-to-the-pan-y. Add the remaining wine and the stock, enough to cover everything. Bring to a simmer (keep stirring!), then reduce to low heat, cover and cook for 30 minutes undisturbed.

It should be getting pretty al dente after 30 minutes, and the liquid level will have dropped below the rice. Season to taste (be generous—about 2 teaspoons if your stock is unseasoned) and add the spring onion, chopped parsley leaves and parmesan. Stir thoroughly to combine, cover and cook for 15 minutes undisturbed, then remove from the heat.

Serve with a splash of oil, a sprinkling of parsley leaves and acidic things like lemon juice and something pickled to balance all that cheese and bacon voluptuousness!

RECIPE NOTES.

Lach actually prefers to use bacon bones, which are leftover pork bones that have been cured and smoked—ask your local butcher. He just throws them in at the start, and when the risotto's ready, the meat will have come away from the bones.

All sorts of mushrooms are great for this, but our favourites are king browns, Swiss browns, saffron milk caps, slippery jacks or morels, depending on the season!

Part of a Lachy risotto is that you are freely allowed to replace ingredients with leftover bits and pieces from the fridge. So, feel free to experiment.

SONIDO!

Stuffed quinoa tomatoes in broth.

LIGHT AND BRIGHT, A LITTLE NUTTY AND SUPER FRESH.

TOMATOES

- extra-virgin olive oil
- 1 cipollini or brown onion, diced (see field notes)
- ½ red capsicum, diced (or 100 g capsicum under oil, page 163)
- ⅓ bunch (40 g) of flat-leaf parsley, leaves separated from stalks, both finely chopped
- 2 teaspoons thyme leaves
- ½ teaspoon sweet paprika
- a big pinch of freshly ground black pepper
- 40 g (⅓ cup) walnuts, roughly chopped
- 2 garlic cloves, crushed
- 1.3–1.5 kg ripe tomatoes
- 1 small zucchini/summer squash, grated
- 2 teaspoons unprocessed honey
- 2 teaspoons apple cider vinegar
- ¼ teaspoon unrefined salt
- 185 g (1 cup) cooked quinoa (as per preparation guide, page 338)
- a few handfuls (about 80 g) of grated parmesan or pecorino

BROTH

- 750 ml (3 cups) vegetable stock (page 341)
- 2 potatoes, diced
- a handful of any leftover herbs

TO SERVE

- sourdough flatbreads (page 134) or similar

Stuffed vegetables have been put on everyone's tables pretty much forever—I don't know if that's true, but in my mind it is. This is how we make them. They are light and bright, a little nutty and super fresh. The broth in the bottom is so delicious and you can easily make it a larger meal by serving it with some good bread for dipping. Only make this dish in the peak of summer and into autumn, when the tomatoes are fresh and real and perfect. They are *everything* in this simple dish. Share it in the sunshine. *-Lentil*

Preheat the oven to 200°C fan-forced.

For the tomatoes, add a generous splash of oil to a large frying pan over medium heat. Add the onion, capsicum, parsley stalks, thyme, paprika and pepper and sauté for 5 minutes until the onion has softened. Add the walnuts and garlic and fry for a few minutes to toast a little.

Meanwhile, using a paring knife, 'core' the tops out of the tomatoes (see diagram over page) and set them aside. Using a spoon, scoop out the middle of the tomatoes into the pan. Place the hollowed-out tomatoes in a deep casserole dish (about 6.5 litre capacity) with a lid.

Add the zucchini/squash, honey, vinegar and salt to the pan, cover and simmer for 5–8 minutes, or until the mixture is juicy and has broken down. Add the quinoa and parsley leaves to the pan, uncover and cook for 3–5 minutes until the mix comes together but is still a little wet. Remove from the heat and stir in the cheese.

Fill the tomatoes with the quinoa mixture, then place the tomato tops back on. You will probably have some stuffing left over, which you can add to the broth.

For the broth, pour the stock into the dish, so it reaches almost to the top of the tomatoes, adding a little water if necessary. Add the potato, leftover herbs (dice any leftover vegetables you have and throw them in now too) and any leftover stuffing. Splash everything with oil, cover and bake for 45 minutes.

After 45 minutes, uncover and turn the oven up to the hottest it goes. Continue to bake for about 15 minutes until the tomatoes are very soft, but just holding their shape, and a little burnt on top. The soup will have formed a crust and the potato will be really soft. If not, continue to bake for 5 minutes or so—the caramelisation of everything is the key to the sweet flavour!

Allow to cool a little before serving—it's super hot! Serve the tomatoes in shallow bowls with the broth, with bread on the side for dipping. This is great served with a fresh salad on the side also.

Recipe continued over page →

→ **Recipe continued from previous page**

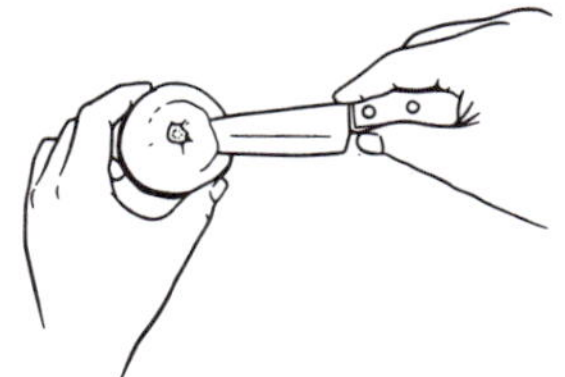

1. Using a paring knife, 'core' the tops out of the tomatoes. Set tops aside.

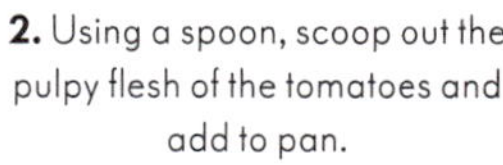

2. Using a spoon, scoop out the pulpy flesh of the tomatoes and add to pan.

3. Fill the hollow tomatoes with stuffing, then place the tops back on for baking.

FIELD NOTES.

On cipollini onions. Cipollini (*chip-oh-lee-nee*) are the sweetest of the onions! They can be red, brown or white, are small, somewhere between a golf ball and a tennis ball, and shaped like a flattened sphere. We encountered these everywhere in Italy, which was such a treat because the only time we've experienced an abundance of them otherwise is when we've grown them ourselves. It's easy to get your hands on some seeds online, they're hardy and you grow them just the same as any other onion. Cipollini are becoming more and more available these days, especially in farmers' markets, so keep your eyes out for *the best* onion around.

SERVES 4–6 // TIME: 30 MINUTES PREPARATION + 3–4 HOURS STEWING

All year

Mumma's barley stew.

- extra-virgin olive oil
- 1 onion, diced
- 2 celery stalks with leaves, finely diced (if in season)
- 20 thyme sprigs, tied with kitchen twine
- 8–10 sage leaves
- 1 cinnamon stick
- 3 dried bay leaves
- 4 garlic cloves, crushed
- 2 tablespoons soy sauce (or tamari)
- a piece of parmesan rind
- a few lamb or beef bones (they need to fit into the pot easily)
- 220 g (1 cup) pearl barley or soaked pot barley (see field notes)
- 150 ml dry white wine
- 1 small sweet potato, diced
- 250 g pumpkin, diced
- 2 medium-large carrots, finely diced
- unrefined salt

My mum was one of seven children, so my grandma (Mumma) was the queen of feeding many people at once, quickly and easily. My aunty tells me, when they were growing up there was always a version of barley stew on the stove. She has memories of riding to school with a pot of it on her lap, and memories of her grandmother making it too. Now there is a pot on her stove, and one on mine. This is my version—the fourth generation/iteration of our family's barley stew. It's warming, savoury, a little umami, herby and super nourishing. Put this on the stove, cook it for hours, feed many. For me, this is food to come home to. The smell of this, the thyme, the onions, the root vegetables, in a moment takes me home, with my family. *–Lentil*

Add a generous splash of oil to a large cast-iron pot over medium heat. Add the onion, celery, thyme, sage, cinnamon and bay and sauté for about 5 minutes until the onion has softened. Add the garlic, soy, parmesan rind, bones and barley (if using pot barley, add it after the vegetables have been browned) and fry for about 10 minutes until the bones change colour, adding a few splashes of wine as needed to stop it from sticking.

Add the sweet potato, pumpkin and carrot and fry for 5 minutes to slightly brown (or if using pot barley, add it now with the soaking liquid and 1 litre of water). Add 1.5 litres of water and cover. Bring to the boil, then reduce to a low simmer and cook for 3–4 hours (no stirring required).

Your stew is ready when it has formed a crust, but still has liquid underneath when peeled back. If not, uncover and reduce until a crust forms (or if you like it super soupy, leave as is). The barley should be soft but not overcooked. Remove the bones and season to taste. Serve with a fresh salad on the side.

FIELD NOTES.

On barley. Barley is a unique grain. Unlike other grains, like wheat and oats, where the inedible outer hull of the grain is really no more than a papery layer, barley hulls are fixed firmly to the inner edible part, which meant ancient farmers had to come up with a special technique—which is a rubbing process—to remove them. Unfortunately, this means that it's quite difficult to not also rub off some of the most nutritious part (outer bran) of the grain too. Both pearl barley and pot barley still go through this process today. However, pot barley is rubbed for much less time and thus still has most of the bran intact, whereas pearl barley is rubbed much more, removing all the bran and some of the *germ* too. So, pearl barley is the barley equivalent of white rice. Whereas pot barley is the more nutritious of the two, like brown rice, and proper preparation calls for a soaking step to improve digestion. So, if you use pot barley for this recipe, be sure to soak it for 12–24 hours first as per the basic grains recipe, page 338.

Eggplant, cherry tomato & borlotti bean salad.

LIKE CAPONATA TAKEN TO FEAST LEVEL.

This dish is so, so tasty. It is amazing hot. It is amazing cold. It was kind of an accident that we ever made it, but ever since we did, we haven't been able to stop! It all came about while we were staying in Sardinia. The air was hot and the produce was *fresh*. We were in the mountains, but we could see the ocean. Perfection.

That morning we went to the local market in the village and found these bright pink and white striped fresh borlotti beans (learn how to grow your own on page 61). And goat's ricotta, still warm, from the charming local cheesemonger. The eggplants, tomatoes and basil were so plump and bright and perfect too. And this dish just kind of created itself and made its way into our late-lunch bowls. A happy bowl of goodness to capture that moment forever.

- extra-virgin olive oil
- 1 red onion, diced
- 1 packed teaspoon thyme (or rosemary) leaves, finely chopped
- 2 eggplants (about 650 g in total), diced
- 500 g cherry tomatoes
- 1½ teaspoons unrefined salt
- 2 cups cooked borlotti beans (as per preparation guide, page 339, with a smashed garlic clove in the water—if using freshly podded beans, skip the soaking step and head straight to cooking)
- 2 teaspoons apple cider vinegar
- ½ packed cup basil leaves, coarsely chopped

TO SERVE

- 200 g fresh cacioricotta (page 148) or ricotta
- basil leaves
- extra-virgin olive oil
- 4 sourdough flatbreads (page 134) or similar

Add a generous splash of oil to a medium, heavy-based frying pan over medium heat. Add the onion and thyme and sauté for 3–4 minutes until the onion begins to soften. Add the eggplant, whole tomatoes and salt and continue to sauté for about 20 minutes, or until the eggplant is really starting to fall apart. Add more oil as needed while it cooks, as the eggplant will continue to soak it all up—that oiliness is absolutely key to the eggplant melting properly! You can lower the heat a little if you feel it needs to slow down.

After 20 minutes, add the beans and toss gently to combine (tossing, rather than stirring, helps the tomatoes hold their shape). Cover, then cook undisturbed for 4–5 minutes until the beans are hot and the ones on the bottom are a little browned. Remove the pan from the heat. Add the vinegar and basil and toss through gently.

Serve in individual bowls topped with the cacioricotta or ricotta, some basil leaves and a final swirl of oil. Serve with flatbreads on the side.

Eggplant & chickpea lasagne.

'THE WAR STARTER', BECAUSE IT'S GOOD ENOUGH TO FIGHT FOR.

RED SAUCE

- extra-virgin olive oil
- 2 onions, diced
- ½ bunch (60 g) of basil, leaves and stalks separated, both finely chopped
- 2 rosemary sprigs, leaves stripped and finely chopped
- 2 teaspoons thyme leaves
- freshly ground black pepper
- 200 g mushrooms, diced
- 4 large garlic cloves, crushed
- 2 tablespoons apple cider vinegar
- 2 tablespoons unrefined sugar (e.g. rapadura)
- ½ teaspoon unrefined salt
- 750 ml (3 cups) chunky passata (see note)

WHITE SAUCE

- 50 g unsalted butter
- freshly ground black pepper
- ground nutmeg
- 50 g brown rice flour
- 500 ml (2 cups) full-cream milk
- 50 g grating cheese (such as cured cacioricotta, page 148, or pecorino)
- unrefined salt

THE REST

- 2 eggplants (600 g in total), cut into 5 mm thick slices
- 300 g (1½ cups) cooked chickpeas (as per preparation guide, page 339)
- 50 g grating cheese (as above)
- freshly ground black pepper

This tastes just like a traditional meaty lasagne, but it's almost completely grain free and is 100% vegetarian. It's a combination of my recipe and my Aunty Terri's recipe. This is something everyone asks for on their birthday and our friend Joe calls it 'The War Starter', because it's so good he would fight for it. Share with many and make memories. *-Lentil*

Preheat the oven to 200°C fan-forced.

For the red sauce, add a generous splash of oil to a deep saucepan over medium heat. Add the onion, basil stalks, rosemary, thyme and a big pinch of pepper and sauté for 3–4 minutes until the onion begins to soften. Add the mushrooms, garlic, vinegar, sugar, salt and a splash of passata, fry for a few minutes, then add the basil leaves and the remaining passata. Add 180 ml (¾ cup) of water to the passata bottle and shake to get out any remaining tomato, then empty into the pan (if using fresh tomatoes, skip this step). Cover and simmer for 30 minutes.

Meanwhile, to make the white sauce, add the butter, two big pinches of pepper and a big pinch of nutmeg to a medium saucepan over medium heat. Once the butter has fully melted, add the flour and fry for a minute or two while stirring. Then slowly add the milk while whisking. Increase the heat to a gentle boil and whisk until the sauce is smooth and thick, about 5 minutes. Turn off the heat and stir through the cheese until melted, then season to taste.

Layer your lasagne in a deep baking dish or casserole dish (37 cm x 22 cm, or the equivalent, with a lid). There are basically three layers. Divide your ingredients accordingly and layer into the dish as follows:

LAYER 1—red sauce, eggplant slices, red sauce, half the chickpeas, white sauce.

LAYER 2—eggplant slices, red sauce, remaining chickpeas, white sauce.

LAYER 3—eggplant slices, red sauce, white sauce, grated cheese, black pepper.

Cover and bake for 20 minutes, then remove the lid and bake for a further 25–30 minutes until golden brown and bubbling. Your lasagne should be fully cooked, with a crisp top, and the eggplant should be super collapsed. Allow to cool a little in the dish before serving. We love to serve it with fresh basil leaves, a drizzle of oil on top, a fresh salad and bread on the side.

RECIPE NOTE.

The freshness and chunkiness of the passata is key in this recipe. So, if you don't have chunky (preferably homemade) passata, use tinned diced tomatoes, or dice 1.5–2 kg ripe fresh tomatoes—just no tomato puree or pureed passata!

The best sardine pasta.

This is a wonderfully simple spring pasta—quick comfort food after a long day. It's all about the dance between the pasta pot and the saucepan, adding little dashes of liquid from the pot to the pan as needed, everything cooking at once, and everything ready at the same time. It's so quick, so tasty and now a staple in our kitchen. Our friend Bug (Geri) said this pasta conquered her fear of sardines. She said, 'I didn't think I liked sardines, but now I'm like, that could have done with more sardines!' We can't make this without thinking of her and laughing a little! *-Matt*

- 400 g dried pasta of your choice (or 500–600 g gnocchi, page 128, or 600–700 g snake beans, see field notes)
- extra-virgin olive oil
- 2 large red onions, diced
- 9 garlic cloves, finely chopped
- 4 large rosemary sprigs, leaves stripped and finely chopped
- 600 g asparagus (about 3 ½ bunches), cut into 1–3 cm pieces
- 250 ml (1 cup) passata
- 3 teaspoons sweet paprika
- 1 ½ teaspoons freshly ground black pepper
- 150 g can sustainably fished sardines in spring water or sardines under oil (page 166), drained (or 300 g fresh sardines, cleaned and filleted) (see note)
- 1 lemon
- 200 g soft goat's cheese (chèvre style) or fresh cheese (page 144)
- ¾ cup flat-leaf parsley and oregano leaves, finely chopped

Cook the pasta (or pasta alternative) in boiling salted water (salty enough to remind you of the sea!) for the recommended time (snake beans will take 4–5 minutes until just tender). Drain, rinse briefly under cold water and set aside.

Meanwhile, add a generous splash of oil to a medium, heavy-based frying pan over medium heat. Add the onion and sauté for 3–4 minutes until beginning to soften. Add the garlic and rosemary and sauté until the garlic is beginning to turn golden. Reduce the heat a little and add the asparagus, passata, paprika and pepper, stir through and simmer, uncovered, for 10 minutes. Don't let your sauce dry out—add a ladle of the pasta water to the pan every now and then as needed.

After 10 minutes, add the sardines to the pan, breaking them up with a wooden spoon or the back of a fork. Squeeze over the lemon and add the cheese, breaking it up so that it melts throughout. Stir until the sauce is creamy. Turn off the heat and add the drained pasta (or pasta alternative). Gently stir through so that the pasta is nicely coated with the sauce.

Serve the pasta in bowls topped with the parsley and oregano and a swirl of oil.

RECIPE NOTE.

This recipe would work fantastically with all kinds of fish, fresh or preserved. Check out our guide to preserving sardines (page 166), or if you'd like to jar/can your own tuna, check out our first book.

FIELD NOTES.

On snake beans. Snake beans have always been pitched as an Asian-style ingredient to us. Well, our minds were blown in Italy, where they were readily available in the markets and a huge part of the cuisine. They are best when young, super soft and creamy tasting. Like this, they make a fantastic vegetable alternative to pasta (see image on page 13). So, the next time you see snake beans in the market, especially the thin baby ones, get on board—you don't even need a zoodler! We now grow our own every year, and if you'd like to give them a go too, see our bean growing tips on page 61.

So good salad.

- 440 g (2 cups) short-grain white rice
- extra-virgin olive oil
- 4 garlic cloves, crushed
- 3 teaspoons unrefined sugar (e.g. rapadura)
- 1 teaspoon chilli flakes (or 2 teaspoons chilli jam, page 172)
- 1 teaspoon ground turmeric
- a big pinch of freshly ground black pepper
- a handful of sage leaves
- 400 g boneless pasture-raised chicken (see note)
- 400 g cauliflower, cut into small florets
- 250 ml (1 cup) milk of your choice (see note)
- zest of 1 large lemon
- unrefined salt

THE SALAD

- 350 g carrots, julienned
- 250 g white cabbage, finely sliced
- 200 g cos lettuce, finely sliced
- 1 packed cup mint leaves, roughly chopped
- ½ red onion, finely sliced

TO SERVE

- all the herbs green sauce (page 124)
- extra-virgin olive oil
- a handful of roughly chopped almonds, toasted
- sliced avocado (if in season)
- finely chopped spring onion

This is inspired by Italian street food—nothing was exactly the same, but at one food van they had a mixed cabbage salad that was jam packed with herbs and served with bread! It was magical.

This has a long list of ingredients, but is in fact a 30-minute meal to feed many. Pretty sure Matt would eat this every night if he could. In truth, it's just seriously delicious—so many good things on a plate, a really balanced, nourishing, mainly-plants meal with lots of herby goodness and perfectly poached chicken (or mushrooms if you choose). This is a big, feed-lots-of-mouths meal—or use the leftovers for easy lunches. *-Lentil*

Place the rice and 750 ml (3 cups) of water in a medium saucepan, cover and bring to the boil. Reduce to a simmer and cook for 15 minutes.

Meanwhile, add a generous splash of oil to a medium, heavy-based saucepan over medium heat. Add the garlic, sugar, chilli, turmeric, pepper and sage and fry for a few minutes until fragrant. Add the chicken and cauliflower and fry for a few minutes until lightly browned. Add the milk, lemon zest and ½ teaspoon of salt and gently bring to the boil. Reduce to a simmer, cover and cook for 10 minutes, then turn the heat off and stand for about 10 minutes to finish poaching.

To make the salad, add all the ingredients to a large bowl. Pour the contents of the pan over the top. Pull the chicken from the bowl, cut into strips, then return to the salad. Massage the salad with your hands for a minute or so to combine well and soften the ingredients a little.

To serve, add a large spoonful of rice to each plate, then a generous portion of salad and some green sauce (we put it in little bowls on the side). Top with a splash of oil, some almonds, a few slices of avocado (if using) and a sprinkle of spring onion, then season to taste. Enjoy! Awesome on a hot summer's day, or anytime of the year really, with a glass of natural white wine.

RECIPE NOTE.

Choose a plant-based milk to make this recipe dairy free. And for a vegan version, simply use whole mushrooms instead of chicken.

SERVES 8-10 // TIME: 30 MINUTES PREPARATION + 6-7 HOURS STEWING

Every Sunday freestyle stew.

THE BEST FOR LEFTOVERS THROUGHOUT THE WEEK.

- extra-virgin olive oil
- 1 large red onion, diced
- 6 garlic cloves, finely chopped
- 1 large fresh or dried hot chilli, finely sliced
- 3 dried bay leaves
- 1 teaspoon fennel seeds
- 1 teaspoon freshly ground black pepper
- a big handful of seasonal herbs (50–80 g) that love a stew (see below), leaves separated from edible stalks, both finely chopped
- 1 kg stewing cut of beef, mutton or goat (see below)
- 2 potatoes, cut into large chunks
- 2 carrots, cut into large chunks
- 2 celery stalks, diced (if in season)
- 750 g leftover seasonal vegetables that love a stew (see below), cut into large chunks
- 250 ml (1 cup) red or white wine
- 500 ml (2 cups) passata
- unrefined salt
- 1 lemon

We eat meat. Not a lot. Not for every meal. But we do. When we were in Italy, it was so refreshing to see the relationship people have with their meat. There is no shame. There is no nastiness. There is just truth and respect. You go to a market and there is a wild boar leg with hair still on it that they are delicately slicing prosciutto from—no one flinches. The poultry still have their heads, necks and feet attached, and all of this makes it into the home stockpot. Everyone, including the children, understands this honest relationship with meat—where it comes from and what it is. Every part of the animal is used. Again, truth and *so* much respect.

Nearly every Sunday, especially through the colder months, it's my job to make the week's stew. This process speaks to me of the oldest and simplest food traditions. Of taking any secondary cut of meat or offal you can get your hands on, rummaging around to pull together a big pile of vegetables that need to be used, adding it all to a pot with water and wine and leaving time to do all the hard work. Use this recipe as the foundation and then build on that with your vegetables and herbs. This is the kind of dish that sets you up for a good week of leftovers (like quick panino, page 235)—rich, warming, nourishing food that cuddles you from the inside out. Served here with the best mash ever—I promise. *-Matt*

Add a very generous splash of oil to a large cast-iron pot over medium heat. Add the onion and sauté for 3–4 minutes until beginning to soften. Add the garlic, chilli, bay leaves, fennel seeds, pepper, any hardy herbs (like rosemary or thyme) and any edible herb stalks (like basil or parsley) and sauté for 2–3 minutes until everything is super fragrant.

Recipe continued over page →

THE BEST MASH
(optional—omit for a dairy-free version)

- 1 kg Dutch cream potatoes, peeled and cut into large chunks
- 60 g unsalted butter
- 2 heaped tablespoons grated pecorino or parmesan
- 150–200 ml full-cream milk
- unrefined salt

STEWING MEAT CUTS

shanks, shoulder, mature osso bucco, intercostals, almost any cut of mutton, tendons and sinews, necks, cheeks or tails. If you can, include cuts on the bone—talk to your local butcher

STEWING VEGETABLES

zucchini/summer squash, pumpkin, green beans, capsicum, turnip, swede, celeriac and parsnip

STEWING HERBS

basil, parsley, marjoram, oregano, thyme and rosemary

→ **Recipe continued from previous page**

Add the meat, nestling it into the mix so that it is browning on the base of the pan. Let the meat brown there for a few minutes, then add all the remaining vegetables and herbs around the meat. Add the wine and boil for about 5 minutes. Finally, add the passata and enough water to cover (in our large cast-iron pot, we just fill to about 2 cm from the top). Bring to the boil, then reduce to the barest simmer, cover and stew for 4 hours until the meat has softened.

After 4 hours, uncover and stew for a further 2–3 hours until the liquid level has reduced by 2–3 cm and the stew is lovely and saucy.

In the final hour, make your mash (if making). Boil the potato in a medium saucepan of salted water until very soft. Drain, then return to the pan. Add the butter, cheese and a very generous splash of milk and blitz with a handheld blender until sticky and silky, adding more milk as needed. This method is a bit polarising, as the handheld blender makes the mash super sticky, but we love it this way—it's our favourite! Season to taste.

When the stew is ready, season to taste and serve over the mash topped with a squeeze of lemon, a drizzle of oil and any extra herbs you may have. Alternatively, make little pies by placing the stew in small ovenproof dishes, topping them with mash, then placing under a hot grill for a few minutes until golden on top.

Pan-fried gnocchi, pea & rocket salad.

An old recipe in our house, but a good one. We always seem to have these ingredients throughout the year in one way or another, whether fresh, preserved in jars or in the freezer. It's what we refer to as the 'pretty salad'—it's just so pretty! It's bright, quick, tasty and a good mid-week meal. If you don't have gnocchi, just substitute with potato.

- 2 capsicums, cored and sliced, or 200 g capsicum under oil (page 163)
- 150 g (1 cup) fresh or frozen peas
- extra-virgin olive oil
- 350–500 g gnocchi (prepared and cooked as per page 128), or equivalent cooked potato or sweet potato, roughly chopped
- 100 g rocket, torn
- a big handful of mint leaves, roughly chopped or torn
- 2 chillies, finely chopped (if in season)
- juice of ½ large lemon
- 60 g (½ cup) walnuts, roughly chopped and toasted
- 2 tablespoons fresh or frozen and thawed pesto (page 124)
- a big pinch of freshly ground black pepper
- 100 g ricotta or fresh cacioricotta (page 148) (or buffalo mozzarella, torn)
- unrefined salt

If using fresh capsicum (skip this step if using preserved), preheat the oven to the hottest grill setting.

Lay the capsicum in a single layer on a large baking tray. Grill for 10–12 minutes, or until just blistering and softening—a little burnt is fine!

Blanch the peas in a small saucepan of boiling salted water until soft, about 1 ½ minutes. Refresh under cold water, drain and set aside.

Add a large splash of oil to a medium, heavy-based frying pan over medium heat. Pan-fry the gnocchi (or potato) for about 3 minutes until just browning. Set aside.

Add everything except the gnocchi (or potato), ricotta and salt to a medium bowl and massage gently. Add the gnocchi and ricotta and toss to combine. Season to taste and serve as is, or it's great served cold.

FIELD NOTES.

On the joys of growing your own rocket. We can't stress enough how great rocket is to grow. It's super easy to do, and if you give it consistent water, you'll be able to keep harvesting it perpetually throughout the growing season, from spring through to winter. And the flavour of home-grown rocket is incomparable to store bought. To get the full flavour of this dish, start your patch today (see page 66 for full instructions)!

SERVES 4-6 // TIME: 20 MINUTES

Simplest red sauce.

- 400 g dried pasta of your choice (gluten free if preferred) (or 500-600 g gnocchi, page 128, or 600-700 g snake beans, see field notes, page 303)
- 1 kg ripe heirloom tomatoes
- 1 large garlic clove, crushed
- a big pinch of unrefined salt
- a big pinch of freshly ground black pepper
- extra-virgin olive oil
- 90 g (⅓ cup) ricotta (or fresh cacioricotta, page 148)
- a big handful of basil leaves, roughly chopped or torn
- grated pecorino, cured cacioricotta (page 148) or parmesan, to serve

Sometimes simple is just so good. So, in the spirit of simplicity, we are only going to tell you that this sauce is just the best—easy, fresh, a little creamy and delicious. Trust us. Also see page 235 for another idea on how to use it.

Cook the pasta (or pasta alternative) in boiling salted water (salty enough to remind you of the sea!) for the recommended time (snake beans will take 4–5 minutes until just tender). Drain, rinse briefly under cold water and set aside.

Meanwhile, roughly chop or pull the tomatoes apart and add to a blender. Add the garlic, salt, pepper and 3 tablespoons of oil and gently blend until juicy, a little combined, but still super chunky.

Pour the tomato mixture into a deep, heavy-based frying pan over high heat. Fry, uncovered, for about 15 minutes, letting the tomatoes stick to the base and burn a little, stirring or agitating very occasionally.

Once the tomatoes have broken down and the liquid has reduced, decrease the heat and add the ricotta, basil and pasta (or pasta alternative) and cook for another minute or so until everything is hot and combined. Remove from the heat, add a generous splash of oil and stir through. Your pasta should have a thick coating of sauce, but not be swimming in it. This is how the Italians (as we learnt) do it!

Serve in bowls, topped with grated cheese. Enjoy!

Blueberry and olive oil torte, page 332.

Desserts.

To celebrate.
Easy to make, wholesome,
everyday desserts.

Peach & cream slabs.

naked rye cookie dough (page 192) (see notes), pressed into a small square or rectangular container (about 8 cm x 11 cm) and cooled in the fridge as per method

24 large basil leaves (or a big handful of toasted, shredded coconut)

PEACHES

8-10 ripe but firm peaches, cut into thick slices

2 ½ tablespoons lemon juice

3 tablespoons extra-virgin olive oil

2 tablespoons unprocessed honey

BUTTERCREAM

1 ½ teaspoons full-cream milk

100 g unsalted butter, at room temperature

2 tablespoons unprocessed sugar (e.g. rapadura)

1 ½ teaspoons vanilla extract

1 teaspoon boiling water

RECIPE NOTES.

You can make these into small 'bites' if you like, by making the slabs smaller. You may also want to do this if you already have naked rye cookies baked.

It's also delicious to simply put the buttercream and biscuits together and make a sandwich.

This recipe is close to my heart. It is my version of a slice my grandmother (Mumma) makes that everyone in my family asks for, savours until it's all gone and then asks for another batch. It's just so good. The funny thing is, none of us bother to write the recipe down, so each time we try to make it we call each other to ask for the recipe. Last time I wanted the recipe, this is how it went: I called my aunty to ask for it, who asked my cousin if she had it, who then called Mumma to ask for it. My aunty called me back, gave me the recipe, then I called Mumma to confirm it!

There are a few steps to this, but it's so worth it. It has a crunchy base, creamy middle and deliciously fresh, fruity topping. I can't put into words how good these are. Just make them for yourself and all the people you love! Note, if you are a member of my family and reading this, no this is not Mumma's recipe. It's my version. You'll have to ask Mumma for hers. *-Lentil*

Preheat the oven to 170°C fan-forced. Grease or line two large baking trays.

Flip the cooled cookie dough onto the bench (you may need to loosen the edges with a knife). It should stay in the shape you cooled it in—a slab. If not, let the dough melt a tiny bit, then wrap in baking paper or a beeswax wrap and shape into a slab. Slice the cooled dough so that it makes 12 individual slabs, about 8–10 mm thick. Place the slabs on the trays, accounting for a spread of about 2 cm, and bake for 12–16 minutes until golden brown on top and a little browned on the edges—the goldenness is key to crispness! Leave to cool on the trays.

Meanwhile, add all the peach ingredients to a small–medium saucepan over medium heat and stir. Cover and simmer for about 10 minutes, stirring occasionally. By this stage the peaches should have softened but still hold their shape well. Uncover and reduce for 5–10 minutes until the peaches look glossy and most of the liquid has evaporated. Place the peaches in the fridge to cool for about 30 minutes.

Once everything has cooled, make the buttercream. Add the milk, butter, sugar and vanilla to a medium bowl and beat with an electric beater until creamy and pale. Add the boiling water and continue to beat until the mixture comes together and is thick, pale and creamy.

Spread about 2 teaspoons of buttercream onto each slab, evenly dividing the mix. Top each slab with two basil leaves (or a sprinkle of coconut) and some peaches, making sure you get all of the sticky honey deliciousness on there. Serve now or place in the fridge to chill (the best, in our opinion!).

These will keep in the fridge for 3 days (after this the cookies start to soften).

So simple chocolate gelato.

NO CHURN, NO COOK, FULL OF GOODNESS.

Gelato always makes me think about all the 'adult children' that we know—especially the person who stabbed their hand with a knife getting the gelato out of the container because they couldn't wait for it to soften, so they tried to get it out with a hot knife, which went through the container and out through the other side into their hand. You know who you are!

This is simply a really good, no-cook, fuss-free chocolate gelato (that does require you to wait a few minutes for it to soften!). Also, don't tell anyone there's avocado in it, because they might think it would be not so great—but I assure you, it's super creamy and delicious *because* of the avo! The strawberry salad isn't essential, but adds an awesome freshness in spring and summer. *-Lentil*

GELATO

- 100 g dark chocolate (70% cacao)
- 300 g ripe avocado flesh (about 2 avocados)
- 200 ml full-cream milk
- 2 tablespoons double cream
- 75 g (⅓ cup) unrefined sugar (e.g. rapadura)
- 35 g (⅓ cup) raw cacao powder
- 2 teaspoons vanilla extract
- a pinch of unrefined salt

STRAWBERRY SALAD (if in season)

- 250 g strawberries (or alpine strawberries), diced
- a handful of mint leaves
- a handful of basil leaves
- a handful of roughly chopped hazelnuts (or 1 tablespoon hazelnut meal)
- 2 teaspoons unprocessed honey
- juice of ½ small lemon

Melt the chocolate in a heatproof bowl over a small saucepan of simmering water, stirring occasionally.

Meanwhile, add the remaining gelato ingredients to a blender and pulse for a few minutes until well combined. The mixture should be thick, aerated and mousse-like, with no chunks of avocado. Add the melted chocolate to the blender and blend for another minute or so until well combined.

Using a spatula, divide the mixture between 4–6 small bowls, or tip into one airtight container and freeze (this will take 2 hours or more).

When ready to eat, take the gelato out of the freezer and sit on the bench for 10 minutes or so to soften a little. We like it a little on the melted side, but you choose how you like it! Your gelato should be super creamy and not icy at all.

While you wait for it to defrost a little, prepare the strawberry salad (if you're making it) by blending all the ingredients on low until *just* combined—it should still be a little chunky.

Serve the gelato on its own or with a few spoonfuls of strawberry salad and enjoy!

Broken cake with natural cherry syrup, fruit & cream.

SERVES 8-12, MAKES ABOUT 350 ML SYRUP
TIME: 35 MINUTES

This dessert is dedicated to Andrew and Kerry—such an important part of our village. Every time we visit Andrew and Kerry's place, over the river from our old farm, there is always something new to try. A new wine, or fermented treat, some sweet thing, or jam, or sauce, or soup, or freshly harvested fruit or nuts. It's the best! We took them our 'stale' cake (page 204), and Kerry instantly pulled out a cherry sauce she'd just made. The two went together like peas in a pod. We love these visits so much, full of coffee, wine, the exchange of big ideas and music. It always feels full of life there. And that's what this dessert is to us—a celebration of life. *-Matt*

- 500 g fresh or frozen pitted cherries
- 1 tablespoon lemon juice
- 1 'stale' cake (page 204), broken into pieces
- a hero fruit of the season (like berries or peaches or figs), fresh or preserved in natural syrup, sliced
- thick cream, fresh cheese (page 144), fresh cacioricotta (page 148) or ricotta
- herbs and edible flowers (like fennel and lemon verbena)

For the syrup, add the cherries to a small saucepan with a splash of water, cover and bring to the boil over medium heat until really bubbly. Reduce the heat a little and try to hold that bubbliness for a minute, then reduce to the barest simmer and cook for 30 minutes.

Once cooked, mash the cherries with a potato masher, stir through the lemon juice and serve hot or set aside to cool before refrigerating.

The syrup will keep in an airtight container or jar in the fridge for at least 2 weeks.

For the rest, the method is yours to imagine and enact. Make it art.

Raw chocolate & espresso mousse.

MOUSSE

- 300 g ripe avocado flesh (about 2 avocados)
- 200 ml milk of your choice
- 75 g (⅓ cup) coconut, raw or rapadura sugar (use raw sugar for the 'cleanest' flavour)
- 50 g (½ cup) raw cacao powder
- 2 teaspoons vanilla extract
- ¼ teaspoon unrefined salt
- 2 tablespoons espresso (replace with milk of your choice for kids)

TO SERVE (optional)

- 1½ tablespoons cacao nibs
- a few handfuls of sliced strawberries (or alpine strawberries) (if in season)
- a handful of roughly chopped hazelnuts
- melted dark chocolate

These are inspired by my friend Mel, who told me one night that I must find her a replacement for her late night 'ten-minute chocolate bowls', which she said were extremely unhealthy look-at-it-and-put-on-five-kilos cake bowls. So, this is my answer to that. These feel super indulgent, but are healthy, creamy and basically taste like delicious chocolate mousse. Again, like the gelato (page 319), don't tell anyone there is avocado in this! These are great dinner party desserts or easy late-night snacks. *-Lentil*

Add all the mousse ingredients to a blender and pulse for a few minutes (the time will depend on the power of your blender) until well combined. The mixture should be thick, smooth, aerated and semi-set, with no chunks of avocado—like a mousse!

Using a spatula, divide the mousse between four small bowls or jars and cool in the fridge for 3 hours or more, but they're best after 12 hours. Once ready, the mix should be thick and set. If you put some on a spoon and turn it upside down it shouldn't fall off!

When ready to eat, serve as is or top each bowl with a sprinkle of cacao nibs, sliced strawberries, hazelnuts and melted chocolate.

RECIPE NOTES.

If it's too thick for your liking, add a little bit of milk at a time until it's at the desired texture.

Once we've emptied the blender, we often add a splash of milk, ice and espresso and blend to make a quick iced coffee for the cook.

FIELD NOTES.

On all the sugars. This recipe really highlights the diversity of flavours of different sugars. Coconut sugar makes a super-fruity mousse. Raw sugar makes a sweet and clean mousse. Rapadura imparts a subtle anise note. The fantastic, truly primitive sugar our friend Bob makes by simply evaporating fresh sugarcane juice brings with it fantastic grassy *and* anise notes. Everyone has different tastes, and each dish is a little different. This is a great example of how it's all about taking the ideas behind the recipes in this book and really making them your own by adjusting to your tastes and local abundance. You pick what works best for you!

Baked plums, sage & warm cheese.

So beautiful, rich and sticky. A simple favourite. The plums go perfectly with the cheese and oat crackers, and are also great cold (make extra to have leftovers!) with ice cream or gelato (page 319), or served with chickpea pancakes (page 218).

Preheat the oven to 160°C fan-forced.

Pull apart the cheese and arrange on a serving plate, then set aside.

Split the plums in half with your hands over a deep baking dish or brownie tin (about 16 cm x 16 cm or the equivalent), allowing the juice to fall into the tin. Remove and discard the stones.

Evenly distribute the plums, fitting them snugly together. Drizzle the oil and honey over the plums. Rub the sage leaves between your hands until fragrant and scatter evenly on top. Pull the butter into small pieces and dot it over the sage leaves. Bake for 25–30 minutes.

After 25–30 minutes, increase the temperature to 250°C fan-forced and bake for a further 10 minutes until the plums are fully soft and surrounded by a sticky sauce.

Pour the hot plums and their sauce over the plate of cheese you set aside earlier. Serve with oat crackers on the side to scoop up the cheesy-plum goodness. Alternatively, they are also great served with chickpea pancakes. Enjoy!

RECIPE NOTE.

These baked plums can easily be made at the same time as oat crackers (page 136) as the required oven temperature is the same.

BAKED PLUMS

- 600 g plums (about 12) (any variety is fine)
- 2 tablespoons extra-virgin olive oil
- 1 tablespoon unprocessed honey
- 15 sage leaves
- 2 teaspoons cold unsalted butter

TO SERVE

- 150–200 g cheese of your choice, we like to use fresh cheese (page 144), fresh cacioricotta (page 148), mozzarella, camembert, brie or blue
- oat crackers (page 136)

Four-ingredient walnut cake.

THIS JUST *SAYS* CELEBRATION.

CAKE

- 6 eggs, separated
- 2 teaspoons lemon zest
- 140 g (⅔ cup) unrefined sugar (e.g. rapadura)
- 230 g (2 cups) walnut meal, toasted (see notes)

RASPBERRY CREAM
(optional—see notes)

- 300 ml pouring cream
- 1 tablespoon unrefined sugar (e.g. rapadura)
- 1 teaspoon vanilla extract
- 250 g (2 cups) fresh or thawed frozen raspberries, plus extra to serve

This is a fluffy, easy, decadent, two-tiered, minimal-ingredient cake. It says family, birthdays, celebrations and Christmas. It feeds many and is a really delicious dessert staple. When we get walnuts, we get them in bulk, either picked from trees around us or from Matt's aunty and uncle's little walnut farm—so it's something we can always make, using what we've got. *-Lentil*

Preheat the oven to 170°C fan-forced. Liberally grease or line two 20 cm round springform cake tins. (If you only have regular cake tins, this will still work, but they must be lined with baking paper.)

Add the eggwhites to a medium bowl and beat with an electric beater. Add the lemon zest and a spoonful of the sugar and beat to stiff peaks. Set aside. Add the yolks to a separate medium bowl and beat to combine. Slowly add the remaining sugar, beating until pale, glossy and creamy, about 5 minutes. Fold the walnut meal into the yolk mixture, then gently fold in the eggwhites in a few batches. Try not to break all the fluffiness. Take your time and fold the mixture together gently until well combined (we go slow, and it takes about 3 minutes).

Divide the mixture evenly between the prepared tins and bake for 20–25 minutes until golden brown. When ready, the cake will be starting to pull away from the edges of the tin and a skewer inserted into the centre will come out clean. Cool in the tins, then transfer to a cooling rack. If you prefer your cake cold, place in an airtight container in the fridge to chill before adding the cream.

Once fully cooled, make the raspberry cream, if desired. Whip the cream, sugar and vanilla in a medium bowl, making sure not to turn it into butter! Gently mash the raspberries in a small bowl, so they're still chunky, then gently stir into the cream until marbled (not fully combined).

To assemble, layer half the cream onto one of the cakes, then place the other cake on top and add a final layer of the cream on top. Add some extra raspberries on top. Share and celebrate. Store any leftovers in an airtight container in the fridge.

RECIPE NOTES.

To make walnut meal, blitz walnuts in a blender until they form a flour (like almond meal in texture). Toast in a dry frying pan over medium heat, stirring occasionally, until just browning, then tip out of the pan.

For a dairy-free version of this recipe, simply omit the raspberry cream.

This cake freezes super well without the cream, so you can always bake the cake bases, freeze and then add the cream when ready to use!

SERVES 8 // TIME: 15 MINUTES + OVERNIGHT SOAKING + FREEZING

GF | DF | V

Almond sorbetto (& popsicles).

THE ITALIAN SLUSHY.

It's 42°C and this is all I want. Thankfully, our dear friend Stellina has prepared us for anything now. She is such a generous woman. So nurturing. So happy. A powerful ball of determined love. Just one of the incredible things she so carefully taught us was the foundation for this recipe—the traditional almond and honey milk of her area. And we have taken that joyful lesson and used it to create our version of the super-refreshing and surprisingly unique soft sorbetti we were served throughout Southern Italy that summer.

So here it is, traditional almond and honey milk meets soft sorbetti, with an option to popsicle-ise (because who doesn't want *that* option?). Get this in your freezer, because next time the thermometer pushes past the high 30s you're going to be thanking past-you for being such a legend. *–Matt*

400 g almonds

115 g (⅓ cup) unprocessed honey

125 ml (½ cup) chilled water or milk of your choice

SPECIAL EQUIPMENT

nut milk bag or cheesecloth

DAY 1

Add the almonds and 1.5 litres of water to a medium bowl and leave to soak overnight.

DAY 2

Drain and rinse the almonds, then add to a blender with 800 ml of water. Blend until a thick liquid forms.

Position your nut milk bag (or a colander lined with a doubled-over piece of cheesecloth) over a bowl. Pour the mixture, scraping everything out of the blender, into the bag/colander. Now, squeeze, squeeze, squeeze to extract all the liquid. You should get at least 800 ml (see field notes for what to do with the leftover pulp).

Return the liquid to the blender (no need to clean the blender from the previous step, as all those little chunky flecks are nice) with the honey. Blend briefly to combine but try not to aerate the liquid too much—you've made Stellina's thick, sweetened almond milk!

NOW, TO MAKE SOFT SORBETTI

Pour the almond milk into ice-cube trays and freeze until frozen solid (about 5 hours or so). Turn the blocks out in to the blender, then add the chilled water or milk and blend. Pour into glasses and serve immediately.

OR, TO MAKE POPSICLES

Add the chilled water or milk to the almond milk while still in the blender and blend again briefly to combine (again, try not to aerate the liquid too much). Pour into popsicle moulds, freeze until frozen solid (about 5 hours or so) and enjoy!

FIELD NOTES.

On what to do with nut pulp.
The hardest thing about nut/seed milks for many people is the pulp left at the end (with this recipe you will get about 4–5 cups of pulp left over). So here are a few of our favourite things to do with the pulp to give you a bit of inspiration!

Dips. When blending dips, add to the mixture (e.g. hummus, carrot dip) to thicken.

Baking. Add to breads, brownies, cookies, macaroons and savoury crackers in place of regular nut and seed meals.

Muesli. Add to toasted or bircher muesli.

Soups. Add to soups to thicken.

Custards. Add to baked custards and rice custards.

Bliss balls. And protein balls.

Feed it to the chickens. If you have chickens, they will love it!

Compost. And if all else fails, your compost will thank you for it (it's all a cycle and great to add back to the earth).

SERVES 6-8 // TIME: 40-50 MINUTES

Blueberry & olive oil torte.

- 250 ml (1 cup) full-cream milk
- 140 g (⅔ cup) unrefined sugar (e.g. rapadura)
- 2 teaspoons lemon zest
- 1 teaspoon vanilla extract
- 100 ml extra-virgin olive oil
- 2 eggs
- 140 g brown rice flour
- 40 g almond meal
- 30 g (3 tablespoons) tapioca (cassava) flour
- 1 teaspoon bicarbonate of soda
- 115 g (¾ cup) fresh or frozen blueberries
- ricotta, fresh cacioricotta (page 148), cream or sour cream, to serve

This is a light and fluffy torte that has an awesome moist deliciousness throughout and is slightly crispy on the outside. We want this to be a liberating cake, one you can make throughout the year, regardless of the seasons, so freeze some blueberries when they are in season! With this cake comes so many memories for us, as it's similar to a torte that a dear family friend always makes us for birthdays, or just because. Mumma Linda, this one is inspired by you. X

Preheat the oven to 160°C fan-forced. Grease or line a 23 cm round cake tin or springform tin.

Add the milk, sugar, lemon zest and vanilla to a small saucepan and warm over low heat, stirring until the sugar has dissolved—do not boil! Add the oil, stir, then turn off the heat.

Whisk the eggs well in a medium bowl. Sift in the dry ingredients, then pour in the milk mixture and whisk super well to form a smooth and runny batter.

Pour the batter into the prepared tin and scatter the blueberries evenly over the top. Make sure you don't drop all the fruit into the middle of the cake, as it will take longer to cook.

Bake for 30–40 minutes until golden and a skewer inserted into the centre comes out clean. The cake should have risen a little and be airy and spongy in texture. Cool in the tin, then remove from the tin and place on a cooling rack.

Serve the cake warm or cold, with ricotta, fresh cacioricotta, cream or sour cream.

RECIPE NOTE.

Don't worry if some of the blueberries sink—it's all part of it!

Cold polenta & grape slice.

A SUPER-PRETTY, ADULTS DESSERT FOR THOSE WITH A MORE SAVOURY PALATE.

- 450 g red seedless grapes
- 2 tablespoons red wine
- 1 tablespoon extra-virgin olive oil
- 1 tablespoon unrefined sugar (e.g. rapadura), or unprocessed honey
- 80 g classic polenta (masa harina, if possible)
- 60 g (½ cup) walnuts and pistachios, roughly chopped and toasted

TO SERVE (optional—see note)

- 250 g red seedless grapes, gently torn apart or halved
- 100 g fresh cheese (page 144), soft goat's cheese (chèvre style), ricotta or cacioricotta (page 148)
- a large handful of walnuts
- 3 teaspoons unprocessed honey
- 1-2 teaspoons extra-virgin olive oil
- a big handful of mint leaves, torn

This slice tastes buttery and creamy but there's no dairy in it—it's sweet from the grapes and super refreshing. Born from a hot day when we just wanted something cold and fresh tasting to share with many, this is an easy dessert that's made for dinner parties. It's also great as an appetiser with a glass of chilled, light red wine.

Grease or line an 18 cm x 18 cm (or equivalent) baking tin or brownie tin.

Add the grapes to a medium, heavy-based saucepan and massage and press with your hands to break the skins. Place the pan over medium heat and add the wine, oil and sugar. Bring to the boil, then reduce the heat and gently simmer with the lid on for 5 minutes.

Add 500 ml (2 cups) of water to the pan and bring back to the boil. Reduce the heat to low and slowly add the polenta while stirring (adding while stirring is key, otherwise you will end up with lumps). You should now have a thick mixture, without polenta lumps.

Simmer uncovered over low heat, stirring occasionally, for about 40 minutes. The mixture should just bubble occasionally.

When ready, the polenta will have thickened, started to bubble more and be just starting to stick to the pan. Stir in the nuts and turn off the heat. Spoon the polenta mixture into the prepared tin and refrigerate until cool and set (2–3 hours or more).

When ready to serve, flip the slice out onto a board, then top with the grapes, cheese, walnuts, honey, oil and mint, if you like. Cut into slices, serve with a light red and enjoy in the sunshine!

RECIPE NOTE.

To make a dairy-free version of this reicipe, simply omit the cheese. For a vegan version, omit the cheese and honey.

FIELD NOTES.

On the traditional way. Traditionally, Italians made something similar using grape must. Grape must is a step in the winemaking process. It's all the parts of freshly crushed grapes—the juice, the skins, the seeds and sometimes the stems, just after crushing. Because not everyone makes wine or has access to grape must, we have used fresh grapes in this recipe instead! But if you *do* make wine, you can definitely replace the grape content of this recipe with must.

References.

We believe you should never stop learning. We are so fortunate to have met mentors who have shared their wisdom and taught us hands-on skills, and every day we experiment and learn from trial and error. While there are many things in life that have to be experienced to be truly understood, luckily, we don't have to figure *everything* out for ourselves. People from all around the world are exploring, experimenting and explaining, and a lot of this knowledge is freely available online. Throughout this book, we've referred to a few of the studies and books that have helped educate us along our journey, so if you want to learn more, you can use this as a starting point.

To find out more about how having abundance and security affects our brain (mentioned on page 12):

Eldar Shafir et al., 'Poverty Impedes Cognitive Function', *Science*, 30 Aug 2013, vol. 341, issue 6149, pp. 976-80.

For further information on the importance of community and connection in human evolution (mentioned on page 15):

Harari, Y.N., *Sapiens: A Brief History of Humankind*, 2014, Harper, New York.

To learn more about what leads to meaning (mentioned on page 16):

See Michael F. Steger's work for the Laboratory for the Study of Meaning & Quality of Life.

To read more about how people who have meaningful relationships live longer, healthier and happier lives (mentioned on pages 15-16):

Boyle P.A. et al., 'Purpose in Life is Associated with Mortality Among Community-Dwelling Older Persons', *Psychosomatic Medicine*, 2009, vol. 71, no. 5, pp. 574-9.

Patrick L. Hill et al., 'Purpose in Life as a Predictor of Mortality across Adulthood', *Psychological Science*, vol. 25, no. 7, pp. 1482-1486.

See also, the Harvard Adult Development Study, one of the longest studies of adult life ever conducted. The research is ongoing. Notable published articles are:

Waldinger R.J. et al., 'What's Love Got To Do With It?: Social Functioning, Perceived Health, and Daily Happiness in Married Octogenarians', *Psychology and Aging*, vol. 25, no. 2, pp. 422-431.

Waldinger R.J. et al., 'Security of attachment to spouses in late life: Concurrent and prospective links with cognitive and emotional wellbeing', *Psychological Science*, vol. 3, no. 4, pp. 516-529.

Appendix.

Key recipes and guides from our first book, used throughout this one. Included here for your reference.

Starting a sourdough culture.

MAKES 1 x 'IMMORTAL' BATCH OF SOURDOUGH CULTURE
TIME: 7 DAYS

Fermenting grains with a sourdough culture takes them to the next level and starting a new culture from scratch is super simple. It's a fun process to watch it grow over about a week. Whether you want a gluten-free, whole-wheat or any other kind of culture, always start it with stone-ground rye flour. Stone-ground rye flour has that special something that makes the good things happen. After your culture is very alive, it can be converted to any flour you desire.

400 g stone-ground rye flour (as freshly milled as possible)

400 ml unchlorinated water (it must be unchlorinated to allow the wild bacteria and yeasts to grow)

DAY 1.

Add 50 g of rye flour and 50 ml of water to a 500 ml jar and mix well. Cover with a damp cloth, place the lid on but don't tighten and set aside in a warm place, about 25–38° C (we put ours on top of the coffee machine).

DAY 2.

After 24 hours, discard all but about 2 tablespoons of the mix, then add the same amounts of flour and water to the jar, mix thoroughly, cover with the (freshly dampened) cloth and lid and return to its warm place.

DAYS 3–5.

Repeat Day 2 instructions each day.

DAY 6.

By now your culture should really be bubbling between feeds. Repeat Day 2 instructions twice (12 hours after the last feed, then again 12 hours later).

DAY 7.

Repeat Day 2 instructions 12 hours after the last feed. Twelve hours later your culture should be forming big bubbles and be ready for making bread.

RECIPE NOTES.

A healthy culture smells a little acidic, like vinegar, a little yeasty, like beer, and also a little sweet and fruity, like banana or pineapple. There is quite a lot of variation, but no matter what, it will smell pleasant. If your culture begins to smell like nail polish remover, takes on funny colours, or just doesn't smell right, it's probably not. Best to discard it and start again!

Maintaining your culture.
Repeat the process of discarding and feeding daily for at least another week to get your culture really alive, and then freeze about 2 tablespoons for a backup just in case your culture spoils/dies down the track. From this point, feed it any wholegrain flour you like—millet, wheat, brown rice, whatever. If you feed it gluten-free flour, it will soon become gluten free.

We usually keep our culture in the fridge in between bakes. It's not considered the 'done thing' to refrigerate your culture, but we've never had a problem managing it this way. Plus, we always have a backup in the freezer just in case, which we can simply bring out and feed to make it come alive again. Just remember, sourdough culture is alive. So, if you *do* have it out of the fridge or freezer, it *must* be kept warm (at a constant 25–38°C) and fed every day.

Using your culture.
Two days before you plan on baking, combine 150 g of flour, 150 ml of water and at least 2 tablespoons of sourdough culture in a 1 litre jar and leave in its warm place. That's enough to culture a 3 kg batch of bread (10% by weight). If you want to bake more or less, feed it appropriately.

Twenty-four hours later, your culture will be ready to use. Never put anything in your starter jar but flour and water (especially don't contaminate it with salt, because it will wreak havoc with your culture) and always leave at least 2 tablespoons of starter in the jar. As soon as you are finished, seal the jar and pop it back in the fridge.

Basic soured grains.

MAKES 3-4 CUPS COOKED GRAINS
TIME: 12-24 HOURS SOAKING + 15 MINUTES TO 1½ HOURS COOKING (DEPENDING ON THE GRAIN)

To us, a simple bowl of steaming grains symbolises absolute nourishment. Soaking grains in water acidified with apple cider vinegar for at least 12 hours in a warm room deactivates enzyme inhibitors—which disrupt your digestion—by simulating germination conditions in the seeds. Apple cider vinegar is our go-to, but you can use any other vinegar, lemon juice, yoghurt or whey to acidulate the water too. Grains cooked after being soaked this way taste sweeter, are more easily digested and contain a world of otherwise unavailable nutrients. All ancient societies came up with a method just like this to deactivate the enzyme inhibitors in their wholegrains so that they would get the most out of their food and enjoy the most vibrant health. While much has changed in the world—it is still as necessary as ever to take the time to do the same.

2 cups wholegrain of your choice

1 tablespoon apple cider vinegar (or other vinegar, lemon juice, yoghurt or whey)

DAY 1.

Add the grain to a jar, bowl or saucepan and cover with the amount of water indicated in the table opposite. Add the vinegar, cover and set aside to soak for 12–24 hours at room temperature (or, even better, keep grains at 25–38°C during soaking for best results—we put ours on top of the coffee machine).

DAY 2.

Tip both the soaked grain and the soaking water into a saucepan (or if you've soaked in a saucepan, just place the whole thing on the stove), cover and bring to the boil. Reduce to the barest simmer and cook for the time indicated in the table opposite, or until all of the water is absorbed and the grains are tender. The cooked grain can be eaten right away or, for best results, set aside off the heat, covered, for a further 15 minutes for a final steam before serving.

RECIPE NOTES.

If using whey to soak grains, please note that it is not as acidic as the other options mentioned, so it's better to replace the water content entirely with whey.

You can also sour grains in straight yoghurt rather than just adding a tablespoon, but use this for baking or eating grains raw, such as in bircher, not for this method.

When cooking grains, never add salt until after they're cooked. The salt will prevent the grain from fully softening.

For an even richer flavour, drain your grains after soaking and measure the liquid. Replace the liquid with the same amount of stock and cook as per the method.

Measures and cooking times for wholegrains.

Cooking times and water absorbency vary a little harvest to harvest, but follow this guide and you can't go too wrong.

1 cup of grain	Cups of water	Cooking time
Amaranth	1½	20 minutes
Barley, hulled (pot barley)	2	50 minutes
Buckwheat	1½	20 minutes
Bulgur (burghul/cracked durum)	2	15 minutes
Einkorn (farro piccolo)	1½	30 minutes
Emmer (farro medio)	1¾	40 minutes
Freekeh (green-harvested durum)	2½	60 minutes
Khorasan	2½	50 minutes
Millet, hulled	1½	20 minutes
Oats (freshly rolled)	3	30 minutes
Quinoa (washed)	1½	15 minutes
Rice, black or brown	1¾	30 minutes
Rice, red	2½	50 minutes
Rye	2½	90 minutes
Sorghum	2½	30 minutes
Spelt (farro grande)	2	50 minutes
Teff	2	20 minutes
Whole wheat	2½	90 minutes
Wild rice	2	50 minutes

Basic pulses.

MAKES 2-3 CUPS COOKED PULSES
TIME: 12-24 HOURS SOAKING + 20 MINUTES TO 8 HOURS COOKING (DEPENDING ON THE PULSE)

Beans, peas and lentils (or 'pulses'), like grains, have enzyme inhibitors that require deactivating. But they also contain oligosaccharides (difficult to digest carbohydrates that are responsible for beans' gassy reputation) and lectins (carbohydrate-binding proteins that render raw pulses absolutely toxic) and removing all of these 'anti-nutrients' is key. Properly prepared, pulses are absolutely awesome foods. They are excellent sources of protein, packed with minerals vitamins, fibre and healthy fats. They have been a mainstay of traditional diets for as long as humans have tilled the land, and we eat them often.

To draw out the anti-nutrients, we soak pulses in *salted* water. It's important not to use an acid here (as you would for wholegrains) because acids cause the proteins in pulses to constrict, preventing them from fully softening. We also never cook pulses in the liquid we soak them in, as that's where all of the oligosaccharides and lectins now are!

1 cup dried beans, peas or lentils of your choice

1 teaspoon unrefined salt

DAY 1.

Place the pulses in a jar, bowl or saucepan and cover with at least 750 ml (3 cups) of water. Add the salt, cover and set aside to soak for 12–24 hours at room temperature (or, even better, keep pulses at 25–38°C during soaking for best results—we put ours on top of the coffee machine).

DAY 2.

Drain the pulses and wash thoroughly under cold running water. Place in a saucepan (we prefer a really heavy cast-iron pot for all pulses, as an even distribution of heat gives maximum butter-softness) with enough water to just cover and bring to the boil. Skim off any foam that forms on the surface and reduce to the barest simmer. Cook for the time indicated in the table opposite, topping up the water if necessary, until butter soft.

There should be barely any water remaining when the pulses are ready. Otherwise, strain the liquid (it is delicious to drink), season the pulses well (the salt makes them even more digestible) and serve immediately, or store in the fridge for up to a week.

RECIPE NOTES.

As with grains, you can substitute the cooking water with stock for a richer flavour.

When cooking pulses, never add acids, like tomatoes, whey, vinegar, yoghurt or lemon juice until after they're cooked. The acid will prevent the pulse from fully softening.

Remember to never cook pulses in the water you used for soaking. Always drain and cook in fresh water.

Cooking times for pulses.

Cooking times vary a little from harvest to harvest, but follow this guide and you can't go too wrong. Cooking times are largely based on the size of the seed (with some exceptions), so that's how we've grouped them.

The below cooking times may seem long, however this is to maximise the digestibility of the pulses and to achieve butter-soft results. Long, slow, even cooking over the fire was how pulses were cooked traditionally, and that is what we are trying to replicate.

Pulse	Cooking time
Beluga lentils	20 minutes
Other whole lentils (puy, brown etc.) and small beans (adzuki, mung etc.)	30-60 minutes
Cowpeas (black-eyed peas), lima beans	50-90 minutes
Dried whole peas	70-120 minutes
Cannellini beans, black beans, borlotti beans, fava beans (dried broad beans), kidney beans, pink beans, pinto beans	2½-4 hours
Great northern beans	3-5 hours
Navy (haricot) beans	3½-6 hours
Black pinto beans, chickpeas	4-8 hours

Sprouts.

MAKES 3+ CUPS
TIME: 3+ DAYS

Sprouting germinates grains, pulses and other seeds completely, turning them into vitamin-rich, super-digestible baby plants. Sprouts are crunchy and delicious, and can be eaten raw or cooked. You can sprout many seeds, but some are tastier than others. Our favourite by far are puy lentils—they taste so fresh and minerally. We also *love* wheat, rye, mung bean and alfalfa.

1 cup grains, pulses or other seeds (e.g. wheat, lentils, mung beans, fenugreek etc.)

DAY 1.

Place the seeds in a 2 litre jar and fill with water. Shake the jar in a circular motion over the sink, and then pour the water out. (This washes away any dirt or grime.) Fill the jar with water again and leave to soak overnight.

DAY 2.

Drain the water but leave the seeds in the jar. Fill with water and drain again. Place some muslin on top, fasten with a rubber band and leave for 24 hours with the opening facing down at a 30–45° angle, allowing any excess water to drain away—on a dish rack over the sink, or in a bowl both work well. It is key for the jar to drain freely while the sprouts grow to avoid mould forming.

DAY 3.

Refresh by filling with water and draining again. Leave for another 24 hours the same way—your sprouts should now be growing!

DAYS 4–6.

Repeat the filling and draining for at least 3 more days until you have sprouts the size that you want them—we usually let them go until the first tiny green leaves appear!

STORING SPROUTS

Store the sprouts in the fridge for over 2 weeks in a fresh jar with no lid. Not using a lid ensures airflow, preventing mould and keeping the sprouts crisp!

Mayonnaise.

MAKES 300 ML
TIME: 10 MINUTES

This goes on everything. It makes even a humble bowl of steamed vegetables and rice taste amazing. Mayonnaise was a mystery to us for so long. We just went without. But it turns out it's super easy. The thing that put us off was the vegetable oils, which we aren't fans of because they are so highly processed. Olive oil becomes bitter when blended, and sesame oil can taste too strong, but finally we hit upon cold-pressed sunflower oil—locally grown and wonderfully neutral, making it the perfect candidate for classic mayonnaise without all of the processed oils.

The secret to this recipe is adding the oil slowly. And sometimes, even though you follow all of the steps, mayonnaise just goes wrong and splits. Don't beat yourself up—go again, and we promise it will work!

3 egg yolks

1 tablespoon apple cider vinegar

250 ml (1 cup) cold-pressed sunflower oil

juice of ½ lemon

1 teaspoon unrefined sugar (e.g. rapadura), dissolved in a splash of hot water

¼ teaspoon unrefined salt

Place the yolks and vinegar in a blender (or in a jar if you prefer to use a hand-held blender) and blend while very slowly adding the oil—this is the key to stop it splitting. The mixture should start to look creamy once you have added about half of the oil. Add the lemon juice and keep blending while slowly adding the rest of the oil. It should now be thick and creamy. If it's not super creamy, add more oil a little bit at a time until it is. Add the sugar and salt and blend again to combine. This will store for up to a week in the fridge.

RECIPE NOTE.

If you don't mind a mildly bitter flavour from olive oil, you can use half sunflower oil and half olive oil—add the olive oil at the end of the blending process to reduce the bitterness.

Vegetable stock.

MAKES ABOUT 2 LITRES
TIME: 8-12 HOURS

Stocks are gateways to easy meals. They have heaps of flavour and are full of nutrients, simply add some vegetables, meat, grains and spices and you have an easy 'one pot wonder'. You can use any old vegetables you have left over from the week, oversized vegetables (they're past their best) from the garden, or any overabundance you have of one vegetable (because you overplanted it in the excitement of planting). Vegetable stock is so easy: throw it all in a pot and leave it for 8–12 hours to cook down, then freeze it for easy meals later.

1 kg mixed vegetables (try to include some root vegetables for the best flavour), cut into large chunks

2 carrots, halved

4 celery stalks, cut into 20 cm lengths

1 onion, halved

3 litres unchlorinated water

1 bunch of parsley (or any other herbs), tied together with twine

5–10 black peppercorns

Preheat the oven to 220°C fan-forced.

Place the vegetables on a baking tray and roast for about 10–15 minutes until browned.

Tip the vegetables into a stockpot and cover with the water. Add the parsley and peppercorns and bring to the boil. Turn the heat right down and simmer for about 8–12 hours with the lid on.

Strain, discarding the vegetables (they will be tasteless as they've given up all their nutrients to the water). Refrigerate or freeze the stock in airtight containers.

Waste bone stock.

MAKES ABOUT 6 LITRES
TIME: 12-24 HOURS

When meat is processed, so many people these days throw away the bones. This is one of the most nutritious parts of the animal and we think it's crazy to ever throw these away. Traditionally, making stock was always a key component of processing any animal, so that all parts of the animal were used. If you don't raise or hunt your own animals, go to a butcher who stocks meat from well-sourced, pasture-raised animals and get some bones or carcasses that would otherwise go to waste.

4 kg bones (meat, chicken, fish, shellfish or game)

8 litres unchlorinated water

Preheat the oven to 220°C fan-forced.

Place the bones on a baking tray and roast for about 10–15 minutes until browned.

Tip the bones into a stockpot and cover with the water, leaving at least a few centimetres of space at the top. Bring to the boil very slowly over a low heat, skimming off any foam as it rises to the top. Turn the heat down and simmer very gently for 12–24 hours with the lid on. (Some say that slowly bringing half of the water to the boil first, then adding the other half cold and bringing it back to the boil causes the meat and bones to contract and release even more goodness. Sometimes we do this, and sometimes we just add it all at once.)

Strain the stock and pick the meat off the bones to eat. Refrigerate or freeze the stock in airtight containers.

RECIPE NOTES (FOR BOTH STOCKS).

For a stronger flavoured and more concentrated stock, take the lid off towards the end and reduce the liquid.

It's important not to add salt to your stock if you intend to soak grains with it or make something like risotto (page 286), as it will prevent your grains from fully cooking (page 338).

Quick lacto-fermentation guide.

Fermentation is an ancient technique and has been keeping humans healthy and fed for thousands of years. Lacto-fermentation preserves by helping the good bacteria (lactobacilli) overpower the bad. *Everything* is preserved in the process, including all of the original vitamins and minerals, plus the natural enzymes, and, as an added bonus, the bioavailability of most of the vitamins and minerals is actually enhanced due to the pre-digestion performed by the good bacteria and enzymes. When we consume the good bacteria present in fermented foods, we are also maintaining the balance of good to bad bacteria in our digestive systems, and happy digestion equals lots of energy for our bodies.

Key ingredients.

Lactobacilli (the good bacteria). Lactobacilli are everywhere, especially in our guts and on plants that grow in or close to the soil (but not when grown using hydroponics or the like). They live by digesting carbohydrates (sugars and starches), and produce lactic acid as a by-product. The lactic acid they produce is responsible for the sharp taste of traditional pickled vegetables, like sauerkraut and kimchi (these good bacteria are also present in other traditional foods, like cultured (sour) cream, yoghurt and sourdough bread), and creates a low pH (acidic) environment that the good bacteria love, but that bad bacteria cannot survive in—hence our food is preserved. Because lactobacilli are naturally occurring bacteria, we don't need to inoculate our ferments with them. We simply have to create an environment conducive to their survival. Basically, we need to make sure that they multiply faster than the bad bacteria.

Unrefined salt. You *can* lacto-ferment without salt, but the right result is certainly more guaranteed when you use it. Lactobacilli are far more tolerant of salt than bad bacteria, allowing them to get to work digesting the carbohydrates in the fermenting food, producing lactic acid and rapidly multiplying. Soon they have produced so much lactic acid that the environment is so acidic that no new bad bacteria can survive—bad bacteria cannot live in a highly acidic environment. You can salt your vegetables dry, or you can soak them in brine. Both have exactly the same effect, it's just that one or the other is usually more appropriate depending on the food.

Key tips.

Over-fermentation. One thing to understand is that you *can* over-ferment your foods, which is why in the recipes we say to refrigerate after 5–7 days fermenting at room temperature. When we say over-ferment, we don't mean they spoil or go bad—in fact, they would technically be even better for your digestion. What it means is that the good bacteria have started to digest the cellular structure of the food you are preserving, resulting in an overly sour taste and, eventually, a mushy texture.

Temperature. Lactobacilli are extremely sluggish below about 12°C, the average temperature of a traditional cellar. So, if you have a cellar, use that to store your lacto-fermented preserves. Additionally, it is key to note that if it is winter and constantly below 12°C when you are trying to ferment, it's not going to work very well. The best time to ferment is late spring to late autumn.

Salt ratios. We always use a 2–5% brine, or 2–5% salt to raw vegetable weight for dry salting—that is to say, 20–50 g of salt to 1 litre of water or 1 kg of vegetables. If, as with kimchi, you are washing the vegetables after salting, go as high as 10%. In each case, this is plenty of salt to get the lactobacilli off to a great start, without making the ferment too salty to eat. Any higher than 5% salt in the finished product and we promise that you'll want to spit it out!

Keeping everything submerged. It is super important that when you lacto-ferment, *everything* remains submerged in the liquid from start to finish. Any produce exposed to the air will eventually grow mould. A white film on the surface of the liquid is fine, that's just a bit of friendly penicillin. But other moulds are less fun. Check on your ferments daily and don't be afraid to top up the liquid level with some unchlorinated water if needed.

Quick hot-bottling guide.

Hot-bottling (otherwise known as canning, jarring and jam making) has only been around for as long as jars, cans, sugar and vinegar have been readily available, but it's a wonderful technique with lots of positives. It works by pasteurising the food to reduce bad bacteria populations to harmless levels, and then holding the food in a vacuum so that no new bacteria can enter, thus maintaining it in a stable state.

Because some bacteria survive pasteurisation (the point isn't to kill them all, but rather to reduce numbers to harmless levels), we always use one of two key ingredients to prevent the survivors from multiplying and destroying all our hard work: sugar and/or vinegar (or another acid). Sugars preserve food by dehydrating bad bacteria via a process called osmosis. Vinegar, and other acids, preserve food by creating an environment with such a low pH (high acidity) that bad bacteria cannot grow. Most vinegars are much more acidic than needed for this task, so as long as your recipe contains at least a 5:1 ratio of fruit/veg to vinegar, your final preserve will be safe.

The final step of course is the bottling iteslf! There are two techniques to bottle safely and successfully:

The 'hot jar, hot liquid, hot lid' method.

1. Sterilise. Place the jars or bottles in a 100°C oven or a saucepan of boiling water (they don't have to be submerged, steam sterilises too!) and leave them there until you're ready to bottle. Sterilise the lids in boiling water only—never in the oven, as the seals will melt. Sterilise other utensils, like funnels and spoons, in boiling water.

2. Fill. Your preserve must be HOT (72–80°C) before bottling. Remove the jars or bottles from the oven or water and fill to 1 cm from the lips. Do this in small batches so that everything is still super hot when sealed.

3. Clean. Wipe the lips of the jars with a clean, dry cloth.

4. Seal. Be careful not to over-tighten the lids, as this may break the seal (it's not how tight you screw the lids on that seals, but the vacuum created when the jars cool). Allow the jars to cool to room temperature on the bench.

5. Check. Once cooled, the lids should have sucked down. If they haven't, the bottling wasn't done quickly enough (so everything wasn't hot enough) or there is a fault in the lid. It's best to re-bottle with a new lid with the 'classic water bath' method, opposite.

6. Store. Store in a cool, dark place. Once opened, store in the fridge.

The 'classic water bath' method.

1. Fill. Fill clean jars or bottles to 1 cm from the lips.

2. Seal. Screw on the lids so that they're firmly in position, but be careful not to over-tighten them, as this may break the seal (it's not actually how tight you screw the lids on that seals, but the vacuum created when the jars cool).

3. Place in the water bath. Place as many jars as fit in a single layer in the biggest, deepest pot you have. Jars must be the same or a very similar height.

4. Add water. Fill the pot with water to within about 5 cm from the top of the shortest jar.

5. Heat. Cover and gently heat the water to 72–80°C. Maintain in this heat range for 15–20 minutes. What we are doing here is pasteurising everything—jars/bottles, contents and lids—all at the same time, so you need to give the contents time to heat to 72°C.

6. Cool. Check that the lids are still firmly in place and lightly tighten if necessary (but again, don't over-tighten them!). Cool to room temperature either on the bench or in the water bath.

7. Check. Once cooled, the lids should suck down. If they don't, there is a fault in the lid. Repeat the steps with a new lid or a whole new jar or bottle and lid.

8. Store. Store in a cool, dark place. Once opened, store in the fridge.

Thank you.

There was just this moment that we really, deeply realised that life is better with our village. It's so much more fulfilling, meaningful and happy when we share all of our experiences and nurture each other. In particular, we thank Italy and all the people who welcomed us into their homes and fed us, for deeply cementing that belief.

After the first book we said (out loud) that we weren't going to do another. Because writing a book can sometimes feel like the most unpredictable roller-coaster you've ever been on— so many feelings at once—painful, exciting, liberating and then towards the end you get 'the fear': what if no one reads it, no one likes it?

But then, you work with beautiful people who tell you lovely things and make sure your words/recipes are as good as they can be, and you actually hear from (real life!) readers, and because of this you feel re-inspired, there is a new flood of ideas and so here we are again.

Thank you to our beautiful and amazing book team for believing in us—Mary, Jane, Lucy, Ash, Marcus, Shantanu; to our recipe testers Emma and Caroline, and to the friends who tested our recipes in their kitchens before they entered the world; Soph, our on-shoot 'everything' person for remaining so patient; Mel, for your amazing illustrations; Peter, for giving this text a last minute proofread; special thanks to our lovely publisher, Mary, for entrusting Matt to design this book; and to our previous book designer, Daniel, for laying such an incredible foundation in the first book for us to build upon.

This book means as much as the first—and it means different things. This one took a village. Almost every part was in some way inspired by, fed to, made by, read by and/or experienced within our village. Thank you to every person who has welcomed us into their home, who has made us feel warm, who has made us feel loved. And there are a lot of you. Life isn't perfect, but every day it amazes us how fun the chaos of life is and how amazing our people are, and how lucky we are to have this village of loved ones surrounding us. Specific mentions to:

IN ITALY

Matt's family in Cirvoi, Guido and Carine, Diego, Stellina and Giuseppe, Annalise and Antonio, Licia—you all welcomed us and nurtured us wholeheartedly.

FROM LENTIL

My family (immediate—with special mention to my dad, aunties, uncles, cousins, second/third cousins)—you are a constant source of chaos, entertainment and inspiration. Thank you for teaching me how to love, what community means, what family means, and despite so much hardship, still showing me what it is to be nurtured; Matt—for accepting me as I am and being the most genuine and patient person I know; Lee and Tara—specifically, for your inability to cook, you inspire me to cook more simply (see gelato, page 319).

FROM MATT

My Italian cousins and my Castlemaine cousins, you make me feel like I fit. Thank you for being you, for being so real and open and free and wild and fiercely honest. My immediate family, for putting up with me even though I may not fit the picture quite so neatly—I love you dearly. Brian and Jessica, always, for patiently and joyously instilling in me the skills that started me on this path in such a meaningful way. And of course, to Lentil—you have conquered mountains I hope I never have to see the foot of. You are a determined, loyal ball of love. You will always be the brightest spark, the loudest voice and the deepest source of joy to me.

FROM BOTH OF US

To our readers, we wouldn't be here without you. To every person mentioned in this book. Sarah and Tom, Hermione and Joe, Siv and Todd, Mel and Nick, Bug and Mike, Kerry and Andrew, Lachy, Benny, Ru, Matt-Matt, Gen and Andy, Monty and Joe and all the wonderful family that comes with you all. Thank you for always taking us as we are, loving us, having fun, sharing meals, ideas and chaos. Thank you. (Phew, that was long, but it really did take a village!)

xoxo Matt & Lentil

Index.

N

O

P

Q

R

S

T

V

W

Y

Z

Imperial/metric conversion chart.

Weights.	
5 g	¼ oz
15 g	½ oz
20 g	¾ oz
30 g	1 oz
50 g	1¾ oz
75 g	2¾ oz
100 g	3½ oz
150 g	5½ oz
200 g	7 oz
250 g	8¾ oz
300 g	10½ oz
350 g	12¼ oz
400 g	14 oz
450 g	1 lb
500 g	1 lb 1½ oz
550 g	1 lb 3½ oz
600 g	1 lb 5 oz
650 g	1 lb 7 oz
700 g	1 lb 8¾ oz
750 g	1 lb 10½ oz
800 g	1 lb 12¼ oz
850 g	1 lb 14¾ oz
900 g	2 lb
1 kg	2¼ lb
2 kg	4½ lb
3 kg	6½ lb
4 kg	8¾ lb
5 kg	11 lb
6 kg	13¼
7 kg	15½ lb
8 kg	17½ lb
9 kg	19¾ lb
10 kg	22 lb
15 kg	33 lb
20 kg	44 lb
30 kg	66 lb
40 kg	88¼ lb
50 kg	110¼ lb
75 kg	165¼ lb
100 kg	220½ lb

Measures.	
5 ml	¼ fl oz
15 ml	½ fl oz
20 ml	¾ fl oz
30 ml	1 fl oz
50 ml	1¾ fl oz
75 ml	2½ fl oz
100 ml	3½ fl oz
150 ml	5 fl oz
200 ml	7 fl oz
250 ml	1 cup
300 ml	10 fl oz
350 ml	12 fl oz
400 ml	13½ fl oz
450 ml	15 fl oz
500 ml	2 cups
550 ml	18½ fl oz
600 ml	20½ fl oz
650 ml	22½ fl oz
700 ml	23½ fl oz
750 ml	3 cups
800 ml	27 fl oz
850 ml	28½ fl oz
900 ml	30½ fl oz
1 L	1 qt
2 L	2 qt
3 L	3 qt
4 L	1 gal
5 L	1¼ gal
6 L	1½ gal
7 L	1¾ gal
8 L	2 gal
9 L	2¼ gal
10 L	2¾ gal
15 L	4 gal
20 L	5¼ gal
30 L	8 gal
40 L	10½ gal
50 L	13¼ gal
75 L	19¾ gal
100 L	26½ gal

Lengths.	
1 cm	½″
2 cm	¾″
2½ cm	1″
3 cm	1¼″
4 cm	1½″
5 cm	2″
6 cm	2½″
7 cm	2¾″
8 cm	3¼″
9 cm	3½″
10 cm	4″
15 cm	6″
20 cm	8″
25 cm	10″
30 cm	1′
40 cm	1′ 4″
50 cm	1′ 8″
60 cm	2′
80 cm	2′ 8″
90 cm	3′
1 m	3′ 3″
5 m	16′ 5″
10 m	32′ 10″
25 m	82′
50 m	164′
100 m	328′
150 m	492′
200 m	656′
250 m	820′
500 m	1640′
1 km	0.62 mi
1.61 km	1 mi

Temperatures.	
140°C	275°F
150°C	300°F
160°C	320°F
170°C	340°F
180°C	350°F
190°C	375°F
200°C	400°F
210°C	410°F
220°C	430°F
230°C	445°F
240°C	465°F
250°C	480°F

A PLUM BOOK

First published in 2018 by Pan Macmillan Australia Pty Limited
Level 25, 1 Market Street, Sydney, NSW, Australia 2000
Level 3, 112 Wellington Parade, East Melbourne, Victoria, Australia 3002

Design by Matt Purbrick
Photography by Shantanu Starick (with additional photography by Lentil Purbrick)
Illustrations by Mel Baxter
Styling by Matt and Lentil Purbrick
Editing by Marcus Ellis
Typesetting by Pauline Haas
Index by Helena Holmgren
Colour reproduction by Splitting Image Colour Studio
Printed and bound in China by 1010 Printing International Limited

A CIP catalogue record for this book is available from the National Library of Australia.

10 9 8 7 6 5 4 3 2 1

We advise that the information contained in this book does not negate personal responsibility on the part of the reader for their own health and safety. It is recommended that individually tailored advice is sought from your healthcare or medical professional. The publishers and their respective employees, agents and authors are not liable for injuries or damage occasioned to any person as a result of reading or following the information contained in this book.

ABOUT THE AUTHORS

Matt and Lentil Purbrick are the couple behind Grown & Gathered—an online world of all things natural, a previous book (*Grown & Gathered: Traditional Living Made Modern*) and a small farm. They are known for promoting seasonal, regional and wholefood ingredients, alongside natural growing principles.

Matt and Lentil began by selling their produce to some of Melbourne's top restaurants, encouraging chefs to adopt principles of sourcing local, real produce and sustainable farming and packaging. Since then, they have embarked on a number of projects, including The Produce Van, where they pulled their van up each week in the streets of Melbourne to sell their homegrown vegetables and talk to people about sustainability and natural food, and The Flower Exchange, where they grew flowers and traded them without exchanging money for a year.

Their inclusive and pragmatic approach to traditional food and sustainability has inspired many people around the world, and they have become educators and advocates for a bright future.

Matt and Lentil currently live in the North Central region of Victoria, Australia, where they spend their time creating, learning and growing natural food. Lentil loves writing and photography, Matt growing food and design. *The Village* is their second book.

www.grownandgathered.com.au